Moments of Rupture:
Space, Militancy & Film

Sandra Schäfer

metroZones 15

Moments of Rupture

Space, Militancy & Film

Traversing Contaminated Spaces—
A Prologue by metroZones

Militancy is not a term that metroZones[1] has worked with. This is partially due to the complexities of translation—the German *Militanz* (radical attitude) has little in common with the Spanish *militancia* (political activism) or the English *militancy*. But it is also owed to the ambivalences of the so-called militant or committed investigation, more so if it happens in highly contested scenarios. To whom or what are we committed? To truth, knowledge, or "resistance"; to our counterparts or collaborators; or to an imaginary public? With regard to how we (should) get involved in the respective fields we explore—either as research-oriented artists, as curators, or as culture-producing researchers—we hold more questions than answers.

But that is exactly what we believe research is: exploring uncertain terrains, beyond simplifying presumptions or dichotomies; engaging with the unknown; leaving academic conventions and all-too-accustomed comfort zones behind. And that is why metroZones is especially interested in Sandra Schäfer's work. Her artistic exploration of how Hezbollah produces urban space and stages remembrance in post-war Lebanon—and how it pursues a corresponding image politics—confronts such uncertainties and ambiguities.

While frequently travelling to Afghanistan and Iran, Sandra Schäfer co-curated the film and discussion programme "Kabul/Teheran 1979ff" at the Volksbühne Berlin in 2003 as part of the metroZones project "ErsatzStadt". She later co-edited a metroZones publication under the same title dealing with "film landscapes, cities under stress and migration", which was published by b_books in 2006. In 2007, Schäfer released *Passing the Rainbow* (a filmic collaboration with Elfe Brandenburger and multiple participants in Kabul), followed by the metroZones publication *stagings: Kabul, Film & Production of Representation* (2009), which addresses political and media images of Afghanistan.

Schäfer joined the artistic research and exhibition project "Global Prayers: Contemporary Manifestations of the Religious in the City", organised by metroZones, Haus der Kulturen der Welt, and neue Gesellschaft

---

1   metroZones was founded in Berlin in 2007 as an independent association for critical urban research. At the interface between art, science, and politics, metroZones' projects combine approaches to research and knowledge production, cultural and curatorial practices, as well as political interventions. The goal is to publicly address—and politicise—urban issues, everyday life, and conflicts. https://metrozones.info

für bildende Kunst from 2010 to 2014. As a result of her involvement, she presented the two-channel video installation *on the set of 1978ff* in 2011. A discussion with the Iranian photographer Hengameh Golestan led to Schäfer's contribution to the metroZones publication *Global Prayers*. Titled "There is no answer to any of these things", this exchange broached the issue of religious street politics during the Iranian Revolution ^{Becker, Klingan, Lanz, Wildner 2014}.

In her present multi-layered study, Schäfer explores how specific urban sites and architecture in Lebanon (whether post-war reconstruction or memorial sites) collaborate with identitarian and ideological constructions through spatial, sensorial, discursive, and material strategies. Schäfer is particularly interested in spatial and visual articulations of the narrative of "resistance", which she neither adopts nor labels as pure propaganda. For instance, she has observed that Hezbollah tends to suppress the commemoration of destruction, instead producing heroic gestures celebrating the future and redemption. Despite the uncanniness evident in such terrains, Schäfer enters the "minefield" without preconceived judgements or a false display of neutrality.

Schäfer applies a methodology of *traversing* as a bodily, artistic, and analytical practice. This includes procedures such as looking and listening, recording and editing, staging, showing and screening, encoding and decoding. She assumes an agency that relates to other agents, whether inhabitants, architects, or visitors. From a metroZones perspective, field research means precisely that: being present and positioning oneself in the field while acknowledging the presence and agency of others—a however fragile and utopian horizontality—without getting lost in a fictitious sameness or assimilation. This approach challenges the binary of otherness and constantly requires the labour of micro-negotiations. In dealing with Hezbollah's power, rules, and practices, Schäfer's work eloquently shows how this negotiation becomes part of the research.

Working in such extremely regulated fields—and with what Schäfer has called "contaminated materials"—also requires a clear awareness of curatorial framing, whether this is the white cube or black box of the exhibition or screening, or the memorial landscape commissioned and maintained by Hezbollah. Both must be understood as part of a powerful cultural and political "fabric" that *produces* rather than just receives or mirrors various audiences, publics, crowds, citizens, and citizenships.

In her methodology of the "militant image" Schäfer develops a strategy of self-positioning. At the same time, she dares to artistically intervene in Hezbollah's landscapes—both the vertical reconstruction of housing and the horizontal panorama of memory—by dislocating objects, working with voids and silences, and using her own body and gaze as a sensor. Closely aligned with the perspective of metroZones, she focuses on clashes and contradictions, for instance, between glorifying martyrdom and the much more intimate setting of mourning; between the purposes of architecture and the everyday.

Schäfer's examination of how specific spatial productions relate to the "empty signifier" of resistance—an interrogation that occurs at the level of both theory and artistic intervention—might also be understood as an approach of *re-reading*. metroZones has worked with this term for some time, since it emphasises the discursive and (therefore) political situatedness of what is said and done in the field, including our own visual and verbal practices. It refers to research as a process of moving back and forth, of resonating, reconstructing, and reflecting.

Finally, for metroZones, the overall purpose of decolonising urban (and) cultural research requires a trans-local perspective on entangled urbanities and spatialities. Any local setting is shaped and traversed by other localities and geopolitical constellations. Schäfer's work explores such "trans-geographical" settings: her focus on Lebanese spaces and narratives is interwoven with Latin American and German discourses and practices as well as the conflicting geographies and temporalities of the region. As a practice of situated knowledge, her close artistic reading provides a de-orientalisation of phenomena such as religious urban cultures. Thus, Islamistic images and memory politics as well as the production of urban space become readable as discursive practices. As tense and ambiguous as they may be, these practices nevertheless enable us to recognise how religion shapes urban settings and, conversely, how the city shapes religious practices.

Introduction

Several years ago, I began to feel an urgency to engage across political and national borders. As a result, I became interested in trans-geographical events, for example, the Iranian Revolution of 1978. Working together with different protagonists to re-read the Iranian Revolution based on films, photographs, and radio broadcasts, I developed the video installation *on the set of 1978ff* Schäfer 2011. The work focused on questions around political Islam, the Marxist left, the role of urban space in this revolution, and how it was translated in Iran's neighbouring countries as well as in the Global North, since I regard the geographies that we inhabit as entangled.[1] When I was invited to participate in a workshop in Beirut as part of the metroZones project the Urban Cultures of Global Prayers[2] in 2011, I conducted research on these questions in the archives of the UMAM Documentation and Research Centre, which is situated at the edge of the Haret Hreik district (Arabic: حارة حريك),[3] where Hezbollah's headquarters are located. This was the first time I encountered the spaces and projects initiated by Hezbollah (Arabic: حزب الله | Party of God).

In Hezbollah's urban, architectural, and museum projects, I often came across the narrative of resistance (Arabic: المقاومة | al-muqawama). Resistance has been part of Hezbollah's identity since it was formed to oppose the Israeli occupation (1982–2000).[4] During the occupation, resistance was a counter-hegemonic struggle that focused on the contested space of southern Lebanon. Since then, Hezbollah's discourse has centred on the resistance/occupation binary. Hezbollah's national and international role has, however, changed since the time of the occupation.

1   I focused, for example, on the effects of BBC broadcasting inside Iran and the micro-political decisions made during the production of news, which temporarily transformed a big institution like the BBC into an amplifier for the Iranian Revolution.

2   "Through science and art, the project *Global Prayers. Redemption and Liberation in the City* investigates new manifestations of the religious in urban space and the influence of urban cultures on the religious. In making use of collaborations between art and science-based researchers, Global Prayers takes a new approach to exploring the images and sounds, spaces and practices that the religious adopts in the age of globalization. It creates trans-regional networks and advances interdisciplinary approaches" (Global Prayers n.d.). Artists and social scientists from Austria, Brazil, Germany, India, Indonesia, Nigeria, Turkey, and Lebanon were involved in this four-year research project. *Global Prayers. Redemption and Liberation in the City* comprised workshops in cities like Berlin, Lagos, and Beirut as well as exhibitions, conferences, and publications (https://globalprayers.info/about/index.html).

3   In this book, the original Arabic, Farsi, or Hebrew is used the first time a word appears and the direction of the writing is from right to left. After this, words are transcribed in Latin letters.

4   Beginning in 1968, southern Lebanon was home to a resistance by Palestinian militants against Israel, a struggle that evolved into the wider Lebanese Civil War. The resistance lasted until Lebanon was invaded by the Israel Defense Forces (Hebrew: צְבָא הַהֲגָנָה לְיִשְׂרָאֵל | Army of Defense for Israel) in 1982, which led to the expulsion of the Palestinian Liberation Organisation (Arabic: منظمة التحرير الفلسطينية).

When I arrived in Beirut, I began to wonder how Hezbollah's architectural, urban, and museum projects contributed to its present discourse of resistance. This became part of a larger body of research about how contested space is produced—urban space as well as trans-geographical or geopolitical spaces—and what role visual politics plays in this.

The following text investigates Hezbollah's spatial and visual politics through my artistic practice in these spaces. Before doing so, however, it undertakes two tangents. The first examines militancy through different theoretical and activist reflections about the relations between power, violence, and liberation. These reflections are what Donna Haraway terms "situated knowledges" Haraway 1988.[5] They are entangled in specific times, struggles, and perspectives from which they develop their theoretical tools. In allowing these different reflections to speak with and through each other, a contradictory space opens up in relation to questions of power, violence, justice, and social transformation. This theoretical reflection helps to analyse the space in which militancy and militant-image production are located on a deeper structural level.

In the second tangent, I analyse examples from film and media of the 1960s and onwards. One focus is on Militant Cinema produced during the decolonisation and liberation struggles of the 1960s and 70s, when filmmakers developed the term "Militant Cinema" to distinguish their practices from "First", "Second", and "Third" Cinema → see chapter 2.1. In my analysis, I place a particular emphasis on the role that film and media played during the radicalisation of the student movement in West Germany. This is a history that I have long wanted to revisit and that I vaguely remember from my childhood, with images of exploded cars and wanted persons broadcast on television and hanging in different institutions. Based on examples of film and media from this period, I develop a methodology of the militant image. Apart from this methodological focus, I consider the struggles and methods of the 1960s and 70s as relevant to ignite a revision of our present. Furthermore, I take the methodology of the militant image as a basis for my later examination of Hezbollah's spaces.

After these two tangents, I demonstrate how the militant image extends into space. I focus on two projects undertaken by Hezbollah:

5   Haraway opposes "situated knowledges" to "the god trick", which describes the distanced act of seeing: "The eyes have been used to signify a perverse capacity—honed to perfection in the history of science tied to militarism, capitalism, colonialism, and male supremacy—to distance the knowing subject from everybody and everything in the interests of unfettered power" (Haraway 1988, 581).

the Mleeta Museum of Resistance (Arabic: متحف المقاومة) in southern Lebanon and the rebuilding of the Haret Hreik neighbourhood after it was bombed by the Israeli military in 2006. Can one talk about militant space in the same way Hezbollah speaks of *al-muqawama* (resistance)? How are such spaces built and inhabited? In examining these questions, I work in an ongoing exchange with a team that is predominantly composed of women and use my body, with its extended media apparatus, as a detector to analyse these spaces. Furthermore, I recognise the artistic professionalism of Hezbollah's media department and regard them in this sense as "peers". In my writing, I introduce terms and methods that I develop from other theories based on my experience working within Hezbollah's context. In a second step, I provide examples of how Hezbollah employs these methods within its framework. Finally, I analyse how I use these methods in Hezbollah's context and how I intervene in their use by Hezbollah.

It took a while until I could work within Hezbollah's framework. This was largely a result of my own doubts around the organisation's politics and the role that I would play in relation to this. For this reason, I continually asked myself several questions while working on this project: Why work in the context of Hezbollah? For whom? And how? I knew, after all, that once I decided to work within this context, I would be dependent on Hezbollah's approval.

This project was, however, preceded by two encounters with Hezbollah's (media) apparatus. In 2011, I visited the Mleeta Museum of Resistance in southern Lebanon with the Urban Cultures of Global Prayers research group. The group consisted of artists and social scientists with different backgrounds, united by an interest in questions related to religion and urban space. During a screening of Hezbollah's agitprop film in the museum's cinema, some members of the audience applauded. I wasn't sure if I was more upset by the agitational narrative of the film—which reminded me of a language of propaganda that I had learned to be suspicious of—or by the reactions of the audience. My irritation and anger continued during a tour led by an English-speaking guide, a young man in casual clothes who was witty and all too familiar with our international crowd and critical remarks, for which he always found an answer. I felt torn between my critique of colonial Israeli politics, the effects of which I also witnessed in Lebanon; my non-acceptance of antisemitism, stemming from my country's history of persecution and genocide; and a confrontation with Hezbollah's violent narratives, which present the history of occupation as an ongoing threat. The lack of space to articulate or even think about these contradictions during the museum visit left a heaviness in my body. The reactions within the group were diverse. In the merchandise shop, some of my colleagues bought a dartboard featuring images of Israeli politicians, thereby entering into complicity with Hezbollah.

My second encounter with Hezbollah's (media) apparatus took place a few days later, during a guided tour through the Haret Hreik district in southern Beirut with the same research group.[6] We had to wait for our guides at the Centre de Lecture et d'Animation Culturel à Haret Hreik. After we had given our passport details, a group of women from Hezbollah entered the room and took photographs of us without asking permission. In reaction to this, some members of the research group immediately took photographs of the photographers. Both instances made me equally uncomfortable. In the case of Hezbollah's photographic act, it remained unclear what the intention was, and we never saw how these images were used. Did Hezbollah publish them on its websites for publicity? Perhaps to show that an international research group was visiting and to demonstrate the openness of the organisation? Or were the photographs filed away for later identification? I regard our group's act of photographing as weak compared to that of the women from Hezbollah, who seemed to know exactly why they were taking pictures of us.

These two acts of image-taking indicated that we had entered into Hezbollah's territory, which worked according to specific rules. And Hezbollah had its own agenda related to our visit. This became even more apparent during our tour. Using a military tone, our guides told us when we were allowed to photograph certain sections of the district, from which angle, and for how long. Hezbollah performed its steadfastness while we were simultaneously made to perform a parody of the researcher's desire to document the space of "the Other". I began to take some images of the reconstructed buildings, but quickly gave up, feeling instrumentalised. The presence of our bodies (and cameras) in the public sphere was regarded with suspicion. In contrast to the Museum of Resistance, the Haret Hreik district was not a space that was meant or made for us.

During these initial visits, I realised that working in Hezbollah's territory would include limitations, manipulations, and rules that would only become apparent during the working process—if at all.

6   Because of our interest in the entanglements of religion and the urban, we visited the buildings in Haret Hreik that had been reconstructed after the July War in 2006.

Understanding what these rules were and how to deal with them thus became an important issue from the beginning. Making restrictions productive and appropriating methods employed by Hezbollah in order to use them differently were just two ways of dealing with this. My video installations *Mleeta* and *Constructed Futures: Haret Hreik* were influenced by these specific conditions. The first installation focuses on the Mleeta Museum of Resistance (or the Mleeta Resistance Tourist Landmark, as it is officially known). During the Israeli invasion of southern Lebanon (1982–2000), Mleeta stood right in the middle of the occupied zone. Thirty-five kilometres from Israel to the south and forty kilometres from Syria to the east, the mountain served as a hideout for Hezbollah fighters, making it the site of serious battles. The summit of Mleeta is now home to the Museum of Resistance, a propagandistic park that reproduces military scenarios. The second video installation centres on the rebuilding of Haret Hreik after the war in 2006. The Shiite-dominated Haret Hreik district in Beirut houses the headquarters of the Hezbollah Party. In 2006, the Israel Defense Forces bombed the neighbourhood, which Hezbollah quickly rebuilt.[7] This reconstruction project is part of a geopolitical struggle in which architecture takes part in the production of space, landscape, and memory.

In my video work and writing, I analyse how these two projects organised by Hezbollah create a memory, an identity, a new power structure, and a political statement within a conflict based on land and occupation. I employ my own body, with its extended filmic apparatus, as a detector. Furthermore, I use the social entity of the film team to work within Hezbollah's territory. In this sense, my practice is part of what has recently been termed "artistic research".

7   The bombing of Haret Hreik was preceded by Hezbollah's attack on an Israeli border patrol, in which three Israeli soldiers were killed and two were taken hostage.

Mleeta

Two-channel video
installation, 12 min, 2016

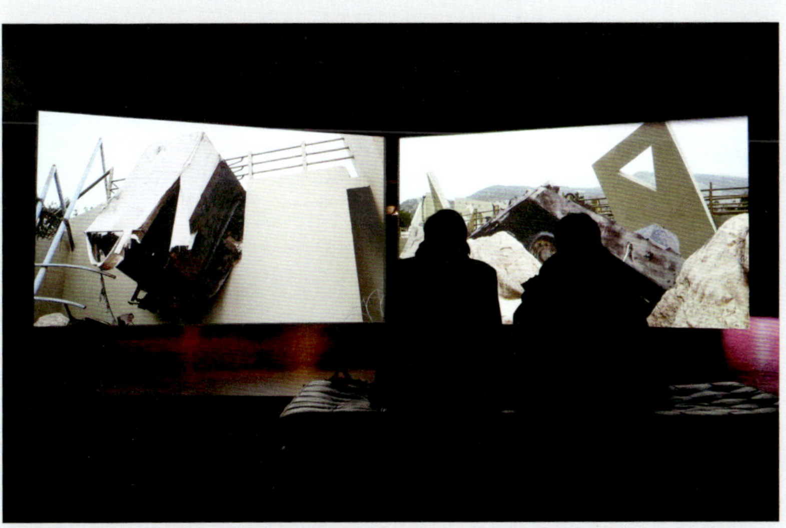

Mleeta at the 66th Berlinale, Forum Expanded, "Traversing the Phantasm",
Akademie der Künste, Berlin, 2016

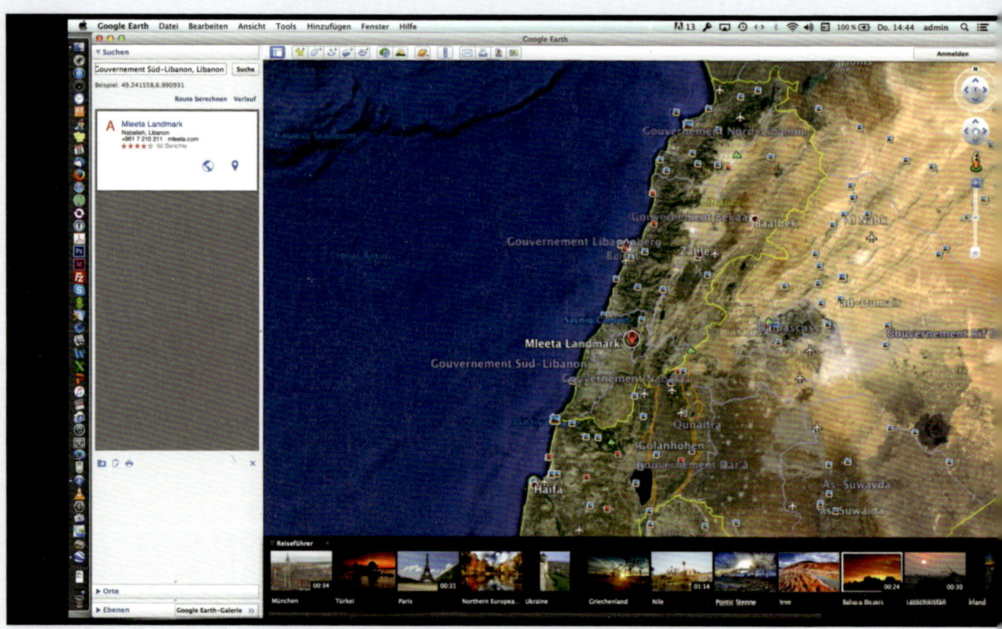

[mouse clicking, irregular electronic sound]

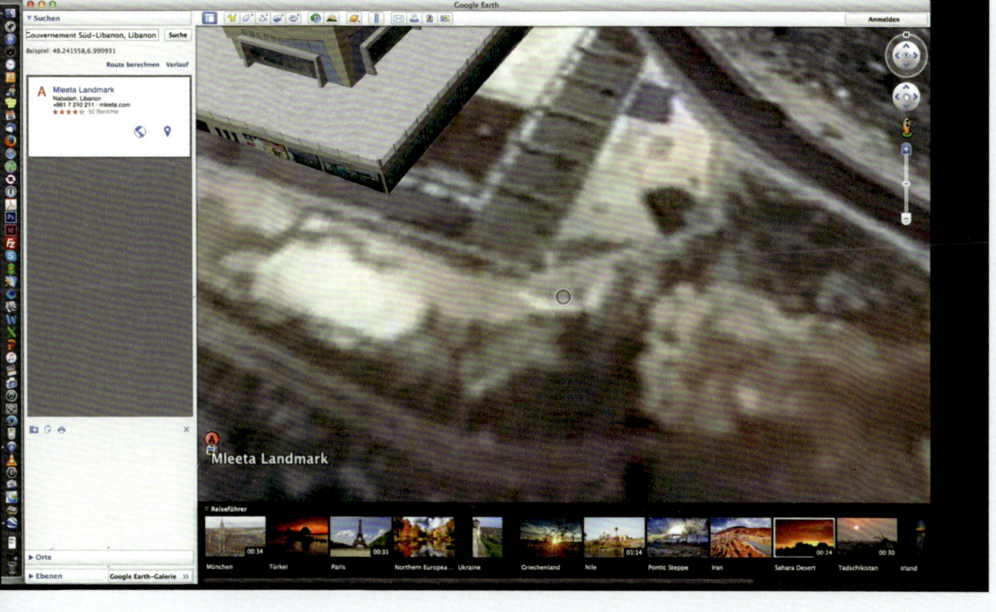

Google Earth   Datei   Bearbeiten   Ansicht   Tools   Hinzufügen   Fenster   Hilfe
Google Earth
Suchen
Gouvernement Süd-Libanon, Libanon   Suche
Beispiel: 49.241558,6.990931
Route berechnen   Verlauf
Mleeta Landmark
Nabatieh, Libanon
+961 7 210 211 · mleeta.com
50 Berichte
Anmelden
Mleeta Landmark
Reiseführer
München   Türkei   Paris   Northern Europea...   Ukraine   Griechenland   Nile   Pontic Steppe   Iran   Sahara Desert   Tadschikistan   Irland
Orte
Ebenen   Google Earth-Galerie

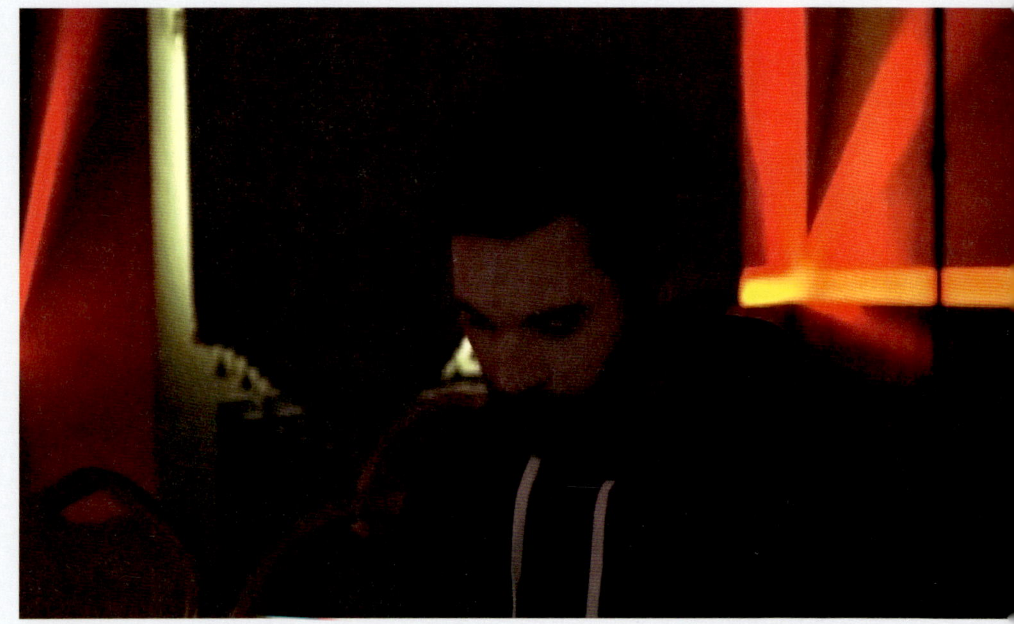

[tapping on mobile phone]

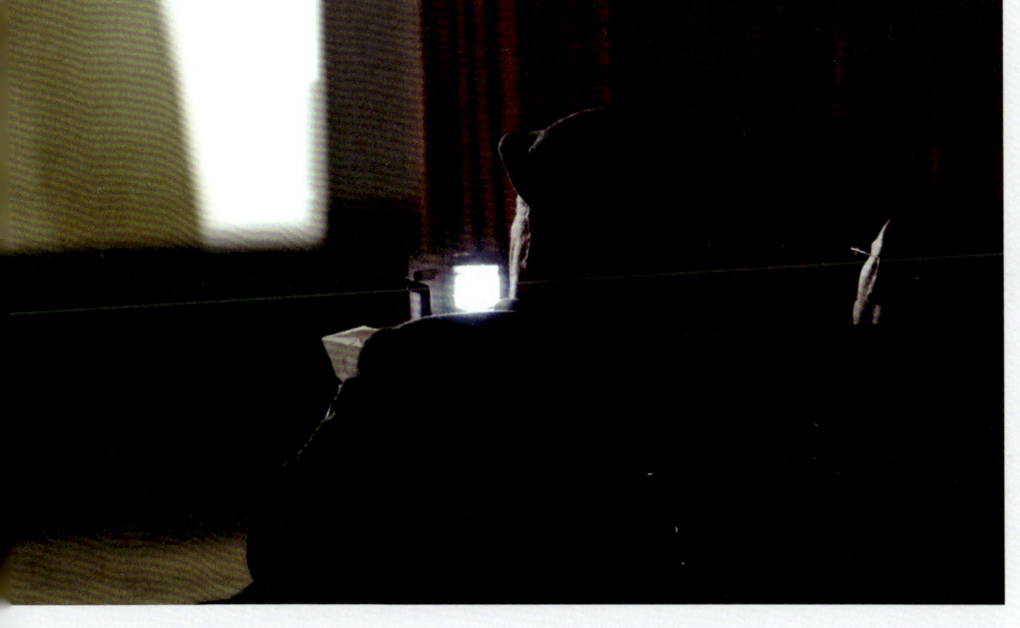

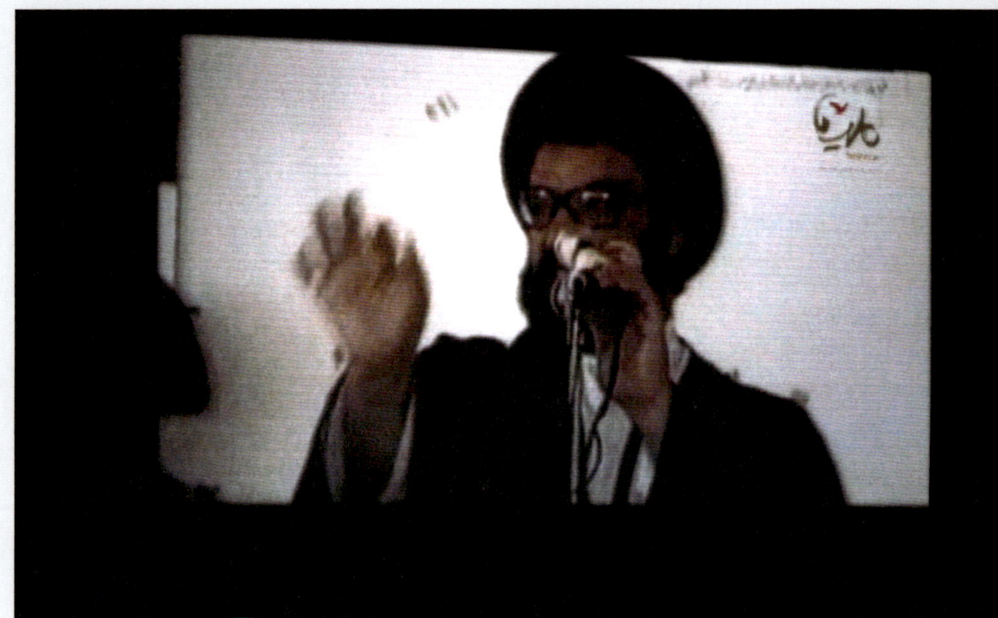

[film soundtrack "scratching" back and forth]

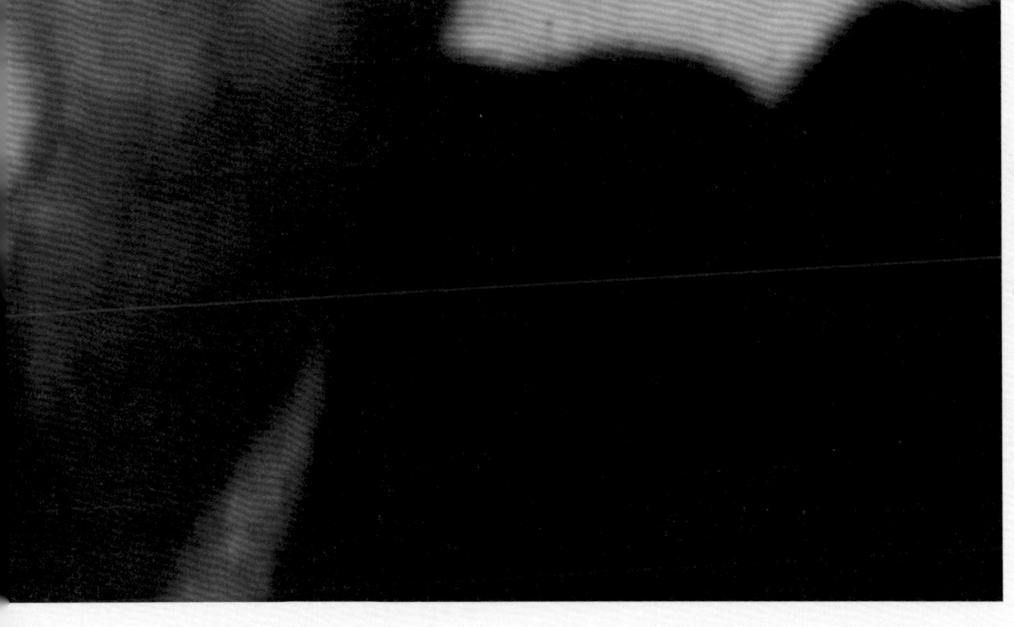

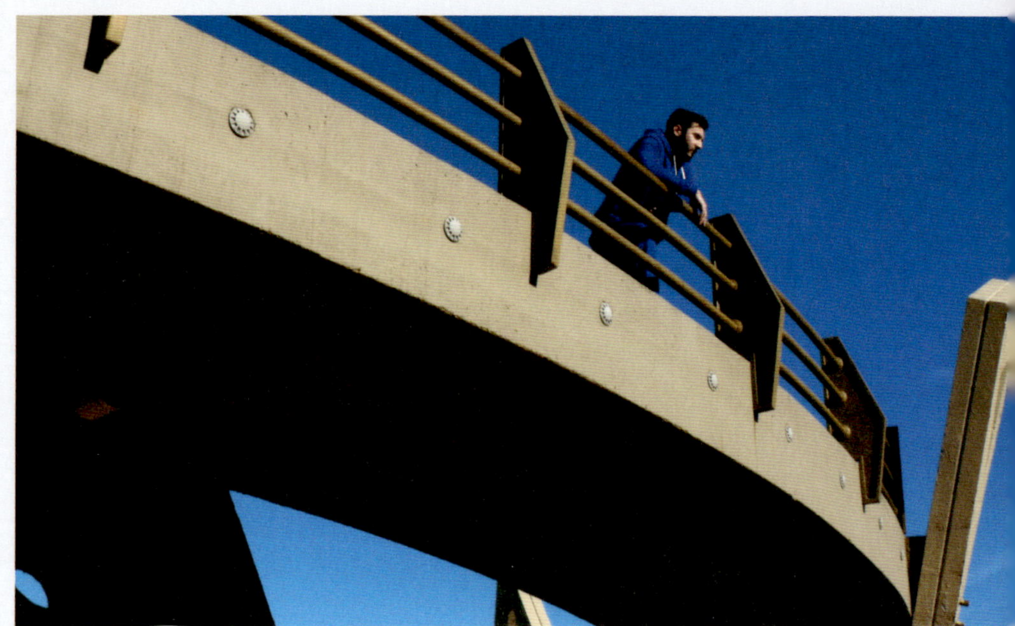

[chirping, footsteps, distant voices]

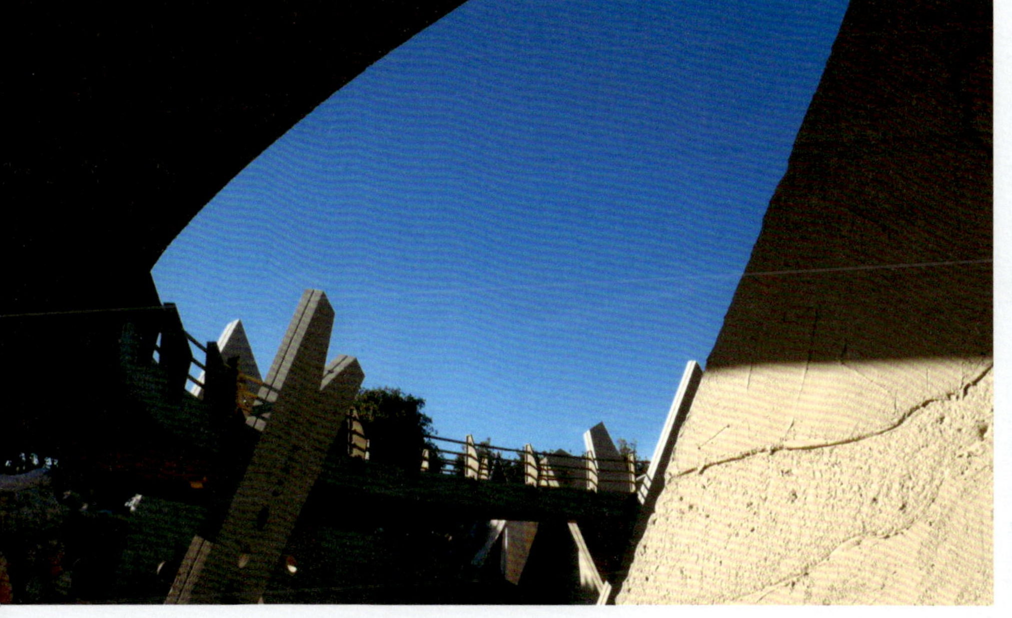

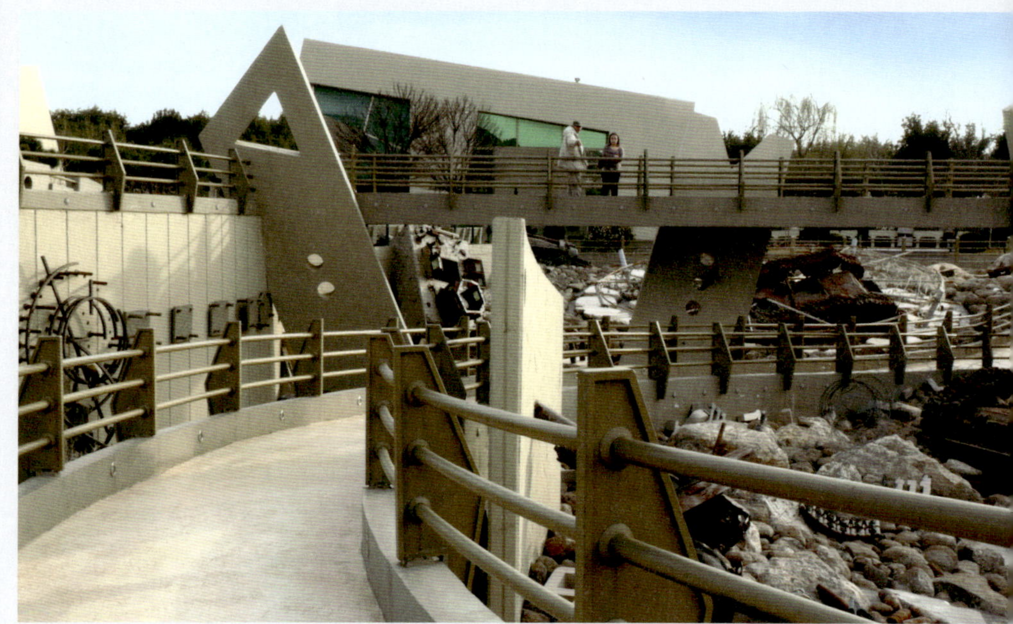

[footsteps, voices of people passing by]

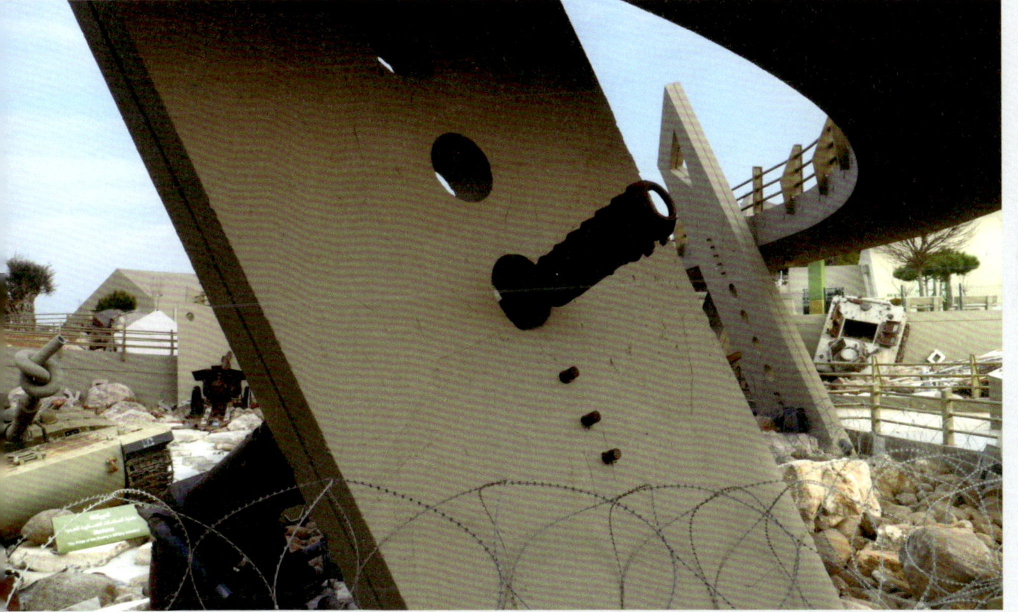

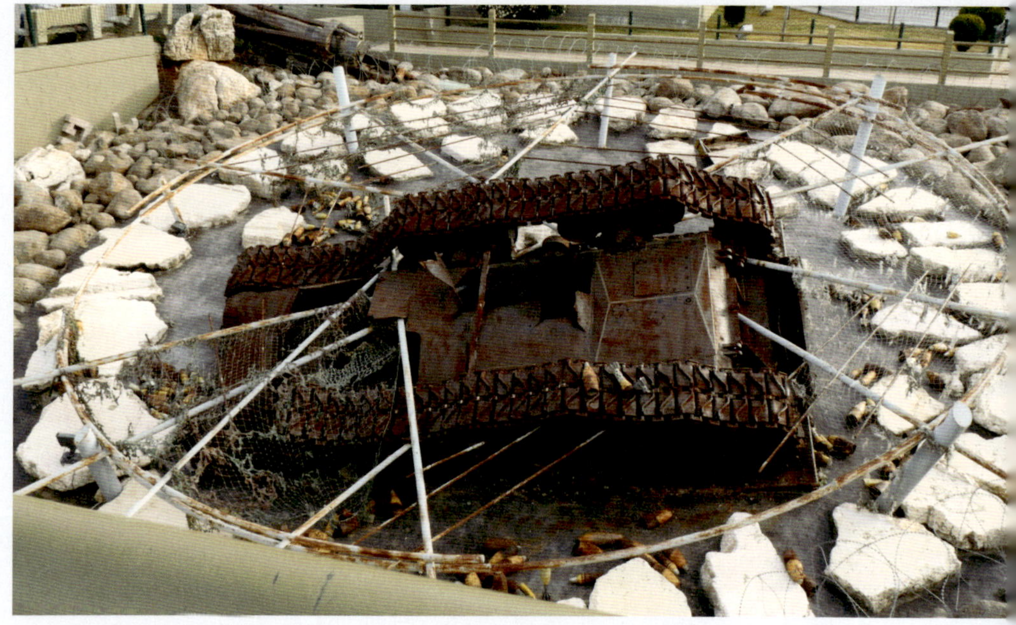

[distant voices]

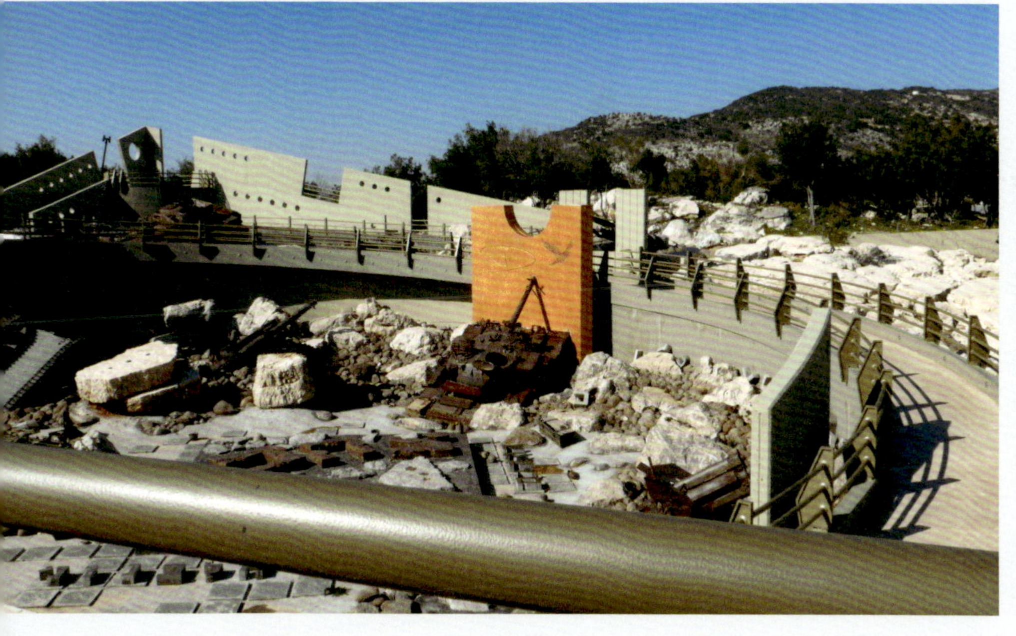

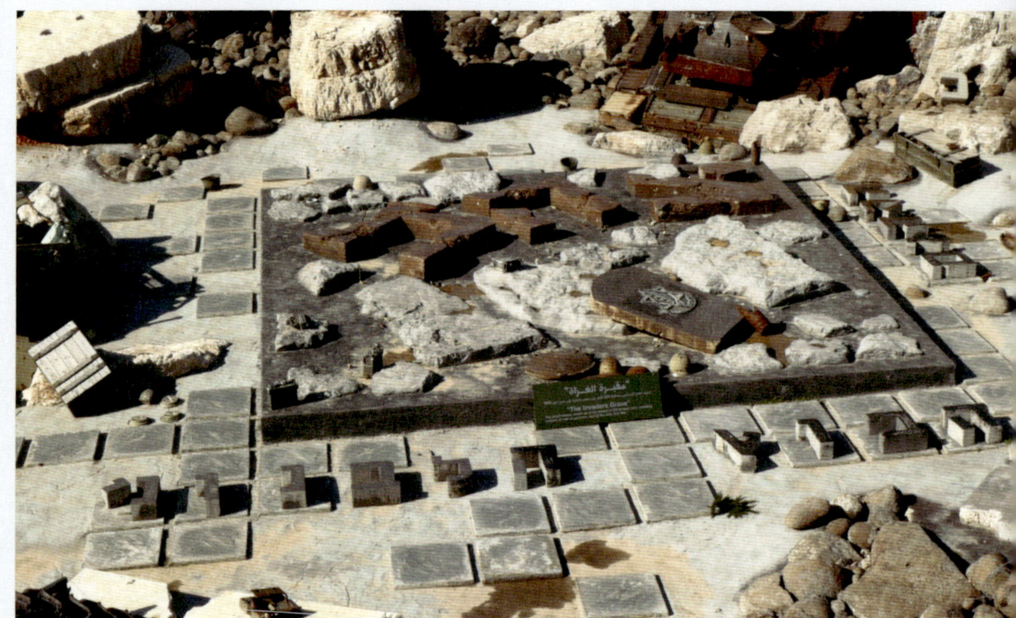

[stones pushed along the ground]

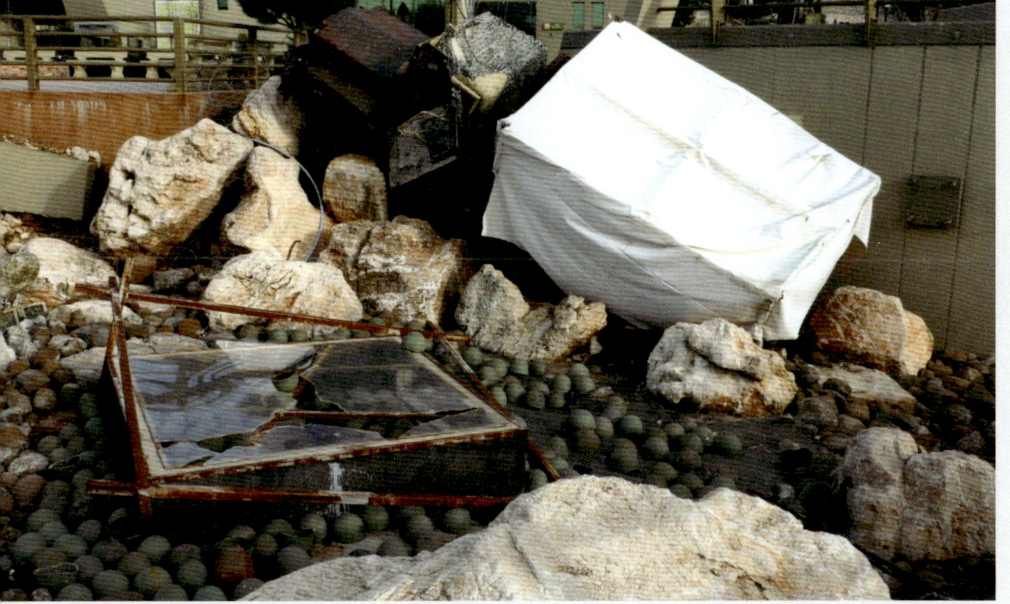

[military airplane flying overhead from left to right]

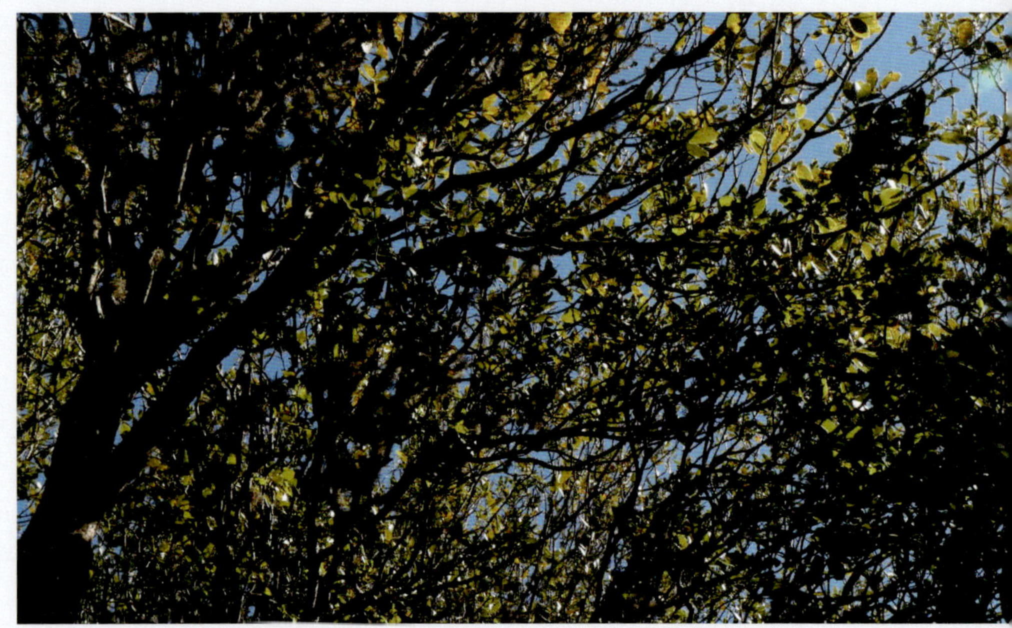

[crickets chirping, leaves rustling in the wind]

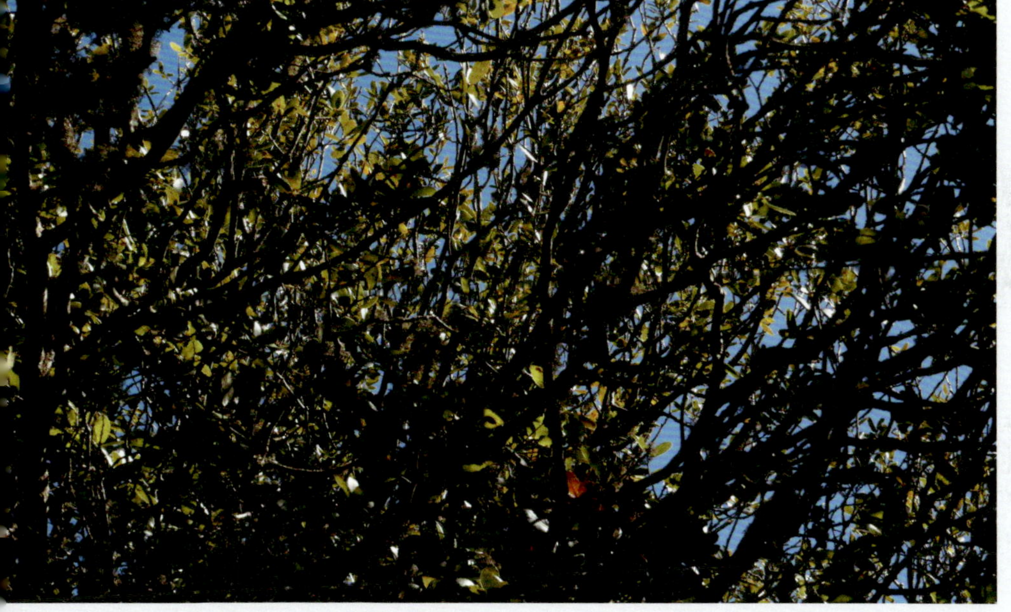

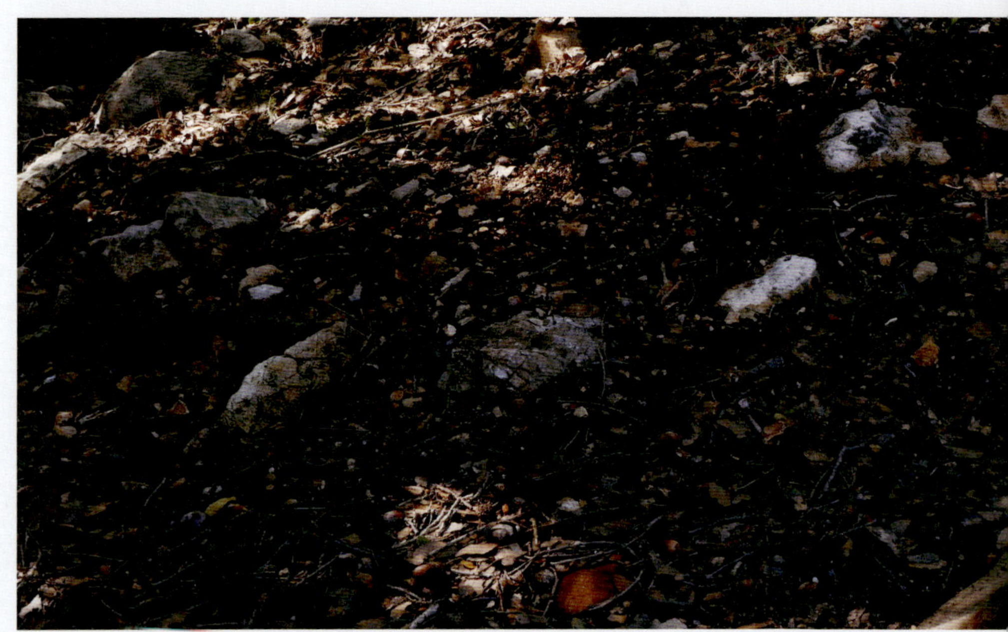

[footsteps running over dry leaves]

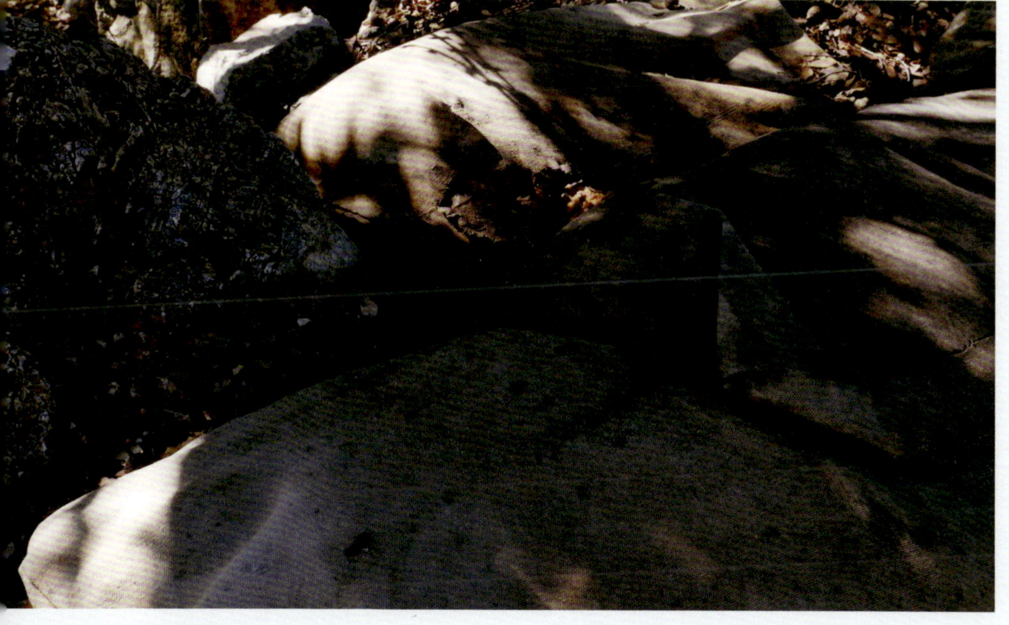

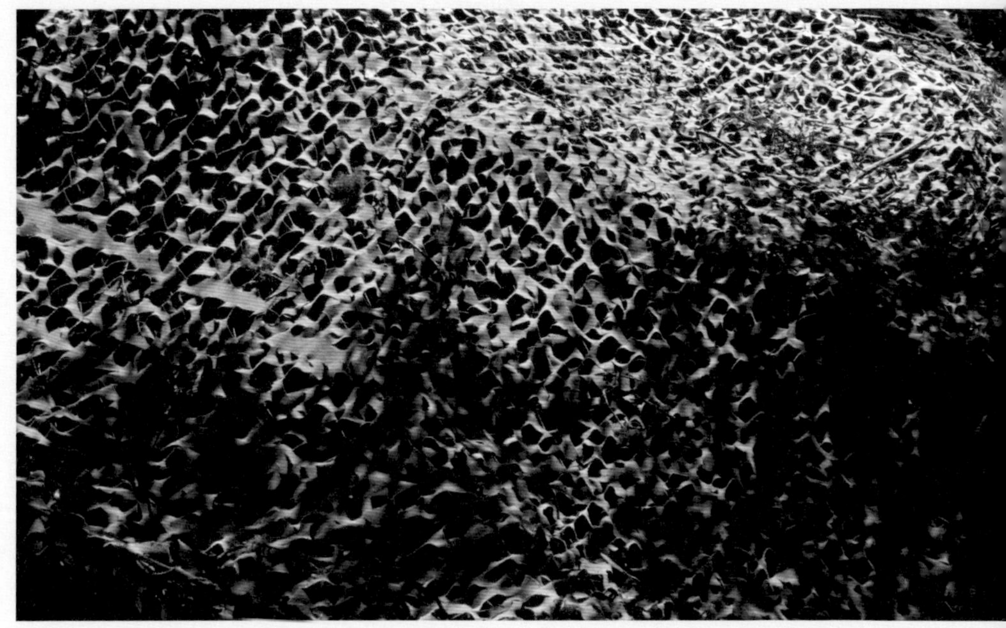

[crickets chirping]

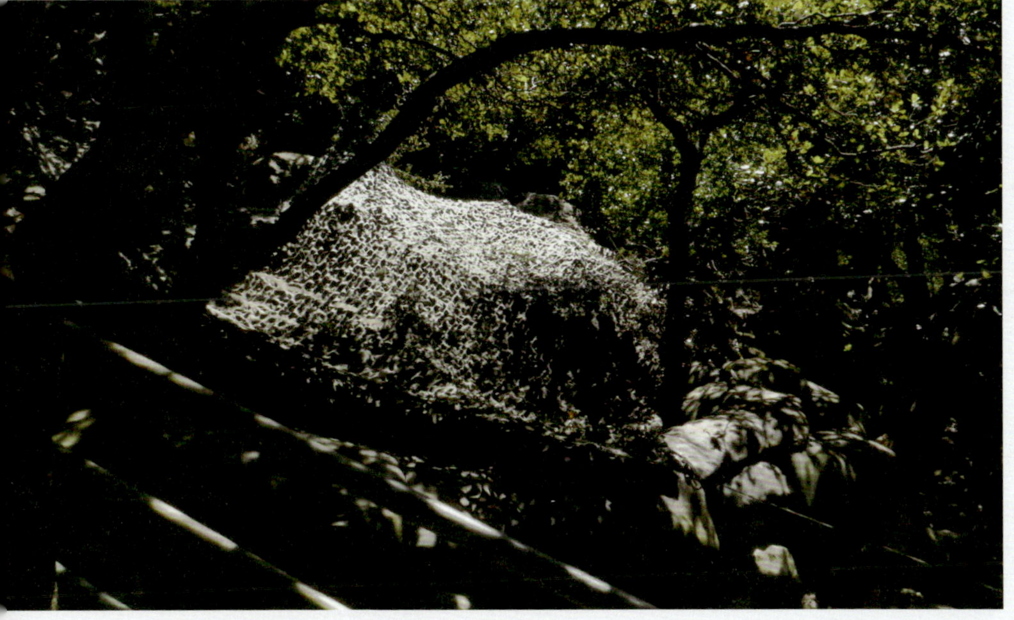

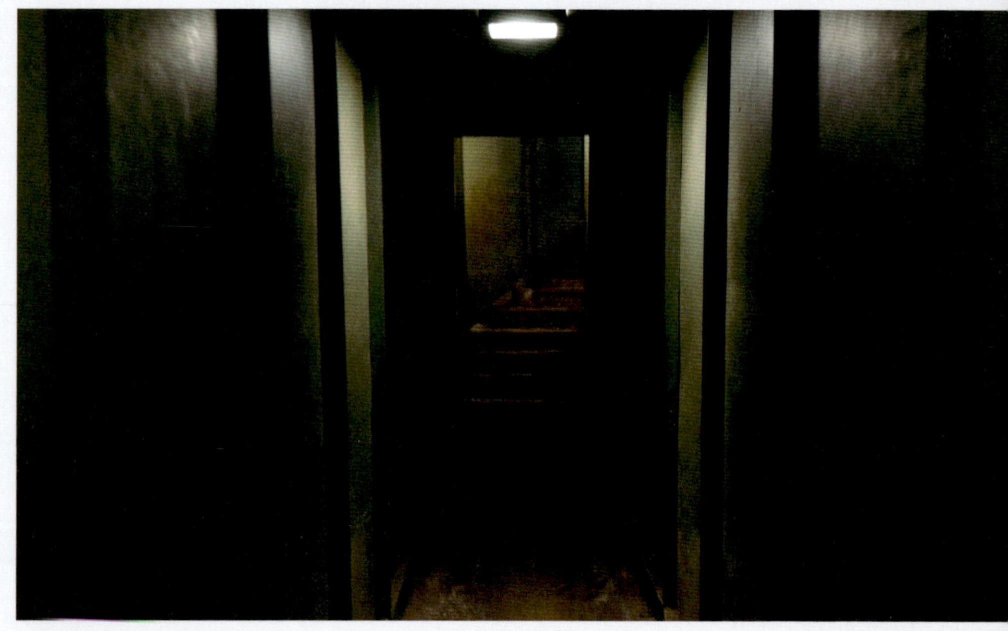

[footsteps]

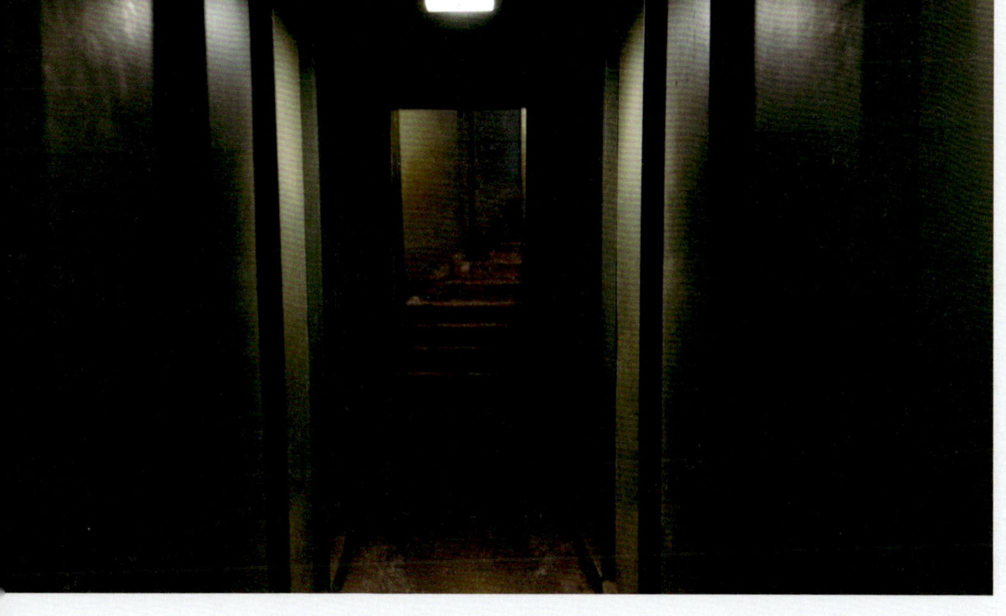

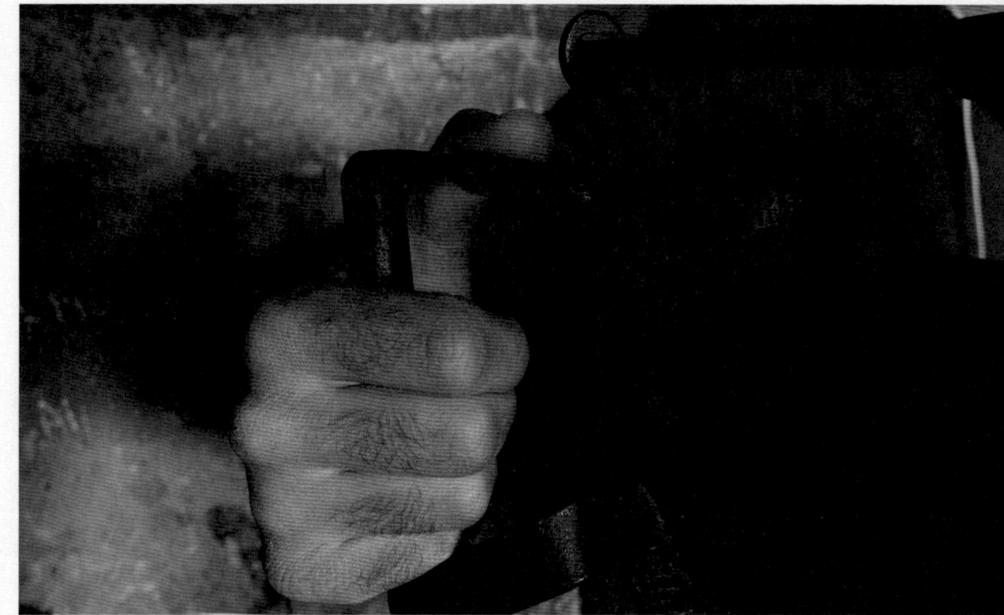

[dry silence]

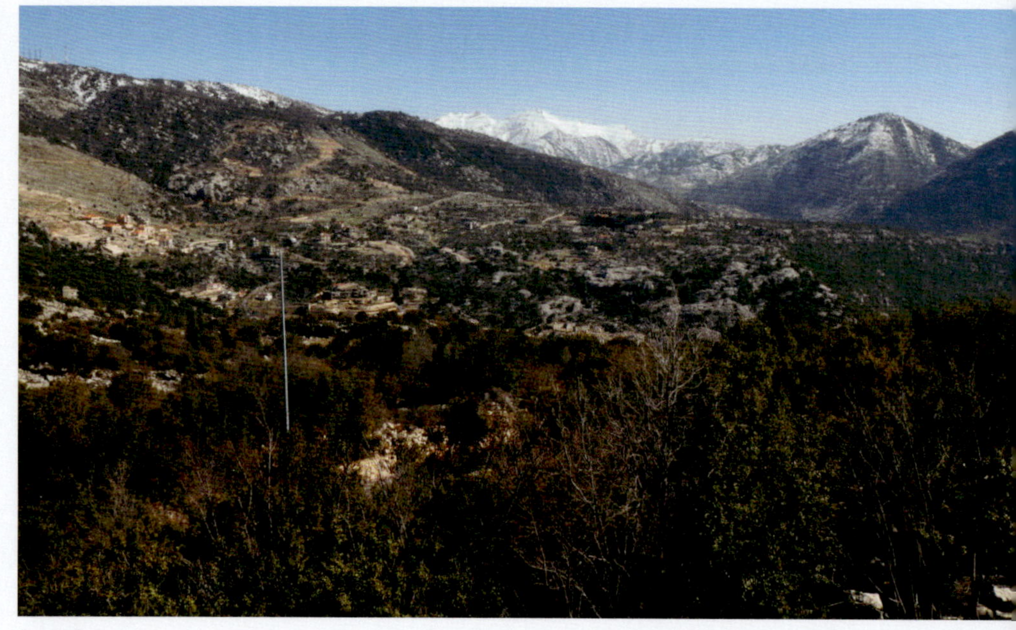

[siren]

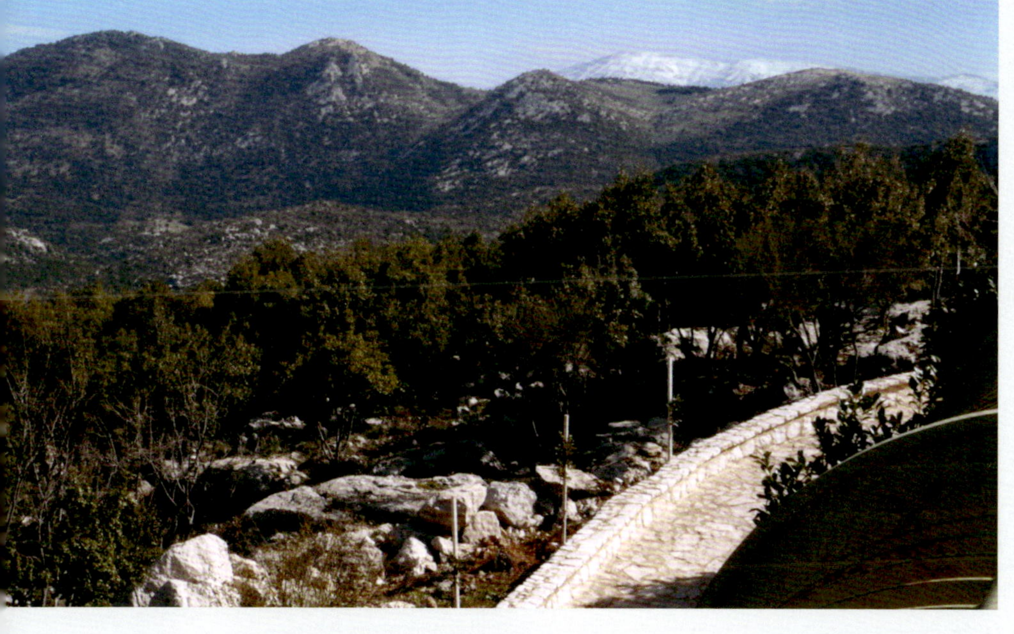

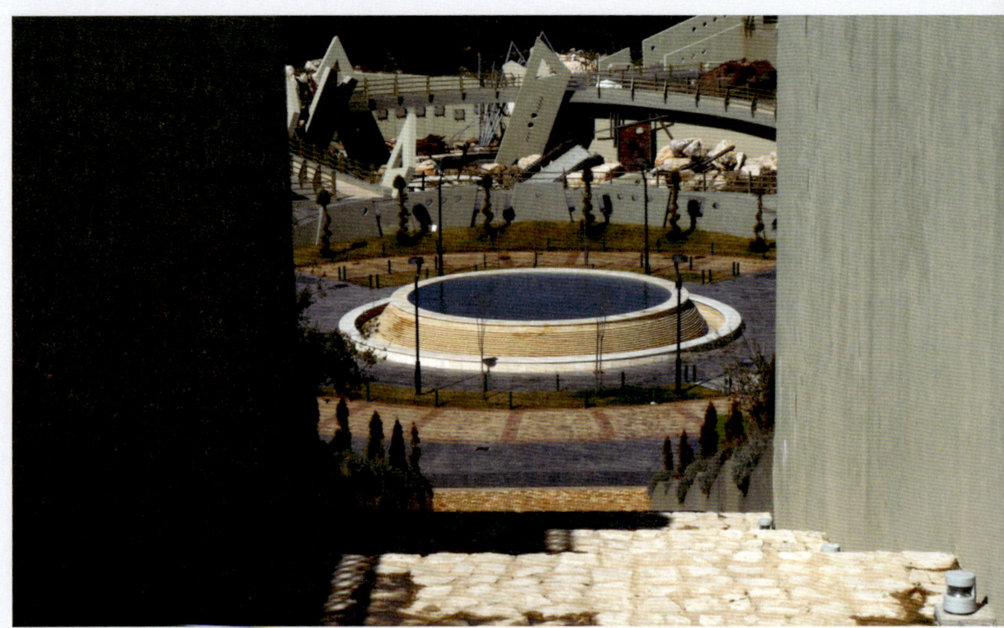

[distant film soundtrack, flag fluttering in the wind, howling foxes, footsteps]

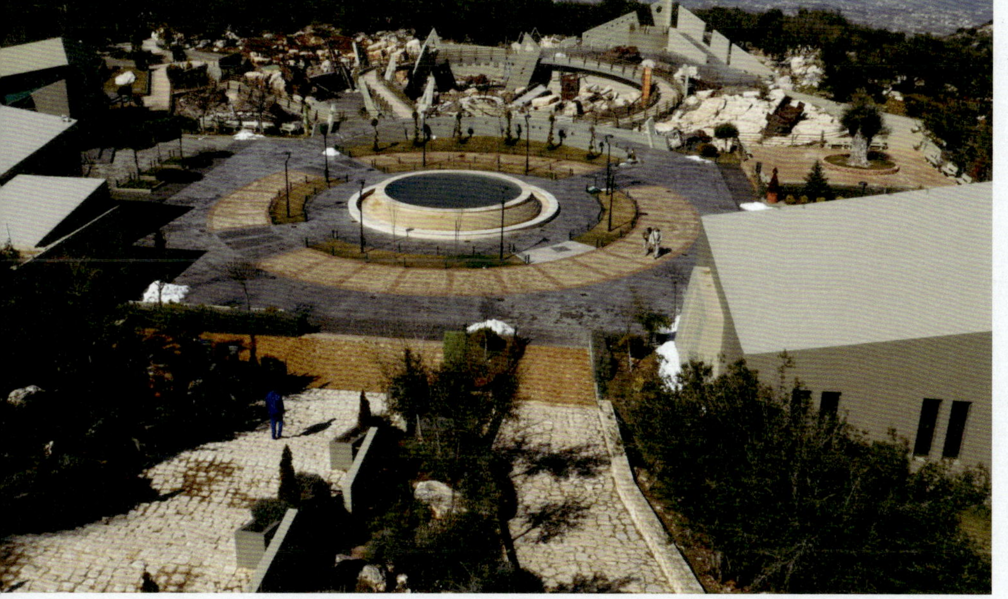

Militancy and Violence

1

"Do not think that one has to be sad in order to be a militant, even though the thing one is fighting is abominable" Foucault, Deleuze, and Guattari 2003, XIII.

Militant-image practice is involved in concrete struggles against existing forms of subjugation. I first want to analyse, on a deeper structural level, where militancy and militant-image production are located. In this chapter, I examine militancy through different theoretical and activist reflections about relations between power, violence, and liberation in texts by Klaus Viehmann, Walid el-Houri, Nick Montgomery and carla bergman, Frantz Fanon, Hannah Arendt, Walter Benjamin, and Judith Butler. This selection of writers and activists represents knowledge from a Western context as well as postcolonial and decolonising thought from Western and non-Western discourses. In allowing these approaches to speak with one another, Western knowledge from during and after the Second World War is placed in proximity to postcolonial and decolonising discourses and practices from the same period of time. This re-reading opens the contradictions inherent to questions of power, violence, and liberation. The contradictions within the militant image are thereby also addressed.

Militancy, a Contested Term 1.1

"Militancy would neither be based on violence nor nonviolence, but on political efficiency and purposefulness" Viehmann 2007.[1]

Klaus Viehmann, a typesetter, writer, and former member of the *Bewegung 2. Juni* (2 June Movement),[2] writes that militancy can be defined as a strategic struggle based on efficiency and purposefulness that includes both violent and nonviolent means. According to the activists

---

1   Translated by Sandra Schäfer. "Militanz wäre weder ein auf Gewalt noch Gewaltlosigkeit, sondern auf politischer Effizienz und Zielgerichtetheit ausgelegter Weg" (Viehmann 2007, 125).

2   The *Bewegung 2. Juni* was an anarchist urban guerrilla group based in West Berlin and active between 1971 and 1980. The organisation grew out of several smaller militant groups and former members of the *Rote Armee Fraktion* (RAF | Red Army Faction). The name refers to the date in 1967 when the student Benno Ohnesorg was shot by the policeman Karl-Heinz Kurras. The *Bewegung 2. Juni* fought against the generation that had participated in the Nazi regime and its continuations after the war. The group organised bombings against public authorities, robbed banks, and was involved in kidnapping representatives of the state and the economy. It managed to free several political prisoners. Unlike the RAF, its members only went underground when they were forced to. The group stopped its activities by 1980. Some of its members joined the RAF or other militant groups.

Nick Montgomery and carla bergman, militancy often evokes an image of machismo, militarism, and violence Montgomery and Bergman 2017, 30–31. In her description of the different generations of the *Rote Armee Fraktion*, Charity Scribner draws a distinction between its militant beginnings and its terrorist activities in the 1970s Scribner 2015, 2.[3] In doing so, she refers to the increasing physical violence of the RAF's actions after 1970. Here "militancy" seems to have a slightly positive connotation, whereas "terrorism" seems to cast a value judgement on violent acts. Viehmann's definition of militancy, on the other hand, has a clearly positive undertone and includes both physical and non-physical violence. First and foremost, however, it is defined as a long-term political commitment. According to Viehmann, militancy is an attitude towards life that can lead to emancipation on an individual and social level Viehmann 2007, 125.

It is interesting to note that during the student protests, both parties—the students and the state—used the term "terror" to denounce the violent behaviour of the other side. The *Außerparlamentarische Opposition* (APO | Extra-Parliamentary Opposition),[4] for example, characterised the prison verdict against the journalist Beate Klarsfeld, who had slapped Chancellor Georg Kiesinger in the face, as "judiciary terror" Der Spiegel 1969, 23.[5] The *Sozialistischer Studentenbund* (SDS | Socialist German Student Union)[6] in Frankfurt used the slogan "Terrorise the terrorists", referring to the state with its executive and political power. The *Frankfurter Allgemeine Zeitung* replied with the declaration: "It is time to break the terror" Der Spiegel 1969, 23, alluding, in turn, to the occupation of universities and the broken windows at Deutsche Bank and the stock exchange building.

The crucial question of whether violence is a legitimate means—and for whom—is central to whether someone is called a freedom fighter or a

3   Compare with the self-definition of the RAF discussed on page 51.
4   The APO expanded with the rise of the student movement in West Germany during the 1960s. It was formed by the *Sozialistischer Studentenbund* (SDS), amongst other groups, in opposition to the grand coalition of Christian Democrats and Social Democrats.
5   Together with her husband, Serge Klarsfeld, Beate Klarsfeld investigated perpetrators of the National Socialist German Workers' Party. Chancellor Kiesinger joined the Nazi Party in 1933. Starting in 1940, he was Deputy Director of the broadcasting department and maintained relations to the *Reichspropagandaministerium* (Ministry of Propaganda). Klarsfeld accused Kiesinger of distributing antisemitic news although he knew about the Holocaust.
6   The *Sozialistischer Studenbund* was a political association of students in West Germany and West Berlin that existed from 1946 to 1970. Until 1962, it represented the university union of the Social Democrats. In 1962, the Social Democrats excluded the SDS from their party. From 1962 until its dissolution in 1970, the SDS was the only socialist university association independent from any party. Beginning in 1966, it joined the West German *Außerparlamentarische Opposition* (APO) and followed an anti-authoritarian socialism.

terrorist. Members of the RAF referred to themselves as an urban guerrilla group whereas the West German state declared them to be terrorists. The use of this term usually implies that the specific group or action in question has been denied a logical cause.

In his research on Hezbollah's culture of resistance, the media theoretician Walid el-Houri addresses an international readership from many countries—including the United States, Canada, France, Australia, and the Arab League—that officially classify Hezbollah as a terrorist organisation.[7] El-Houri compares this classification with Michel Foucault's definition of madness as a pathological category that helps to stabilise the system of the "reasonable" party. In this sense, the classification of the terroristic Other plays a stabilising role in existing systems of power Houri 2012, 8. It does not, however, grasp the actual contradictions and complexities of the organisation. The writers Mona Harb and Reinoud Leenders point out the limitations of two common analyses of Hezbollah within academia: those characterising it as a terrorist organisation and those highlighting only its civic achievements. According to Harb and Leenders, both approaches fail to understand the diverse strategies and aspects of Hezbollah's way of working: the many links between its civic and military work, as well as its comprehensive policy network Harb and Leenders 2005, 192.[8]

The Red Army Faction defined itself as an urban guerrilla group engaging in "a revolutionary method of intervention" to fight against the state apparatus, imperialism, and fascism ID-Verlag and RAF 1997, 41. In adopting the concept of urban guerrilla warfare, it followed the Latin American model. Its name refers, however, to the Red Army of the Soviet Union, one of the allies that liberated several countries, including Germany, from fascism ibid.. Alluding to the RAF as a military organisation was a provocation and is, in my view, problematic. The army represents the state as one of its law-keeping forces. The name thus contradicts the group's initial tactical guerrilla practice. The RAF was, however, pushed into a military practice by the pressure of the police—with its new "grid inves-

---

7   The European Union, New Zealand, and the United Kingdom have proscribed Hezbollah's military wing as a terrorist organisation. Germany also differentiates between the military and political activities of Hezbollah. Journalist Ronen Steinke explains that one of the largest Lebanese exile communities in Europe lives in Germany; among them are 950 active members of Hezbollah. The German embassy in Lebanon is in contact with Hezbollah. The Foreign Ministry in Germany hesitates to damage its relations with Hezbollah and lose its role as a negotiator—particularly in the conflicts between Hezbollah and Israel (Steinke 2019).

8   Hezbollah, however, has a much more multi-dimensional perception of its enemies (Harb and Leenders 2005, 181–82). This does not, however, deny the organisation's antisemitic and racist discourse.

tigations" and other methods.[9] This was not the case for organisations like the *Bewegung 2. Juni*, the *Revolutionäre Zellen* (RZ | Revolutionary Cells),[10] or the feminist group *Rote Zora*,[11] because their members only went underground if they were forced to. Otherwise, they lived legally, carried out their professions, and pursued their militant activities. In doing so, they stayed in close contact and exchange with their political base.

In the 1970s, with the radicalisation of groups like the RAF, the *Bewegung 2. Juni*, and the *Tupamaros München*,[12] the use of physical violence as a means to change the violent system of the state was highly debated. Some members of the West German left saw violence as a tactic of the state and claimed that the left would never be as successful in its deployment Fischer 1977.[13] The use of physical violence for political ends is still widely contested among activists today, triggering, for example, a controversial discussion after the 2001 protests against the G8 summit in Genoa Attac Koordinierungskreis 2001; Fischer 1977.

> "'Militancy' is a loaded word for some, evoking images of machismo and militarism. For us, militancy means combativeness and a willingness to fight, but fighting might look like a lot of different things. It might mean the struggle against internalized shame and oppression; fierce support for a friend or loved one; the courage to sit with trauma; a quiet act of sabotage; the persistence to recover subjugated

9   The "grid investigation" was developed under the direction of the German policeman Horst Herold, who was President of the Federal Office of Criminal Investigation between 1971 and 1981. As a student, Horst Herold was a member of the leftist *Sozialistischer Deutscher Studentenbund* (SDS). He therefore knew the contexts and frameworks within which the RAF operated. During his mandate, he reshaped the techniques and methods of criminal investigation.

10   The *Revolutionäre Zellen* was an extreme leftist group that belonged to the autonomous movement and was active in West Germany between 1970 and 1990. The group was organised in a decentralised way. Its members did not live underground and were part of legal political organisations. Its militant activities included attempted assassinations and attacks.

11   *Rote Zora* was a radical leftist and feminist organisation in West Germany. Initially part of the *Revolutionäre Zellen* before separating in the 1980s, *Rote Zora* legitimised armed struggle with feminist theory. Similar to the *Revolutionäre Zellen*, its members lived legally, which is why many of their militant activities went unpunished.

12   The *Tupamaros München* was a radical leftist group in West Germany that borrowed its name from the *Tupamaros* in Uruguay. Beginning in 1969, the group committed several attacks on the University of Munich and institutions of the police.

13   In 1977, there was, for example, a discussion about the use of physical violence among the *Spontis*, a West German leftist group that regarded the spontaneity of the masses as the primary revolutionary element. One of its members, Joschka Fischer—who later became the German Minister of Foreign Affairs and a leading member of the Green party—argued that the use of violence should never be legitimised by the violence of the police. In doing so, Fischer claimed, one internalises violence and becomes the same as the police. Instead, liberation from violence is necessary so that it cannot become powerful inside the movement itself (Fischer 1977, 56–57). It is strange to read Fischer's text if one is familiar with his later role in state politics.

traditions; drawing lines in the sand; or simply the willingness to risk. We are intentionally bringing joy and militancy together, with the aim of thinking through the connections between fierceness and love, resistance and care, combativeness and nurturance" Montgomery and bergman 2017, 30–31.

Similar to Viehman, Montgomery and bergman highlight the process-oriented transformation of militancy that takes place on an individual and social level ibid., 34. In their book *Joyful Militancy*, militancy is described as a situated practice that does not start from prefabricated ideas, abstract ideologies, or moral commitments. Instead, it is a necessity felt in everyday life in relation to others. Montgomery and bergman state that "rather than boiling joyful militancy down to a fixed way of being or a set of characteristics, we see it arising in and through the relationships that people have with each other. This means it will always look different, based on the emergent connections, relationships, and convictions that animate it" ibid., 77. In relating the term "joy" to militancy, Montgomery and bergman contradict the common image of the militant as sad, bitter, and violent. They draw a distinction, however, between joy and happiness. The latter has become the ultimate goal of life in neoliberal capitalism, which regards unhappiness as a disorder. In contrast to happiness, joy can include a variety of contradictory emotions like rage, despair, fear, happiness, tenderness, and power. It is part of a process that is "transformative, dangerous, painful, and powerful but also somewhat elusive" ibid., 64–65. In practice, joyful militancy appears as relations between people that open a space in the existing system of subjugation.

Power, Violence, and Decolonisation   1.2

"What makes man a political being is his faculty of action … to embark on something new" Arendt 1970, 82.

The joy of action is exactly what the philosopher Hannah Arendt admires in the student movement, along with the fight against the bureaucracy of the university ibid., 15–16. According to Arendt, there are no longer opposing classes. Instead, there is a system; and it is the system of bureaucracy that challenges people to act violently because "in a fully developed bureaucracy there is nobody left with whom one can argue, to whom one can present grievances, on whom the pressures of power can be exerted. Bureaucracy is the form of government in which everybody is deprived of political freedom, of the power to act; for the rule by Nobody is not no-rule, and where all are equally powerless we have a tyranny without a tyrant" ibid., 81. Arendt writes her reflections on power and violence after her experience of racial persecution during the Second World War and after following the Eichmann trial, in which Adolf Eichmann, a pivotal figure in implementing the "Final Solution", retreated in his role to that of a bureaucrat who was only obeying the rules Arendt 2006. Furthermore, Arendt witnessed nuclear armament during the Cold War, the protests of students in Europe and the United States, and the struggles of the American civil rights movement.

> "The colonized man finds his freedom in and through violence"
> Fanon 1963, 86.

In his analysis of decolonisation, the psychiatrist and philosopher Frantz Fanon presents a distinct position towards the use of violence by the colonised to liberate themselves from the colonisers. Born in the French colony of Martinique, Fanon joined the Free French Forces during the Second World War to fight against the Vichy regime. After the war he studied psychiatry and medicine in Lyon, where his doctoral thesis on the psychological effects of colonial subjugation was rejected by the university. In 1952, he published his research as a book under the title *Black Skin, White Masks* Fanon 2017. One year later, he moved to Algeria to work as a psychiatrist and joined the National Liberation Front (FLN | Arabic: جبهة التحرير الوطني).[14] Shortly before his death, his most recognised book, *The Wretched of the Earth* Fanon 1963, was published.

In this book, Fanon highlights the division of society introduced by the coloniser, who dehumanises the indigenous subject and "turns him into an animal" ibid., 42. Different practices, both institutional and non-institutional, help to stabilise the colonial system by channelling and transforming the anger of the oppressed. One such institution is the church, which preaches a belief in fate that "removes all blame from the oppressor; the cause of misfortunes and of poverty is attributed to God" ibid., 42, 54–55. According to Fanon, even dance can play a permissive role by channelling and transforming aggression into bodily movement. Fanon concludes that "the circle of the dance is a permissive circle: it protects and permits" ibid., 57. Although dance, possession, and different practices of singing or producing sound can play this role, they also contain the

14   Today the FLN is a socialist-oriented party in Algeria. It was established in 1954 as one of the main nationalist movements during the Algerian War (1954–1962). This war led to Algeria's independence from France in 1962. The FLN became the sole legal and ruling political party of the Algerian state. After mass protests in 1988, Algeria became a multi-party state.

possibility of resistance. This brings to mind certain scenes from Gillo Pontecorvo's film *La battaglia di Algeri* (The Battle of Algiers, 1966) that depict the resistance that broke out in December 1960, three years after the French claimed to have eliminated the leadership of the National Liberation Front through the use of torture, disappearance, and execution. In the film, protesters appear in the streets accompanied by the sound of women ululating. Ululation is a practice in which women join together to make a high-pitched vocal sound, forming a vibrant sound pattern that fills the space. In Arabic cultures, women often perform this practice to articulate happiness or moments of passage. Ululation is used, for example, during marriages, when the bride leaves her family and enters the groom's home. However, it is also used in Palestine when the body of someone who has been killed by the Israeli military is brought back to the family. In the case of *La battaglia di Algeri*, ululating becomes a collective act of resistance. Pontecorvo edits the film in such a way that this sound accompanies scenes of protest until Algeria is ultimately liberated from the French colonisers at the end of the film.

According to Fanon, violence is a necessary means for the colonised to destroy the colonies [ibid., 86]. However, he highlights the irrational aspect of violent action [ibid., 41]. Furthermore, his writing emphasises that independence is not sufficient to guarantee liberation for African peoples [ibid., 36]. Fanon asserts that the process of decolonisation changes the colonised completely: "It brings a natural rhythm into existence, introduced by new men, and with it a new language and a new humanity. Decolonization is the veritable creation of new men" [ibid., 36]. This process differs from Négritude,[15] which opposes the French colonising system by engaging in a racial identity for black people worldwide. According to Fanon, however, Négritude simply mirrors the racialisation of the coloniser [ibid., 214]. Fanon describes the collective act of violence as having a unifying effect at the level of the group and, at the same time, a cleansing effect at the level of the individual. This experience of unity, he asserts, is the basis for building a new nation [ibid., 94].

The filmmaker and journalist Philip Rizk describes the Egyptian revolution of 2011 as "an uprising of discontent against the political reality within the neo-colonial condition" [Rizk 2014]. In 1961, Fanon already analysed this neo-colonial condition as a risk [Fanon 1963, 44]. He emphasised that

15   The ideas of Négritude were developed by francophone intellectuals in the 1930s, including Aimé Césaire from Martinique, Léopold Sédar Senghor from Senegal, and Léon Damas from French Guiana. In an attempt to revolt against the racism and injustice of colonisation, they turned the word *négre*, a derogatory term exclusively used by the French, into Négritude. According to Aimé Césaire, the acceptance of "Blackness" could help to decolonise the mind.

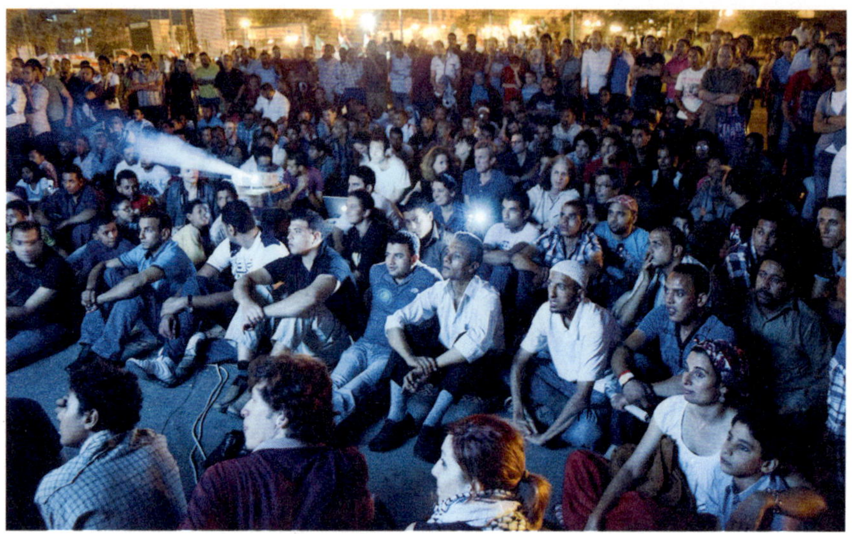

Tahrir Cinema (Arabic: سينما التحرير), 14 July 2011, photograph: Sherief Gaber, Mosireen

after colonialism, a new elite takes over the leading role of the coloniser. In this process, the new leadership collaborates with the coloniser's international enterprises and organisations, thereby exploiting the local resources and workforce ibid., 73. Rizk points out that the Egyptian revolution was preceded by protests against the devastating working conditions experienced by precarious workers, which he distinguishes from the classical working class Rizk 2014. Furthermore, the 2011 uprising was carried out by a diverse group of people—not just by a young middle class, as is often mistakenly reported.[16] And although the internet played a crucial role in distributing information, the most important site of the revolution was the street. The sociologist Asef Bayat asserts that for ordinary people who have no access to institutional positions of power, the street is the most important site for politics. It represents the space where people can protest their concerns and share them with a wider public Bayat 2012, 210.[17] Bayat highlights the spatial aspect of revolutions. He explains that in Cairo, for example, Tahrir Square (Arabic: ميدان التحرير | Liberation Square) became the centre of the uprising because it was easy for big crowds to gather there. Furthermore, it was close to al-Azhar mosque (Arabic: جامع الأزهر) as well as the intellectual cafés and bookshops in Kasr

16   Since interviews for international and national news were predominantly conducted with young, educated, English-speaking members of the middle class, this impression could easily emerge.

17   I refer to the revised German version of Bayat's book *Life as Politics* from 2010, as this edition includes texts that focus on the Egyptian revolution of 2011 (Bayat 2010).

el-Nil (Arabic: قصر النيل) and Tal'at Harb (Arabic: طلعت حرب)—including the historical Café Riche, where the Egyptian revolution of 1952 was
planned. Additionally, Tahrir Square was easily reachable by public trans-
port and people could disappear into its small surrounding streets if the
police dispersed the crowd [ibid., 197-206]. During the revolution, the non-profit
media collective Mosireen[18] (Arabic: مصرّين | We are determined) used
Tahrir Square and the space of the street to screen works about the protests. From 8 July through 1 August 2011 (when the project was dissolved
by the Egyptian military police) the collective ran the Tahrir Cinema on
the square. Additional screenings were organised in the streets of different neighbourhoods, where, as an alternative form of distributing information, Mosireen showed videos about specific local conflicts. These
became part of the 858 Revolutionary Archive, which was released in
February 2018 and contains 858 hours of video footage [858 Initiative n.d.]. Raw
and unedited, it excavates histories that the current regime has tried
to silence from the public sphere and erase from collective memory. The
collection includes videos of disturbing violent acts that contradict the
revolution's international representation as a relatively peaceful protest.

> "Power and violence are opposites; where the one rules absolutely,
> the other is absent" [Arendt 1970, 56].

Hannah Arendt is critical of Fanon's legitimisation of violence as a necessary means to achieve liberation and decolonisation [ibid., 65]. Although
Arendt agrees with Fanon's idea that collectively experienced violence
makes the individual disappear and that confronting death intensifies and
alters the experience of collectivity and the self, she claims that this is des-
tined to change once the threat of death has disappeared. Nevertheless, examples like the revolution in Cuba, where the same guerrilla fighters later
continued to work in the government, demonstrate the opposite. Arendt's
criticism of Fanon as well as her dismissal of the Black Power movement
[ibid., 19-20] testify to her presumption of the cultural superiority of Europe.[19]

---

18   Mosireen's activities comprise filmmaking, filmmaking workshops, an archive, and distribution. During
      the Egyptian uprising, it collected videos by many different producers about specific events. These
      were then screened in local neighbourhoods and contexts (Mosireen Collective n.d.).
19   As Judith Butler points out, Arendt's Eurocentrism becomes apparent in a letter written to Karl Jaspers
      during the Eichmann trial. In this letter, Arendt introduces a hierarchy that distinguishes between Euro-
      pean and Arab Jews (J. Butler 2013b, 139). Arendt writes: "My first impression. On top, the judges, the
      best of German Jewry. Below them, the persecuting attorneys, Galicians, but still Europeans. Every-
      thing is organized by a police force that gives me the creeps, speaks only Hebrew and looks Arabic.
      Some downright brutal types among them. They would follow any order. And outside, the oriental mob,
      as if one were in Istanbul or some other half-Asiatic country. In addition, and very visible in Jerusalem,
      the peies and caftan Jews, who make life impossible for all the reasonable people here" (Arendt 1992,
      434-36).

According to Arendt, Fanon's approach of deriving violence from life is problematic: "Fanon concludes his praise of the practice of violence by remarking that in this kind of struggle the people realize 'that life is an unending contest', that violence is an element of life" [ibid., 69]. Although Arendt admits that being moved is necessary, she argues that violence can be rational and effective only if it is used for short-term aims [ibid., 79]. In placing violence and power in opposition to one another, Arendt introduces an important distinction. According to her, violence can destroy power, but it can never create it. Because power always requires the support of many, it needs a base—even in totalitarianism: "No government exclusively based on the means of violence has ever existed. Even the totalitarian ruler, whose chief instrument of rule is torture, needs a power basis—the secret police and its net of informers" [ibid., 50].[20] Furthermore, Arendt argues that the use of violence varies according to its means. She criticises pseudo-scientific military methods that assume their goals can be calculated.[21] Guerrilla warfare, on the other hand, can potentially defeat a well-equipped army.

Power, being "consent based", is, according to Arendt, always nonviolent. She thus argues that the foundation of the state and the exercise of collective freedom and the law are nonviolent. Violence, on the other hand, is always coercive. Arendt therefore refuses the strategy of militancy, as it pertains to a small group attempting to impose its opinion on a larger one. Nevertheless, she argues that revolution can be a means to change a system because the basis for the new system can be the consent of the many—and therefore uncoerced. Arendt develops a theoretical system according to which violence is defined as coercive and power is defined as nonviolent. If the law were based on violence, it would be illegitimate.

Here it is worth considering Walter Benjamin's "Critique of Violence" [Benjamin 1999]. In contrast to Arendt, Benjamin suggests that something like fate can precede the law. As a consequence, the law can be violent. This contradicts Arendt's concept of the law as an alternative to violence. It is understandable that Arendt develops her ideas and formulates a vocabulary that separates violence and the law after being confronted with the Holocaust and the Second World War. However,

---

20   This process is analysed in Gilles Pontecorvo's *La battaglia di Algeri* with regard to the role played by the French colonisers in Algeria (Pontecorvo 1966).

21   Arendt points out that during the Cold War—the peace policy that continues war by other means—nuclear war cannot be considered a continuation of politics, but is, instead, a universal suicide (Arendt 1970, 9–10).

her vocabulary does not recognise a troubling aspect inherent to the democratic system of the law, which Benjamin analyses in his "Critique of Violence".

Violence, Ruptures, and Looking Back 1.3

"Law-making is power-making, and, to that extent, an immediate manifestation of violence" Benjamin 1999, 295. Benjamin's text was written before the Second World War, which is why it doesn't anticipate fascism's assault on the rule of law and parliamentary institutions, the millions murdered in German concentration camps, and the development of nuclear weapons. However, in 1920, one year before Benjamin finished his essay, the first "general strike"[22] in German history defeated the Kapp Putsch[23] lead by conservative and pre-fascist groups. This strike was followed by huge workers' protests in the Ruhr district. The "Red Ruhr Strikes" were crushed in April 1920 by military and para-military troops.

In his "Critique of Violence", Walter Benjamin demonstrates that the law can't be treated as an alternative to violence. For Judith Butler, "Benjamin's text is notoriously difficult" J. Butler 2013b, 71 because it introduces a set of distinctions. Benjamin differentiates between two systems of law: natural and positive law. In natural law, the use of violent means to reach just objectives is not considered to be an issue Benjamin 1999, 277. The problem with this is obvious: the discourse between the radical left and authoritarian conservatism becomes indistinguishable Zelik 2014, 1. In contrast to natural law, positive law is predominantly concerned with the question of whether something has happened in the framework of the law and does not criticise its ends Benjamin 2003, 278.

Benjamin highlights that for the liberal, state violence as such is not the problem; rather, it is the question of whether those who exercise the law are eligible to do so. To develop this further, Benjamin analyses the right to strike. He points out that apart from the state, organised labour is

22   This action did not include a strike in the individual households of reproductive labour and is in this sense not really a general strike. As the author Silvia Federici points out: "This is why we need to understand the double character of this work [reproductive labour], so that we refuse that part of the work that reproduces us for capital … I think that one of the most important discoveries the women's movement made was that we could refuse some of this work without jeopardising the well-being of our families and communities" (Vishmidt 2013).

23   The Kapp Putsch was an attempted coup that took place on 13 March 1920. It aimed to undo the German Revolution (1918–1919), overthrow the Weimar Republic, and install a right-wing autocratic government.

the only entity that is legally able to execute violence. According to Benjamin, the right to strike can be accepted by the state because not working is an act of escaping the violence of the employer rather than practising violence ^{Benjamin 1999, 281}. The strike is seen as legal if it forces the employer to pay higher salaries, but it is illegal if it aims to overthrow the state. It is, therefore, not the means that are decisive, but the intentions or the ends. In military law, Benjamin continues, the results of war can be the basis for peace in the law-making process that follows. He concludes that violence and the law are inseparably tied ^{Benjamin 2003, 283}.

According to Benjamin, "all violence as a means is either law-making or law-preserving" ^{ibid., 287}. Law-preserving violence, which is performed by the police and the judicial system, is always a demonstration of power. It is an institutionalised, daily effort to bind subjects to the law. Law-making violence, on the other hand, occurs when a polity comes into being and the law is created. Whereas Arendt understands revolution as a means to instate law and to express the consent of the people, Benjamin assumes that the law originates in something called "fate". Judith Butler argues that "law is thus a specific consequence of an angry act that responds to an injury, but neither that injury nor that anger are circumscribed in advance by law ... Fate establishes the coercive conditions of law through manifesting the subject of guilt; its effect is to bind the person to the law" ^{J. Butler 2013b, 78–79}. Benjamin concludes that "law-making is power-making, and, to that extent, an immediate manifestation of violence" ^{Benjamin 1999, 295}. Law-keeping violence is, in a way, a side effect of law-instating violence.

For Benjamin, power and violence are always entangled in an action that aims for specific ends. Enacting the aim will always be an act of power and violence. Benjamin offers the proletarian general strike as an example of an event that can disrupt this circle. Unlike the political strike, the general strike does not aim to create a new juridical order; it is a means without ends. It therefore belongs to the messianic ^{ibid., 291}. Benjamin calls it "anarchistic" ^{ibid., 291–92}. Anarchism should not be misunderstood as "anything goes", as it still follows the commandment "Thou shalt not kill" ^{ibid., 298}. According to Benjamin, anarchism is neither the establishment of another political system nor an alternative to positive law. For Judith Butler, however, "it constantly recurs as the condition of positive law and as its necessary limit" ^{J. Butler 2013b, 86}.

I would nevertheless argue that although violence is not the appropriate tool to reach justice, it is, in certain political situations, a legitimate and necessary means of resistance. But how is it possible to escape the entanglements of law and violence? How is it possible to interrupt this continuous circle of violence that, according to Benjamin, even a revolution cannot stop?[24]

Judith Butler develops an answer to these questions in her book *Parting Ways* and draws a link between the messianic in Benjamin's "Critique of Violence" and "Concept of History". Butler's reflection was published during a period in which she faced immense hostility after her nomination for the 2012 Adorno Prize in Frankfurt. She was denounced for allegedly attributing Hamas and Hezbollah to the progressive left during a 2006 teach-in at the University of California, Berkeley and for supporting the Boycott, Divestment, and Sanctions (BDS) campaign against particular Israeli institutions and products. She was thus accused of being antisemitic Schlüter 2012. In answering these accusations, Butler explained that she associated Hamas and Hezbollah with the "global left" because both organisations define themselves as anti-imperialist. She did not, however, support these organisations; her understanding of nonviolence would make that impossible J. Butler 2013a. She also pointed to her book *Parting Ways*, which addresses the question of Israel and Palestine and insists on nonviolence ibid.. In this polarised climate, however, her elaborate critique of Zionism and her support of Palestine make her appear as a militant figure. Her critique challenges the normative frames of Zionism as well as its colonial subjugation of Palestine and is therefore unacceptable for some. Facing these hostilities despite her longstanding intellectual engagement made Butler feel deeply hurt, as she stated in the magazine *Die Zeit* ibid..

According to Butler, the messianic is not meant as a future-to-come, but as "chips" and "sparks" that appear in the present. The messianic creates what Benjamin calls a *Jetztzeit* (now-time) Benjamin 2003, 395. Butler points out that "to achieve the now, or to somehow allow the now to take place, happens only on the condition of a certain expiation" J. Butler 2013b, 92. She refers to the general strike as an example. The general strike is only possible if forgiveness takes place and relieves workers and citizens from the bonds of the oppressive state in order to bring the system to a halt. This implies negating the state in its completeness and freeing oneself from the bonds of guilt that it attempts to create. For this to happen, citizens and workers first have to say no to the state.

---

24   Benjamin claims that revolution is not the road to justice, as it is not able to step out of the circle of establishing a new order based on violence and power. Instead, revolution provokes rebellious reactions that attempt to establish a new law (Benjamin 1999, 300).

"There is no document of culture which is not at the same time a document of barbarism" _{Benjamin 2003, 392}.

In Benjamin's text, the messianic appears in the figure of a storm. The storm from paradise doesn't bring a new future. Instead, it compels the angel to look backwards and allows it to see the accumulated wreckage left behind by progress. Progress and barbarism are intertwined; one doesn't exist without the other. As Benjamin points out: "There is no document of culture which is not at the same time a document of barbarism. And just as such a document is never free of barbarism, so barbarism taints the manner in which it was transmitted from one hand to another" ibid., 392.

Progress constitutes a unilinear notion of time that establishes homogeneity and continuity as the substance of history. Benjamin wants to identify moments in which the history of the oppressed emerges in a flash, interrupting the continuum of history that is called progress. He opposes the homogeneity that seeks to monopolise temporality in the form of continuous history. In the flash, the past does not appear as it really was. Instead, it is recognised by historical subjects in a situation of danger ibid., 391.

Rather than naming a human being or a body, the messianic refers to another time—one that comes from the past. Remembrance works for Benjamin in an inverse relation to progressive history. Judith Butler describes it thus: "Such a memory belongs to no one, cannot be understood as anyone's cognitive possession; it is circulating, shattered, lodged in present time; it seems to be a memory carried by things, or the very principle of their breaking up into pieces, perhaps in the form of part-objects, partially animated and partially inorganic and strangely divine; something flashes up from this non-concepualizable amalgam, something that is decidedly not substance" J. Butler 2013b, 106. In the flashes of these moments of rupture within linear and progress-oriented history, militant-image production can emerge. These moments, in which sparks from the oppressed past break through the continuum of progress-oriented time, create a "now-time".

"There are no stories in the riots. Only the ghosts of other stories" Akomfrah 1986.

The 1985 riots in Birmingham and London can be regarded as a flash from the past appearing in the present. In their film *Handsworth Songs* (1986), the Black Audio Film Collective (BAFC)[25] brings the colonial past into close proximity with the riots of black youths in Birmingham's Handsworth neighbourhood. Replying to a journalist's request for a story of the riots, a black woman asserts: "There are no stories in the riots. Only the ghosts of other stories" ibid.. In her statement, she refers to the broken continuities between the present racism in Britain, the riots, British colonialism and imperialism, and the repressed histories of Western modernity.

Handsworth Songs opens with a scene of a black janitor in a museum of machinery from the Industrial Revolution. Repeated several times throughout the film, this scene recalls the Industrial Revolution's complicity with slavery. The film also includes images of African-Caribbeans who arrived in London after the Second World War due to British recruitment and immigration campaigns in the former colonies. We see them leaving ships in fashionable suits and dresses, their faces full of anticipation. A young African-Caribbean migrant sings: "London, this is the place for me, London this lovely city. You can go to France or America, India, Asia, or Australia, but you will come back to London." The song is a hopeful and joyful expression of tenderness towards the capital of England. Years later, this hope will, for many, have disappeared.

The film is careful about how it works with speech and how it includes the voices of those who are usually met with indifference in Britain's dominant white society. Two young men describe the arrival of a new chief inspector in Handsworth: "This new chief inspector that has arrived in Handsworth, he has changed a lot of things ... He started to say that the blacks are drug-pushers and we are using every job on the street ... and call us hooligans and criminals. And since the chief inspector has been here ... he can come and put us in a corner and we can't do anything about it." A young woman states: "The youths are angry. Not only the unemployment ... everybody can feel that. Right? It is the harassment that is going on with the black people in the area" ibid.. *Handsworth Songs* is a dense, poetic, and analytical essay that does not represent the riots. Instead, it traces the radical reactions of young black males within a larger framework of British politics and a history of white domination. "BAFC's use of the archive is an act of witnessing and of remembering and by extension an ethical challenge to dominant society. It is never

---

25 The Black Audio Film Collective was founded in 1982 by John Akomfrah, Lina Gopaul, Reece Auguiste, Avril Johnson, Trevor Mathison, Edward George, David Lawson, and Clare Joseph (Clare Joseph left in 1985 and David Lawson joined that same year). It was active until 1998. As described by the writer Kodwo Eshun, the group claimed "the right to theorise the forms an aesthetic might take in the future" (Eshun 2007, 86). Its filmmaking thus cannot be reduced to a reaction against social crises and hegemonic media representations.

simply a question of constructing a counter narrative to the dominant one, which is still to acknowledge its prior authority, but undermining its very structure through exposing its aporias and contradictions" Fisher 2007. In *Handsworth Songs*, the BAFC develops a poetic form that includes images, music, and spoken word; giving space to the unsayable for a future-to-come.

Theoretical reflections and activist methods differ from one another depending on the individual contexts and struggles they are part of. Militancy, as a situated practice, thus develops from a specific situation and need. By introducing a selection of examples, I have outlined how image production becomes part of the struggle against subjugation. In the following chapter, we will see how the methods of militant-image production are developed in concrete contexts. I will deepen the analysis of such images and develop a methodology of the militant image focusing on particular struggles and the techniques and methods that were developed to address them.

2

The Militant Image

"Expansively, capaciously, exorbitantly: the militant image comprises any form of image or sound—from essay film to fiction feature, from observational documentary to found-footage cinépamphlet, from news-reel to agitational reworkings of colonial film production—produced in and through film-making practices dedicated to the liberation struggles and revolutions of the late twentieth century" Eshun and Gray 2011, 1.

How do moving images bring self-consciousness to struggles against given forms of power? In the following chapter, I introduce a methodology of the militant image based on an analysis of film and media from the 1960s and onwards.[1] During the decolonisation and liberation struggles of the 1960s and 70s, filmmakers developed the term "Militant Cinema" Getino and Solanas 1969; Godard 2016.[2] This was done with an awareness that the radical and political role of film goes back much further, to early twentieth-century filmmakers like Dziga Vertov or Sergei Eisenstein and their use of montage Wayne 2001, 25–33.

In the so-called Third World,[3] decolonisation and anti-imperialism aimed to find new ways out of colonialism and dependence on Western

1   For further reading on militant film and "Third Film", please see: (Eshun and Gray 2011; Gabriel 1982; Wayne 2001). For more on the militant image in artistic practice, see: *The Militant Image Reader* edited by Urban Subjects (Urban Subjects 2015), which was published following the exhibition *The Militant Image* at Camera Austria and a workshop at steirischer herbst (2014). For more information about militant images in the context of Lebanon, please see Zeina Maasri's research on political posters during the Lebanese Civil War (Maasri 2008); the film *Shu'our akbar min el hob* (A Feeling Greater Than Love) by Mary Jirmanus Saba (Jirmanus Saba 2017); Doreen Mende's research on the entanglements of visual practices between the GDR, Lebanon, Palestine, and North Africa (Mende 2013); the film *Off Frame aka Revolution Until Victory* by Mohanad Yaqubi, which works with found documentary footage shot by the Palestine Film Unit (PFU) during the first two years of the Lebanese Civil War in addition to material created by filmmakers and activists from Syria, Italy, the UK, Lebanon, France, Germany, Argentina, and others between 1968 and 1982 during the Palestinian revolution (Yaqubi 2016; 2012); Reem Shilleh's and Mohanad Yaqubi's text on the same topic (Shilleh and Yaqubi 2015); performances by Rabih Mroué and Lina Majdalanie; and projects by the artist Walid Raad, to name just a few.

2   Jean-Luc Godard's manifesto *Que Faire?* was initially published in 1970.

3   The term "Third World" was coined in 1952 by the demographer Alfred Sauvy, who derived it from the Third Estate preceding the French Revolution. According to Sauvy, the Third World comprises those countries that represent the majority of the world but are without rights (Sauvy 1952). At the Bandung Conference in 1955, 23 countries from Asia and Africa adopted the term. Although the Third World was understood as a union of poor countries fighting for better economic conditions, it included the struggle against colonialism and racism and positioned itself as neither aligned with the First World NATO-member states nor associated with the Second World countries of the communist bloc. In 1966, the term was replaced with "Tricontinental" at the Tricontinental Conference in Havana. "Tricontinental" derives from an anti-colonial perspective that ignores set colonial borders. The new term aimed to shift the focus from economic underdevelopment (which the "Third World" was increasingly associated with), emphasising, instead, the process of decolonisation.

capitalism. Cultural production accompanied these revolutionary struggles to bring "a natural rhythm into existence, introduced by new men, and with it a new language and a new humanity" Fanon 1963, 36. In their expansive reader *The Militant Image: A Ciné-Geography*, Kodwo Eshun and Ros Gray state that culture had the potential to create this new language and "to act as an agent of the social transformations that produced these new forms of subjectivity" Eshun and Gray 2011, 8. Eshun and Gray apply Irit Rogoff's concept of relational geography[4] to the different "ciné-cultures" that emerged from and participated in the militant politics of anti-colonial struggle and revolutionary decolonisation in the late twentieth century. Using a selection of well-chosen texts, they analyse the culture of Militant Cinema and "its interdisciplinary practice of mapping the affinities, proximities and affiliations of ciné-cultures" ibid., 2.[5] In returning to instances of Militant Cinema from the second half of the twentieth century, Eshun and Gray engage in a recirculation of these practices, igniting "a revision of the historiography of the present" ibid., 3.

In this context, I use the term "militant image" to include a diverse assortment of moving images encompassing film, television reportage, and contributions to talk shows. Not all of the materials I introduce were classified as militant films or images by their makers. I will therefore explain why I identify these as such. Since militant-image production is an aesthetic practice, I analyse its aesthetics and methods to develop criteria for my own artistic research and practice. The selection is fragmentary and relates to different struggles and periods. I will not undertake an in-depth analysis of individual films and will, instead, focus on analysing the techniques used in their particular historical and political frameworks.

4   The writer and curator Irit Rogoff characterises the networks and exchanges that unfold between different groups, individuals, and activities in Africa, Latin America, and African-American communities in the United States as "a sphere of global exchange and circulation that challenges both the hegemonic supremacy of the colonizer's culture and acknowledges the complex internal network of inter-African migrations and influences and exchanges" (Rogoff 2003, 54). Rogoff develops the concept of "relational geography" for the linked narratives and exchanges that move away from the authority of the nation state as a central point of reference to a more cumulative practice (Rogoff 2003, 56). She highlights that "[several] radical European thinkers of the mid twentieth century … single out the Algerian independence struggle to mark out their own political awakening and radicalization" (Rogoff 2003, 54).

5   Eshun and Gray's reader was published as a special issue of *Third Text*, thus inscribing the journal's practice into this concept. Inaugurated in 1987, *Third Text* is an intervention into the hegemonic art context, challenging the "eurocentric and ethnocentric notions of aesthetic criteria that marginalised —and at times continue to neglect—the work of culturally diverse practitioners" (Third Text 2014). *Third Text* focuses primarily on practices in the Global South, the history and theory of Militant Cinema, revolutionary aesthetics, cultures in transition, and an analysis of neo-colonialism.

The selection includes films from the beginning of Militant Cinema in the 1960s, audiovisuals produced during the radicalisation of the student movement in West Germany in the 1960s and 70s, and films from today. I derive seven criteria for the militant image from analysing these materials. These include open and disruptive form, making film politically, empathy and trans-geographical entanglements, showing is doing, anonymisation and camouflage, beyond "with or against", and militant scripts.

Militant Cinema by Octavio Getino and Fernando Solanas   2.1

> "Our time is one of hypothesis rather than of thesis, a time of works in progress—unfinished, unordered, violent works, made with the camera in one hand and a rock in the other" Getino and Solanas 1969, 9.

In the late 1960s, the Argentinian filmmakers Octavio Getino and Fernando Solanas coined the term "Militant Cinema" in relation to their own filmic practice. They regarded this as the most advanced category of "Third Cinema", a division of filmmaking associated with the liberation struggles of the so-called Third World. Getino and Solanas distinguish Third Cinema from "First Cinema", which they characterise as spectacle for the entertainment of the bourgeoisie (for example, the cinema of Hollywood).[6] "Second Cinema" decolonised the filmic form and reached its limit in the French Nouvelle Vague. Getino and Solanas state that "the Second Cinema filmmaker has remained 'trapped inside the fortress' as Godard put it, or is on his way to becoming trapped" ibid., 4. In contrast to First and Second Cinema, Third Cinema isn't part of the system; instead, it tries to fight it. Contrary to Third Cinema, however, Militant Cinema aims not only to decolonise culture, but "leads to the destruction of neo-colonialism, to the national liberation of our countries and the national construction of Socialism" Getino 2011, 53.

In Argentina, a new military government came to power in 1963. Due to opposition, it implemented widespread censorship that affected the local film industry, particularly the production of Second Cinema. In order to produce their militant films outside of the film industry, Getino and Solanas, together with Gerardo Vallejo, founded the *Grupo Cine Liberación* (The Liberation Film Group).[7] Their filmic practice forms

---

6   "The cinema as a spectacle aimed at a digesting object is the highest point that can be reached by bourgeois film-making" (Getino and Solanas 1969, 4).

7   Formed in the late 1960s, the *Grupo Cine Liberación* was part of the Third Cinema movement along with Raymundo Gleyzer's *Cine de la Base* in Argentina, the Brazilian *Cinema Novo*, the Cuban revolutionary cinema, and the Bolivian film director Jorge Sanjinés (Ranzani 2004).

the basis of their writing about Militant Cinema. Both their films and their texts are characterised by "uncertainty, experimentation, and exposing oneself to failure" Getino and Solanas 1969. Since their aim is to change reality, Getino and Solanas regard their films as inconclusive.[8] This emphasis on process concerns several aspects of their filmmaking. The film *La hora de los hornos* (The Hour of the Furnaces, 1966–68) includes scenes that focus on the occupation of the textile mill La Bernalesa. Female workers speak with pride and enthusiasm about how they managed to keep production running without their employer. This echoes Getino and Solanas's consideration of spectators as co-authors and living protagonists. Those who view the film are seen as part of the struggle, since they risk their lives to attend the screening. In watching the film, they become part of it. Furthermore, screenings are meant to be interrupted in order to allow for discussions, questions, articulations of doubt, or proposals as real change happens in the world Getino 2011, 49. This is why *La hora de los hornos* is divided into subchapters; the film can be stopped according to the needs of the audience/protagonists. Getino and Solanas refer to these screenings as "ciné-events". They compare the ciné-event to Fanon's notion of a "liturgical act, a privileged occasion for human beings to hear and be heard" Getino and Solanas 1969, 11. The film is thus completed if it includes discussions among the spectators.

"Any spectator is a coward or a traitor" Frantz Fanon in: Getino and Solanas 1968. With the statement quoted above, the second part of *La hora de los hornos* attacks the passive role of the spectator and challenges the audience to become active. It marks an urgency to bring about change and to take sides. Although the statement is addressed to the workers, farmers, and students experiencing oppression and exploitation in 1960s Argentina, today's audience is very different. I would argue, however, that this remark travels through time and acts to challenge the spectator's position in the present. It holds out a mirror in which the audience may recognise itself. Simultaneously, this form of time travel can recirculate the Argentinian decolonisation struggles of the 1960s. In doing so, the film can intervene in the normalising processes of the neoliberal project; processes that have erased and ignored the history and potential of these struggles. Watching *La hora de los hornos* confronts today's audience with an

---

8   "It is only in the present moment of each screening that these formulations are verified, discussed and brought up to date … To propagandise or raise consciousness is not only to transmit facts and ideas, but also for these to be used by the masses in the construction and practice of what still has not been completed" (Getino 2011a, 47).

analysis of colonial exploitation and neo-colonialism: its different protagonists, local and transnational political and economic entanglements, and violent intimidation of opposition. This knowledge of the injustice and betrayals of the past allows the present to become porous. According to Walter Benjamin, past struggles can appear in the present. The film thus contains the potential to ignite struggles in the now.

La hora de los hornos is diverse in its documentary style and keeps changing its aesthetic throughout its different parts. The six-minute prologue in part one starts with a black screen thanking farmers, workers, students, intellectuals, and revolutionaries for their collaboration. A rhythmic drum soundtrack crescendos accompanied by flashing images. We see protesters in one scene and policemen and soldiers beating them in another. Statements and words are dispersed between the images: "Invent", "Ideology", "Colonized man frees himself through violence." The further division of the film into subchapters makes part one of the trilogy appear fragmentary. Between the commentary running through the film there are interviews with indigenous people. Their discussion of the discrimination they have experienced takes place in long sequences that occur at a slower pace and from a different speaker's position. A segment about the luxurious lifestyle of the oligarchy precedes these sequences. In another section employing parallel montage, the glamour and cliché of advertising is interchanged with brutal scenes of cows and sheep in a slaughterhouse. The bloody corpses of the animals stand in stark contrast to the slick surfaces of advertising images. The accompanying easy-listening soundtrack lends an even more polemic undertone to these scenes. Ironically, Solanas worked in advertising and used the money he made in this field to finance the film's production [Mafud 2007].

In the last scenes of part one, corpses are laid out. People mourn and say farewell. A photographer stands on a table to photograph the dead body of Ernesto Che Guevara. The voiceover states that "the man who chooses his own death is also choosing his own life." Death is framed as a choice in the struggle for liberation; one that is better than staying alive and accepting oppression. For three minutes the camera rests on Che Guevara's face, accompanied by the music from the beginning of the film. The portrait of Che Guevara recalls the iconography of Jesus: both figures suffer in place of others. In previous parts of the film, Christian iconography is criticised in depictions of monuments and sculptures in the cemetery of the oligarchy. Underscored by a soundtrack of

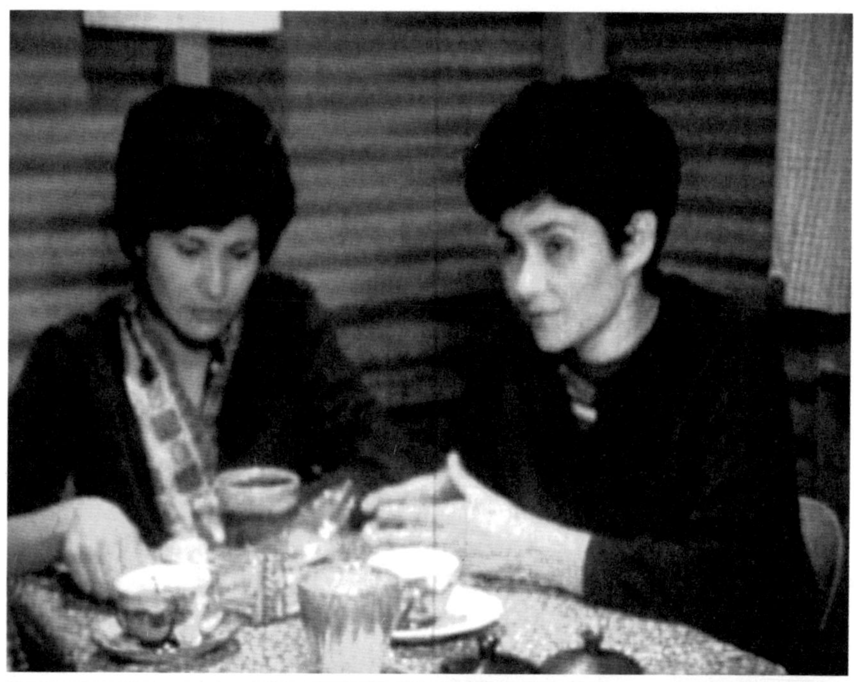

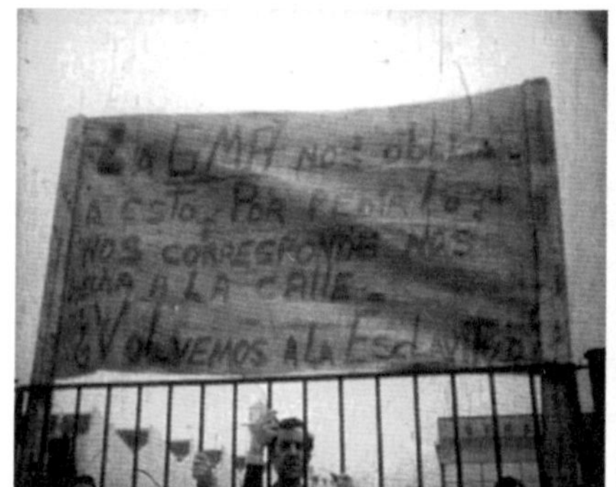

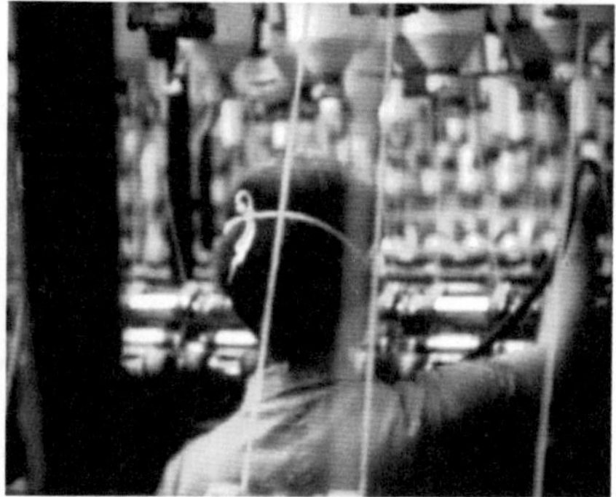

Film stills from *La hora de los hornos* by Octavio Getino and Fernando Solanas, 1966–68

opera music, thunder and lightning make these Christian icons tremble. Getino and Solanas's own use of Christian iconography in relation to a struggle they are in solidarity with is both an act of claiming this iconography and changing it according to their own terms. This also applies to the filmmakers' decision to include a wide range of references to struggles they empathise with. The film is full of quotations from other activists and writers imagining a collective revolutionary space. These figures include the writer Aimé Césaire, the writer and psychoanalyst

Frantz Fanon, the guerrilla leader Che Guevara, the revolutionary and politician Fidel Castro, and the writer and politician Juan José Hernandéz Arregui, who are quoted alongside clips of films by Fernando Birri, Joris Ivens, and Nemesio Juárez.

A revolutionary space of reference is opened through methods of parody and educational commentary, including the voices of indigenous people, and employing parallel montage to contrast the differences between rich and poor. This creates a diverse filmic form. The making of this film[9] correlates with Fanon's idea that the liberation struggle is in a continuous reciprocal relationship with the production of culture and the development of new forms Fanon 1963, 245–46. Fanon polemically states that in order to keep the colonised within the hierarchy of the white racial universe, "the colonialist specialists do not recognize these new forms and rush to the help of the traditions of the indigenous society. It is the colonialists who become the defenders of the native style" ibid. 242.

La hora de los hornos was produced and distributed clandestinely. Anonymity protected the filmmakers against the repression of the state and became a protocol for future films that were published anonymously. While this anonymity protected the filmmakers, it also highlighted the collective working process and the participation in a shared struggle Mafud 2007. The practice of collective authorship was common in the 1960s and 70s. Although *La hora de los hornos* was shown covertly, it reached an audience of 25,000 people in Argentina during eight months in 1970. The film was screened as part of multiple actions and activities initiated by Militant Cinema groups that were linked transnationally between Cuba, Mexico, Venezuela, Colombia, Brazil, Chile, Peru, Uruguay, Bolivia, and Argentina Getino 2011b, 53.

What Is to Be Done? 2.2

"Making film politically is to be militant" Godard 2016.
In 1970, only one year after Getino and Solanas condemned the *Nouvelle Vague* as a trap inside the fortress of culture Getino and Solanas 1969, 4, Jean-Luc Godard drafted his manifesto *Que Faire?* (What is to be done?) Godard 2016. In 1968, the French filmmakers Jean-Pierre Gorin and Jean-Luc Godard founded the Dziga Vertov Group.[10] They saw film as a revolutionary

---

9   For further reading about the making of *La hora de los hornos*, please see: (Brenez 2014).

10   The name refers to the Russian filmmaker Dziga Vertov, the inventor of *cinéma vérité*. Besides Godard and Gorin, members of the group included Jean-Henri Roger, Paul Burron, and Gérard Martin. They made their works with 16mm film, the format for documentary and television, and declined to name individual authorship.

Que faire?

1. Il faut faire des films politiques.
2. Il faut faire _politiquement_ des films.
3. 1 et 2 sont antagonistes, et appartiennent à deux conceptions du monde opposées.
4. 1 appartient à la conception idéaliste et métaphysique du monde.
5. 2 appartient à la conception marxiste et dialectique du monde.
6. Le marxisme lutte contre l'idéalisme, et la dialectique contre la métaphysique.
7. Cette lutte, c'est la lutte de l'ancien et du nouveau, la lutte des idées nouvelles et des anciennes.

35. Faire 2, c'est produire la connaissance scientifique des luttes révolutionnaires et de leur histoire.
36. Faire 2, c'est savoir que faire des films est une activité secondaire, une petite vis de la révolution.
37. Faire 2, c'est se servir des images et des sons comme ~~les dents~~ les dents et les lèvres pour mordre.
38. Faire 1, c'est seulement ouvrir les yeux et les oreilles.
39. Faire 2, c'est lire les rapports de la camarade Kiang-Tsing.
40. Faire 2, c'est _militer_.

Que faire? (What is to be done?), Jean-Luc Godard, 1970

means to increase awareness of the contradictions inherent to the capitalist system and to underscore the necessity of change. In his manifesto, Godard articulates his famous distinction between political film and "making film politically". While the former simply represents political issues, political filmmaking "makes concrete analysis of a concrete situation, produces knowledge of revolutionary struggles and their history, studies contradictions between the relationships of production and the productive forces [and] use[s] images and sounds as teeth and lips to bite with" Godard 2016. In making films politically, the form of distribution is just as important as the production. Making film politically becomes "a small screw in the revolution." Godard concludes his manifesto with the statement that "making film politically is to be militant" ibid..[11] This implies that when a filmmaker makes film politically, he or she participates in the political struggle. In this sense, Godard's approach demonstrates similarities to Getino and Solanas's idea of Militant Cinema.

11   Godard drafted this manifesto in London while working with the Dziga Vertov Group on the experimental documentary *British Sounds* (1969).

"It is true that even to silence, we never listened in silence. We wanted to crow victory right away, and furthermore at their place" ^{Godard and Miéville 1972}.

In 1970, the Dziga Vertov Group filmed activist camps run by the Palestinian Liberation Organisation (PLO | Arabic: منظمة التحرير الفلسطينية) in Jordan, Lebanon, and Syria while activists were preparing for their next deployment. The film titled *Jusqu'à la victoire* (Until Victory) was never finished. Many of the PLO activists died soon thereafter, in violent conflicts with the Jordanian army.[12] The Dziga Vertov Group disbanded in 1972. Four years later, Jean-Luc Godard and Anne-Marie Miéville used the visual material from *Jusqu'à la victoire* in their film *Ici et Ailleurs* (Here and Elsewhere, 1976), which thematises the ambivalent relationship between film and political struggle: within the personal context and elsewhere. In this film, Godard and Miéville self-critically question the techniques of image production favoured by the Dziga Vertov Group in service of the liberation struggle in Palestine. The off-voice in *Ici et Ailleurs* explains that the problem with *Jusqu'à la victoire* was that the sound was turned up so high "that it almost suffocated the voice which it was supposed to be retrieving from the image" ^{ibid.}. A male director asks a female protagonist: "Can you say it one more time? Would you straighten your head a little? Yes, like that." The female commentary continues: "You have chosen for that take a young intellectual, sympathizing with the Palestinian cause, who is not pregnant but accepts to play the part. Furthermore, she is young and beautiful. About that, you stay silent. But from secrets of this type to fascism, there is only one quick step" ^{ibid.}. The idealism inherent to the fascist forms of representation Godard and Miéville mention here—of which they find signs in *Jusqu'à la victoire*—creates a theatre in which performers are made to act in certain ways. However, this form of representation fails to listen to a situation, a person, and their speech.

The distinction that *Ici et Ailleurs* makes between "here" and "elsewhere" is introduced in an image of a French nuclear family sitting in front of a television in their living room. The "elsewhere" is represented by images of Palestinian guerrilla fighters. The film opposes two realities of daily life, both of which are described as simple images. The commentary asks: "Where did the inability to see or hear these very simple images come from?" ^{ibid.}. The film concludes with the statement: "Learn to

---

12   This conflict between PLO activists and the Jordanian Armed Forces (JAF | Arabic: القوات المسلحة الأردنية) took place between 16 and 27 September 1970 and was named "Black September" (Arabic: أيلول الأسود).

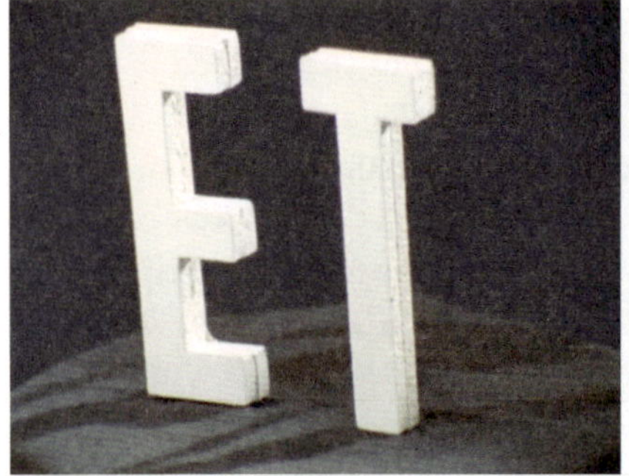
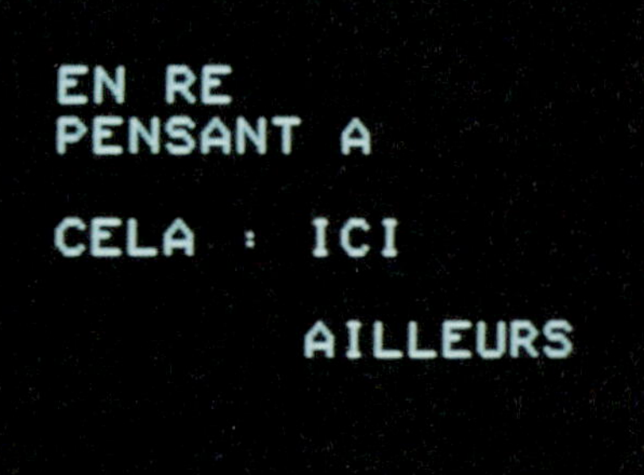

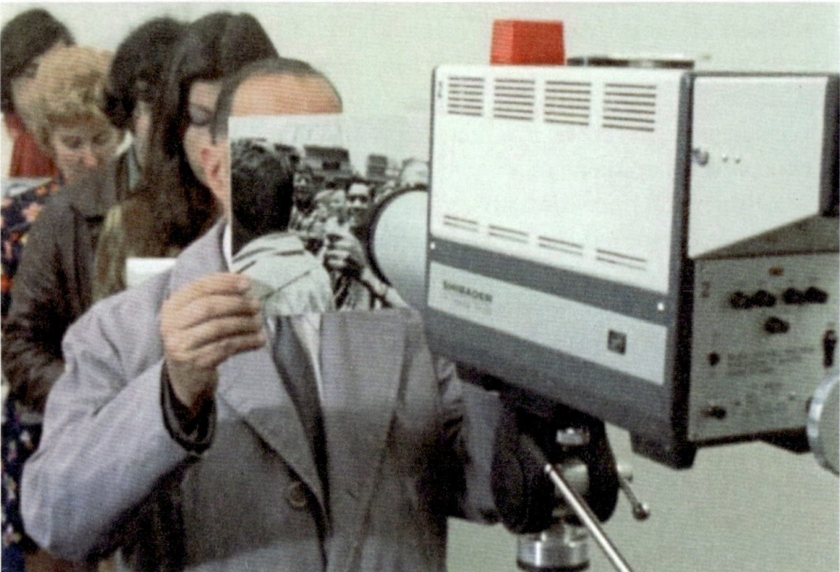

Film stills from *Ici et Ailleurs* by Jean Luc Godard and Anne Marie Miéville, 1972

see here, in order to understand elsewhere. Learn to understand speech in order to see what others do. The others, the 'elsewhere' of our 'here'" [ibid.]. With this conclusion, Godard and Miéville insist on the necessity to follow speech. But they also point to the importance of understanding the "here" before grappling with the "elsewhere".

How to understand "elsewhere" forms a central question in my work within the framework of Hezbollah in Lebanon. My position is, however, not on the side of Hezbollah. Nevertheless, I have to position myself and engage in a reading of Hezbollah's speech. Using film, I react to this speech and frame it. In contrast to Godard and Miéville, I do not put the "elsewhere" in such an awkward proximity to the "here". Instead, I use the medium of video to shift the space of "elsewhere" to different contexts, thus making it accessible.

Empathy and Trans-Geographical Entanglements

2.3

> "Of course, it triggered a reflex in many, this fascistoid state, as we always called it, now it revealed itself. It was the outing, so to speak, of the propensity to violence inherent to this apparent democracy" Giefer 2010.

The student protests against the Shah's visit to Berlin on 2 June 1967 were met with a brutal reaction by the police, culminating in the death of the student Benno Ohnesorg. This event set the scene for the radicalisation of political movements in the 1960s and 70s in West Germany—the *Bewegung 2. Juni* was even named after the date. The investigative film *Berlin, 2. Juni* (Berlin, 2 June, 1967) documents the Shah's visit and the battles that ensued. Made by the students Hans-Rüdiger Minow and Thomas Giefer, the film shows the students' disbelief and shock at the violence they encountered. Several youths trace their experiences of the demonstration: "For us the 2nd of June offered the possibility to see the whole of the Third World assembled in Berlin," states Rudi Dutschke. Another student explains: "I can't show my face because the Persian secret service is very strong in the Federal Republic" Minow and Giefer 1967. Numbers affixed to policemen in a photograph indicate the independent investigation undertaken by students into Ohnesorg's murder.

Bahman Nirumand, a member of the Confederation of Iranian Students (CISNU), was one of the organisers of the protest. Nirumand's book *Persien, Modell eines Entwicklungslandes* (Iran: The New Imperialism in Action) had already been published in West Germany Nirumand 1967. For the first time, many students became aware of American and British involvement in Iranian politics, the exploitation of Iran by Western countries, as well as the brutal oppression of opposition. The paperback book spread this knowledge widely and entanglements between Iran and West Germany became visible on a political and economic level.

In *Berlin, 2. Juni,* viewers see the *Jubelperser* (Cheering Persians) become *Prügelperser* (Beating Persians) Minow and Giefer 1967. Unhindered by the German police, members of the Iranian secret service (SAVAK | Farsi: سازمان اطلاعات و امنیت کشور | Organisation of National Intelligence and Security) beat protesters with batons. When the police finally intervene, it is not to protect the protesters but to support the members of the secret

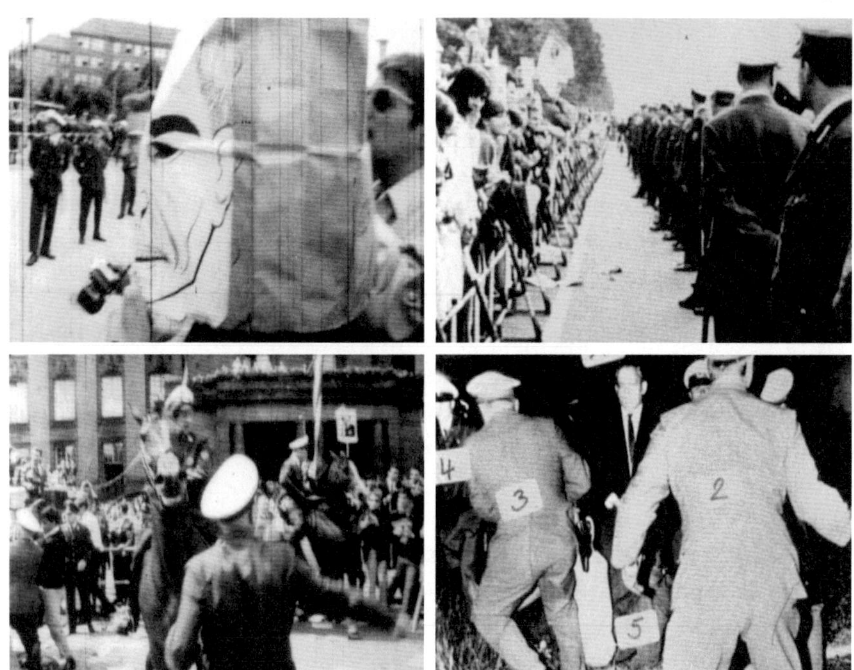

Film stills from *Berlin, 2. Juni* by Hans-Rüdiger Minow and Thomas Giefer, 1967

service. Filmmaker Thomas Giefer states that the violence the protesters encountered ultimately "led to false conclusions, to wrong analyses" Schäfer 2011. The false conclusions he mentions do not refer to the radicalisation of students as such, but to the military logic that some leftist groups used in their later activities.

Before the film's completion, Minow and Giefer travelled to universities throughout West Germany with a projector and film clips Giefer 2010. Their recordings—and later their completed film—helped students grasp what had happened. In this investigative sense, Minow and Giefer's work is a militant film. Even today, it helps us understand the events in 1967 that triggered the radicalisation of the student movement. For this purpose, film serves as a better medium than individual recordings or slides, which can more easily be made to "disappear".[13]

In many ways, 2 June 1967 foreshadowed both the radicalisation of the student protests and the role of the state. In a television report, the

13 At the 2019 Radical Film Network meeting in Berlin, Volker Pantenburg's talk "Versions of Radicality, 1969/1970: Farocki, Meins, Straschek" compared the investigative methods employed by Minow and Giefer with the forensic methods we encounter today, for example in the work of Forensic Architecture in London (Forensic Architecture n.d.).

journalist Ulrike Meinhof comments on the Federal Republic's complicity with the Iranian government, stating that "one cannot welcome the head of a police state without sympathising with a police state" Périot 2015.[14] In the televised news magazine *Abendrundschau*, images of the protests are accompanied by a commentary that justifies the violence of the police as a comprehensible reaction to the uproar. There is no mention of the Iranian secret service and their riot sticks. Referring to this textual framing, Meinhof states that "the images of the *Abendrundschau* expose the text as lies" Périot 2015.[15]

The name of the *Bewegung 2. Juni* directly refers to this protest in Berlin, but references to the so-called Third World go deeper. Organisations like the RAF and the *Bewegung 2. Juni* were inspired by Latin American urban guerrilla groups like the *Tupamaros*[16] in Uruguay. Former RAF member Stefan Wisniewski explains that members thought the movement would only have a chance if it maintained an awareness of movements related to the Global South. Wisniewski states that "without Vietnam, without the changes in the Third World, the RAF would not have become what it then became. Our bearers of hope were the *Tupamaros* and the Black Panthers" Wisniewski 2003, 21.[17]

"The regime of violence that subsumes black people is different from the regime of violence that subsumes exploited workers and hyper exploited postcolonial subordinates" Wilderson III 2017.

In a talk given at the exhibition space District Berlin in September 2017, the writer and filmmaker Frank B Wilderson III was highly critical of the RAF's embrace of the Black Liberation Army.[18] Wilderson explained that black people cannot refer to a third term to legitimise their struggle.

14 Translated by Sandra Schäfer. "Dass man nicht einen Polizeistaatschef empfangen kann ohne mit dem Polizeistaat zu sympathisieren" (Périot 2015).
15 Translated by Sandra Schäfer. "Die Bilder der Abendrundschau strafen den Text Lügen" (Périot 2015).
16 The *Tupamaros,* also known as *Movimiento de Liberación Nacional-Tupamaros* (MLN-T) or the Tupamaros National Liberation Movement, was a left-wing urban guerrilla group in Uruguay in the 1960s and 70s. The movement robbed banks, gun clubs, and businesses in the early 1960s in order to distribute stolen food and money among the poor in Montevideo. As the government became increasingly oppressive, the group began to undertake political kidnappings and assassinations.
17 The murder of Malcom X in 1965 triggered massive riots by black people throughout the United States. Two African Americans from California, Huey Newton and Bobby Seale, founded the Black Panther Party for Self-Defense in 1966 to realise Malcom X's ideas. The organisation was active during the 1960s and 70s and legitimised armed resistance against social oppression.
18 The Black Liberation Army (BLA) was founded by members of the Black Panther Party in the United States in 1970. As a reaction to the infiltration and sabotage of the Black Panther Party by the police and the FBI, some members were convinced that working underground and with different means had become necessary. The BLA consisted of several groups and collectives without a centralised leadership (Umoja 1999). It was active until 1981.

Unlike the RAF's use of the term "labour" or the Irish Republican Army's[19] use of the term "land", the black person exists outside of such categories due to slavery. In the same way, he or she is not considered within the category of human subjectivity. The black person is not the dialectical "other" to the human subject but the "ground" that makes its existence possible through characteristics such as liberty, citizenship, and belonging to a wider social body Wilderson III 2014, 35. Wilderson takes up Mikhail Bakhtin's notion of the "chronotope"—which describes how time and space are represented in language—and elaborates that the time-space agglomeration and "thickening" is non-existent for black people, rendering them unable to constitute themselves in a wider history. Blackness is thus a-historical.

According to Wilderson, slavery is not just a historical phenomenon: it is inherent to the situation of black people today. This is why a deeper social transformation is needed Hartman and Wilderson III 2003. However, Wilderson regards solidarity with the black struggle by non-black people as highly problematic. Any such act of solidarity puts non-black people in the place of black subjects, thereby turning black people into objects ibid., 190. This difference between black and non-black subjects and their struggles in, with, and against the state stands in absolute contrast to Hannah Arendt's thinking. Nevertheless, Wilderson's pessimistic analysis is an important contribution to understanding today's racism in the United States. Furthermore, it can be read in the tradition of Frantz Fanon's thinking in *The Wretched of the Earth*, particularly his notion that colonialism needs to be destroyed by the colonised Fanon 1963. Although Wilderson does not provide suggestions about how to change the present situation, he is right to insist on the difference between the struggles of, for example, the RAF in West Germany and the Black Liberation Army in the United States.

"'Empathy' is too good a word to leave to any other side"
Farocki 2016, 105.

How can empathy with a seemingly far-away conflict like the Vietnam War be visualised in film? Harun Farocki devotes *Nicht löschbares Feuer* (Inextinguishable Fire, 1969) to this question. The film was made at the end of the 1960s in West Berlin, after the student protests against the Shah's visit in 1967 were met with brutal police reactions that triggered

---

19   The Irish Republican Army (IRA) is one of several Irish paramilitary movements that believe Ireland should be an independent republic.

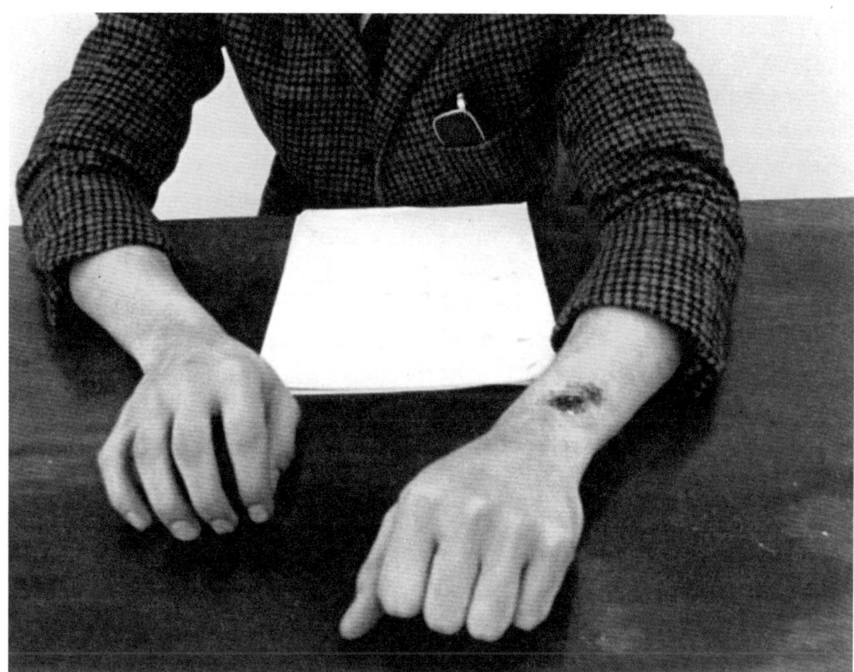

Film still from *Nicht löschbares Feuer* by Harun Farocki, 1969

the radicalisation of the student movement and the foundation of groups like the *Bewegung 2. Juni* and the RAF. At the time the film was made, Harun Farocki was a film student at the Deutsche Film- und Fernseh-akademie Berlin (DFFB). He had recently been expelled from the school and re-accepted following protests by his peers.

In this film about the production of napalm in the United States and the effects of its use during the Vietnam War, Farocki asks: How can we maintain our responsiveness? And how can an image be produced about the Vietnam War amidst the circulating images of atrocity? In the first scene of the film, Farocki sits behind a table—like a news presenter—and reads a report by a Vietnamese man about his experience of a napalm bomb explosion.[20] Farocki asks how the effects of napalm can be communicated without making the viewer close their eyes to the picture, the memories, and the facts. He states that he can only give a hint of how napalm works; then he stubs out a cigarette on his arm.

20   This report was presented by Tai Binh Dan at the International War Crimes Tribunal in 1967. The tribunal was a private body organised by the philosopher Bertrand Russell and hosted by the philosopher Jean-Paul Sartre. Its aim was to investigate and evaluate American foreign policy and military intervention in Vietnam.

A voiceover adds that a cigarette burns at 400 °C, whereas napalm burns at 3,000 °C.

We don't see or hear any reactions from Farocki when he performs this auto-aggressive act approximating the impossible task of representing the effects of napalm. Nevertheless, the concern triggered by watching the cigarette burn the filmmaker's arm allows us to imagine the effects, even if the image only gives a hint of an idea. In the second part of the film, Farocki appropriates the style of a Brechtian *Lehrstück* (learning play) to analyse how American researchers, factory owners, secretaries, and workers are involved in the production of napalm and how they legitimise their activities. In doing so, Farocki highlights how certain methods are used to make the overall production process less comprehensible for those who participate.

In her work, Judith Butler focuses on the normative frames that structure an image. She highlights that if the image, in turn, structures how we register reality, it is involved in our interpretative acts. Butler's concern is with "how [the image] shows what it shows. The 'how' not only organizes the image, but works to organize our perception and thinking as well" J. Butler 2009, 71. In this sense, images "act on us" ibid., 67–68. They relay affect and interpret reality. It is possible, however, to show the frames, to expose and thematise the mechanisms of restriction. Butler calls this process "the disobedient act of seeing" ibid., 72. This is exactly what Farocki accomplishes in *Nicht löschbares Feuer:* both through its division into two parts and via the auto-aggressive act of inflicting pain.

Harun Farocki's way of working is characterised by a distancing and analytical approach. In his 2008 text *Einfühlung* (Empathy), he writes that the word "empathy" belonged to "the other side" in the 1960s and that Brecht taught him "not to gawp so romantically" Farocki 2016, 104. Here the "other side" refers to the entertainment industry whereas Brecht's method refers to the epic theatre, specifically its use of the *Verfremdungs-effekt* (alienation or distancing effect). According to the alienation effect, the actor doesn't completely identify with her role. Although she performs in a realistic way, the familiar is meant to become unfamiliar. In this process, emphasis is placed on the reciprocal relationship between human action and social conditions. Taking an attitude of observation and reflection, the viewer sees that these actions and conditions can be different.

Farocki writes: "'Empathy' is too good a word to leave to any other side. 'Empathy' is a finer expression than 'identification', and the German word *Einfühlen* has a transgressive overtone. A compound of *Eindringen* (to penetrate) and *Mitfühlen* (to sympathise). Somewhat forceful sympathy. It should be possible to empathize in a way that produces the effect of alienation" Farocki 2016, 105. The author and filmmaker Antje Ehmann—who was Farocki's longstanding partner—reflects on the role of empathy in Farocki's observational films: "This kind of empathetic watching and listening to words and images is not only non-judgemental and unintentional, it is not a *feeling* at all: it's an active practice" Ehmann 2016, 23. As an active practice, empathy shows similarities to what Farocki calls the "listening out" of images during editing—a process described in his film *Soft Montage* Farocki 1995. This approach is the opposite of the Dziga Vertov Group's "theatre method", which is used in *Jusqu'à la victoire* and suffocates the voices of those who speak. In contrast, Farocki's way of working requires attention and an analytical approach that does not confuse empathy with affirmation or identification. The active practise of listening and watching is an important part of my own filmic work, as discussed in chapter 5.

How does one engage in social change? Referring to the radicalisation of some of his fellow students, Farocki states: "I would always find an excuse to make films. To join a terrorist organization was out of the question. My daughters had just been born in 1968 and I had completely different concerns. Certainly, there were others who had children and abandoned them in order to become terrorists. Sauber and Meins were particular radical artists and this is the paradox, they profoundly believed in art. They couldn't just modify things a little bit. They had to choose a heroic counter-life. They couldn't say: Okay, then let's just make films for the community college in Neukölln" Farocki and Goll 2016, 57. As a film student, one of Farocki's peers, Holger Meins, made a careful, intimate, and respectful filmic study of the daily life of a homeless man named Oskar Langenfeld, with whom he spent several weeks Meins 1967. In his filmmaking, it was important for Meins to participate in Langenfeld's life. Meins later chose to join the RAF and go underground. When he was incarcerated in Wittlich, he protested against the conditions in the prison by going on hunger strike. He thus used his body as the only means of resistance he had left; even if it meant killing himself.

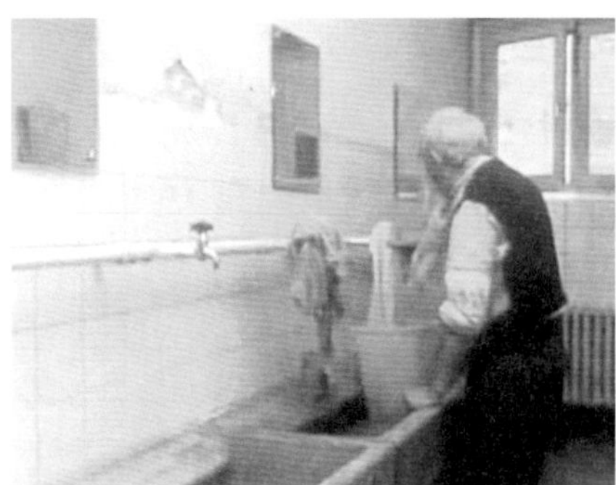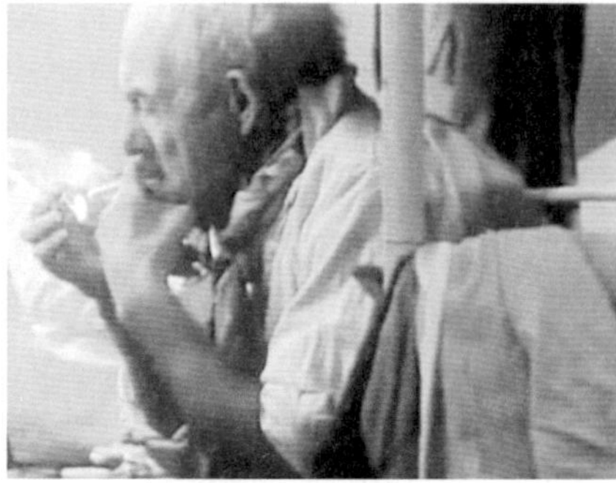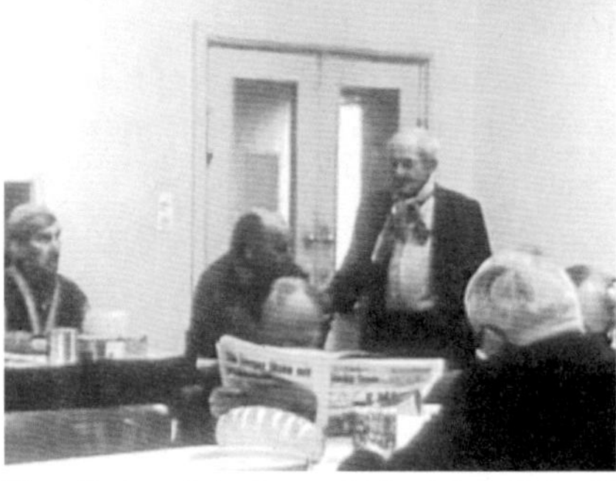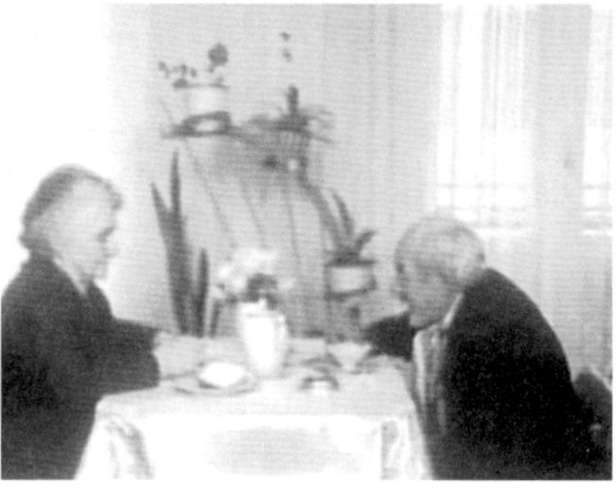

Film stills from *Oskar Langenfeld* by Holger Meins, 1967

"I am more willing to risk imprisonment or any other negative outcome, personally, than I am willing to risk the curtailment of my intellectual freedom and that of those around me whom I care for, equally as I do for myself" Poitras 2014.

How might a disobedient act of seeing function within the surveillance system of the United States? When Edward Snowden, a former employee of the Central Intelligence Agency (CIA), recognised the architecture of surveillance and repression that he was contributing to, he decided to inform the public. Snowden stepped out of the system and leaked classified information in collaboration with the filmmaker Laura Poitras, journalists Glenn Greenwald and Ewen MacAskill of *The Guardian*, and journalist Barton Gellman of *The Washington Post*. Laura Poitras's 2014 film *Citizenfour* documents this process. In making the film, Poitras acts in complicity with Snowden, intervening in the normativity of surveillance and allowing, in Judith Butler's sense, "a seeing in the non-seeing". In the documentary, Snowden explains that he is more willing to risk imprisonment than the curtailment of the intellectual freedom represented by the internet Poitras 2014. Snowden continues that

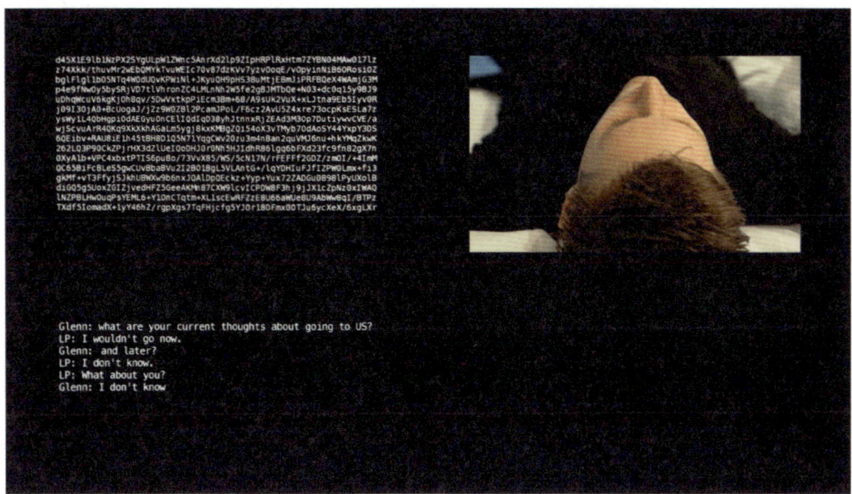

Film stills from *Citizenfour* by Laura Poitras, 2014, arranged by Sandra Schäfer

he finds it more powerful not to conceal his identity, thereby showing that he is not afraid of the state. In doing so, his act encourages other members of the public to do the same. Beyond this, he asserts that by showing his identity he "is inverting the model that the government has laid out" ibid..

In conversation with Laura Poitras, the artist and theorist Hito Steyerl states that the variety of skills that were necessary for Poitras to make this film—including encryption, filtering information, tactical opacity and transparency, and crossing borders—constitute an aesthetic Poitras and Steyerl 2015, 311. Although Steyerl focuses on the extended skills required to make *Citizenfour*, Snowden's own strategic actions, the journalistic techniques of distribution, and the collective activity of the group are also important to consider. All of these techniques, including the participation of the filmmaker and the journalists, constitute a militant practice.

Militancy is, however, also active on a different level due to the fact that Edward Snowden, like WikiLeaks founder Julian Assange, challenges the idea of nationality and citizenship. Both Assange and Snowden attack the core of the judicial and political system because of "their dismissal of national and political belonging" de Lagasnerie 2016, 121.[21] In doing so, Assange and Snowden reject the ways in which they are produced as citizens by

---

21   Translated by Sandra Schäfer. "Eine Ablehnung ihrer nationalen oder politischen Zugehörigkeit" (de Lagasnerie 2016, 121).

the state. Thus, within the order of constitutional law, they are counter-subjects. Assange takes refuge in the Ecuadorian Embassy in London whereas Snowden escapes from Hong Kong to Russia. They refuse to submit to "their" state and opt instead to change their political community. Their activities cannot, however, be defined as disobedient, because the disobedient subject still accepts the legal system that is applied to his or her actions.

In Poitras's recent documentary film *Risk* (2017), she accompanies Julian Assange and the WikiLeaks team over a period of six years. Due to its long production period and the circumstances of its making, the film has an eclectic style. In making *Risk*, Poitras entered difficult territory. It is common knowledge that those who work within the context of WikiLeaks are monitored by different secret service agencies. During the six years of filming, the organisation also made a number of problematic decisions initiated by Assange as its leader. In a personal, diaristic style, Poitras comments on the making of the film. The documentary starts in 2011, after WikiLeaks released thousands of diplomatic cables as well as secret video footage of an American helicopter crew gunning down civilians in Iraq. This footage was leaked by Bradley (later Chelsea) Manning, who spent several years in prison for this act.[22]

The film emphasises the topic of sexism. This occurs, for example, in scenes featuring a conversation between Julian Assange and a female lawyer. In their dialogue about Assange's alleged sexual assault of two women in Sweden, Assange blames the accusers of being part of a radical-feminist conspiracy and acting as a "tag team". To avoid his rendition to Sweden, Assange applies for asylum in Ecuador and takes refuge at the embassy in London. One of his collaborators, Jacob Appelbaum—who, as part of the independent hacker scene, helped develop the software Tor[23]—is also accused of bullying, abuse, and sexual misconduct. A short scene at the HOPE hacker conference shows internal discussions about this abuse within the hacking community. It seems difficult to go public with this accusation, as political opponents could potentially use it as an argument not only against Appelbaum but against the whole community.

22 In 2017, Chelsea Manning's sentence was commuted as one of President Obama last actions in office. In May 2019, she was imprisoned for contempt after refusing to testify before a grand jury investigating Julian Assange.

23 Tor is a free software program that protects its users against traffic analysis, a form of network surveillance that threatens personal freedom and privacy. "Tor protects you by bouncing your communications around a distributed network of relays run by volunteers all around the world: it prevents somebody watching your Internet connection from learning what sites you visit, and it prevents the sites you visit from learning your physical location" (Tor 2018).

In the film, Assange accuses Poitras, who did not initially tell him about the files she received from Snowden, of betrayal. Although Snowden's controlled distribution of files does not align with WikiLeaks's approach to releasing documents, Assange and WikiLeaks member Sarah Harrison helped Snowden escape from Hong Kong to Russia. Afterwards, Harrison could not return to England and has since stayed in Berlin. The risk of engaging in these affairs is significant and comes at a high personal cost.

As an isolated enemy, Assange attempts to copy the system in order to fight it from the inside and the outside. In 2016, WikiLeaks intervened in the American elections. Although Assange denies it, there are indications that files pertaining to the presidential candidate Hillary Clinton were given to him indirectly via the Russian secret service. In her commentary, Poitras is open about her distrust of Assange. Throughout the film, the network around this egocentric figure becomes more and more dispersed and Assange and his collaborators gradually become more isolated. Living and working in this isolation puts pressure on each person involved. Sometimes empathy and enmeshment are abused. Nevertheless, the film leaves many things opaque. Poitras enters a swampy terrain of entanglements. Assange's state of exception—as described when he lists his enemies in an interview scene with Lady Gaga—is only one of many moments in the film that are difficult to bear.

I regard Poitras's decision to enter the world of WikiLeaks—despite its consequences for her own life—as a militant act. Poitras doesn't completely identify with Julian Assange or WikiLeaks. Instead, she articulates her critique and ambivalence towards the organisation and, in particular, its leader. In Poitras's film, empathy is a complicated thing.

Showing Is Doing **2.4**

> "Is it possible to make films in Germany today? Is it possible from a philosophical point of view? My starting point was actually: Is it possible to make images in Germany? Is it possible to have a visual imagination?" Périot 2015.[24]

The audiovisuals produced in West Germany during the radicalisation of the student movement are hardly present in the German context

---

24   Translated by Sandra Schäfer. "Ist es möglich, heutzutage in Deutschland Filme zu machen? Ist es möglich von einem philosophischen Standpunkt aus? Mein Ausgangspunkt war eigentlich: Ist es möglich in Deutschland Bilder zu machen? Ist es möglich die bildliche Vorstellungskraft zu haben?" (Périot 2015).

today. They are a muted, cut off, or carefully orchestrated part of recent German history. The dominant narratives of state power, of the peace-seeking 1980s and the dizziness of the reunifying 90s, blur and overshadow the radical outbursts, paranoia, and violence of the 60s and 70s. For this reason, Jean-Gabriel Périot's compilation film *Une Jeunesse Allemande* (A German Youth, 2015) appears even more unique and important. The particularity of Périot's film is that it traverses the media landscape of that time, collecting and recirculating diverse material, particularly from the beginning of the student uprising and its radicalisation. In doing so, Périot's montage of found footage draws on a large collection of sources: student films by Helke Sander, Harun Farocki, Skip Norman, Thomas Giefer, Hans-Rüdiger Minow, Holger Meins, Claudia von Alemann, Gerd Conradt, and Helma Sanders-Brahms; various agitprop films; scenes staged with Gudrun Ensslin in Ali Limonadi's experimental film *Das Abonnement* (The Subscription, 1967); television reports and shows involving Ulrike Meinhof; official televised speeches made by Chancellor Helmut Schmidt; and a scene from Rainer Werner Fassbinder's contribution to the collective film *Deutschland im Herbst* (Germany in Autumn, 1978). Périot's film thus extends to a much wider space of articulation in which the radicalisation of the 1970s was embedded.

Significantly, the filmic and political work of Ulrike Meinhof is one of the threads running through Périot's film. Meinhof was a student of education as well as an editor and journalist for the magazine *konkret* before she joined the Red Army Faction in 1970. In several television appearances, she intelligently and eloquently represents the critical voice of the young generation. She is introduced in a talk show on the topic of *Die ausgehöhlte Autorität* (The Undermined Authority) as follows: "Her authority is based on the arguments she formulates as a journalist" ibid.[25] In a commentary, she admits that the public role she plays only partly corresponds to her needs: her opinion is co-opted in a *Kasperletheater* (Punch-and-Judy show) that forces her to say deadly serious things with a smile on her face ibid..

Périot introduces Meinhof through the diversity of her political and journalistic work. He thus puts her later activities into a wider framework of political, social, and artistic engagement, working against the distorted image of the terrorist body; particularly the monstrous

---

25   Translated by Sandra Schäfer. "Ihre Autorität beruht auf den Argumenten, die sie hervorbringt als
      Kolumnistin."

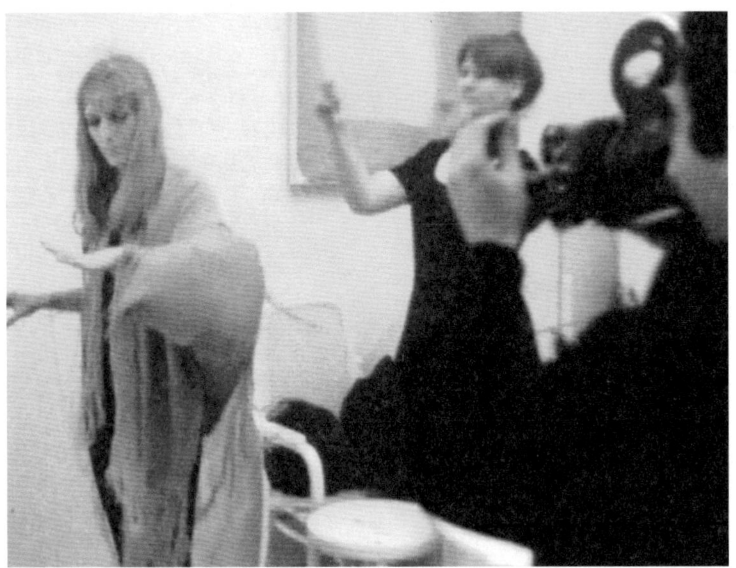

Gudrun Ensslin in Ali Limonadi's experimental film *Das Abonnement*, 1967

representation of the female terrorist body.[26] Meinhof's journalistic work often focuses on the topic of labour. In a 1965 television report for NDR, for example, she denounces the lack of workplace safety and criticises the court's dismissal of a worker's complaint against his employer. Meinhof also approaches this topic from a feminist perspective, touching upon the reproductive labour in her own life. In one interview, she states that for women like her—who work in the public sphere—the problems of reproductive labour are the same as for any other woman. This is why, she asserts, the private is political.

Meinhof's critique of the limitations of her journalistic and filmic work becomes apparent in her correspondence with the producer of *Südwestfunk*, Dieter Waldemann. In this correspondence, she self-critically reflects on the making of *Bambule* (1970), her filmic collaboration with Eberhard Itzenplitz.[27] Based on Meinhof's long-term research into West German educational institutions, *Bambule* is a feature film about

26   Irit Rogoff, for example, points out that according to traditional thinking, it is impossible for femininity and terrorism to inhabit the same body, as the female body is associated with reproductive labour (Rogoff, 2003, 48–63).

27   Eight years later, Margarethe von Trotta made the feature film *Das zweite Erwachen der Christa Klages* (The Second Awakening of Christa Klages, 1978), which is based on the experiences of Margit Czenki (who also took part in the film). Czenki later worked on von Trotta's *Die bleierne Zeit* (Marianne and Juliane, 1981), which tells the story of the sisters Christiane and Gudrun Ensslin. In 1987 Czenki made the feature film *Komplizinnen*, which is influenced by her experiences in prison.

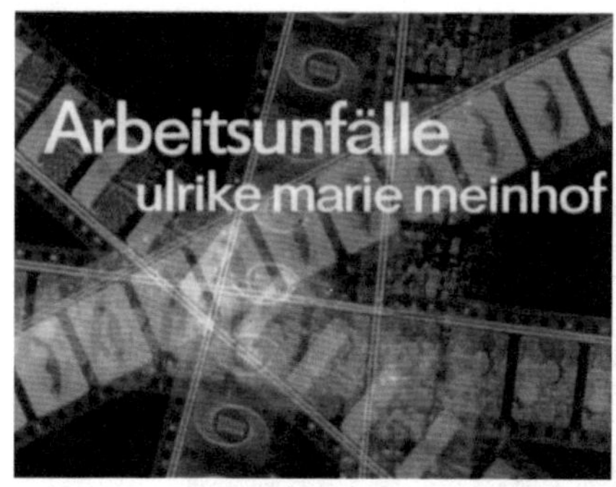
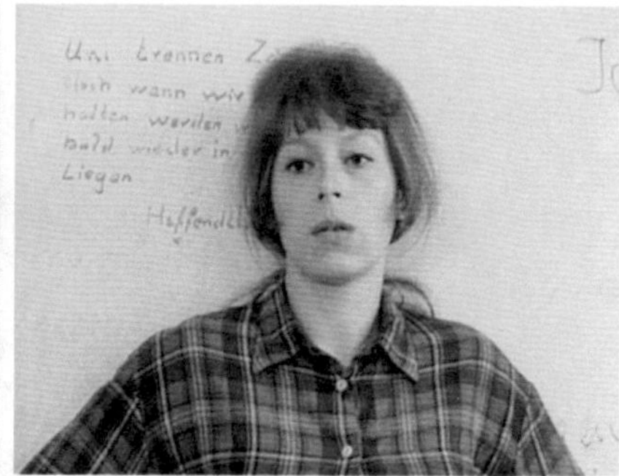

Arbeitsunfälle, reportage for NDR by Ulrike Meinhof, 1965

Bambule by Ulrike Meinhof and Eberhard Itzenplitz, 1970

the authoritarian structures in a boarding school for girls. In her correspondence with Waldemann, Meinhof questions the effectiveness of this filmic project to initiate concrete change. After shooting was completed, she writes: "It has only now become clear to me that a rebellion in the institution—the organisation of the youths themselves—is of a thousand times more value than any film … Do you understand? That's what I realised: that with this film I establish nothing but an aesthetic relation to the problems of these proletarian youths, just as any other writer would do. I realised that this is claptrap, revolutionary claptrap" Mohr 1996.[28] Meinhof continues: "There will only be change if the oppressed themselves act. Those who want to support them must do so practically. They have to help the oppressed organise themselves, act, and enforce their demands … It is important to participate at an individual level" ibid.[29] In these statements, Meinhof's subsequent decision to leave her intellectual work of writing and filmmaking and devote herself to the RAF becomes clear.

In June 2016, Meinhof and Itzenplitz's film was shown as part of the project "No Play–Feminist Training Camp". In this context, Meinhof's writing about *Bambule* was also distributed. Her film and writing thus became part of No Play's practice as "a queer understanding of feminism

28   Translated by Sandra Schäfer. "Nur ist mir jetzt wirklich klar geworden, daß ein Aufstand im Heim, die Organisierung der Jugendlichen selbst, tausendmal mehr wert sind als zich Filme … Verstehst Du? Das hab ich kapiert, daß ich mit diesem Film nichts als ein ästhetisches Verhältnis zu den Problemen dieser proletarischen Jugend herstelle, wie jeder andere Schriftsteller auch – daß das Gewäsch ist, Revolutionsgewäsch" (Mohr 1996).

29   Translated by Sandra Schäfer. "Ändern wird sich nur etwas, wenn die Unterdrückten selbst handeln. Wer sie dabei unterstützen will, muss es praktisch tun, muss den Unterdrückten selbst helfen, sich zu organisieren, zu handeln, ihre Forderungen durchzusetzen … Es kommt darauf an, selbst mitzumachen" (Mohr 1996).

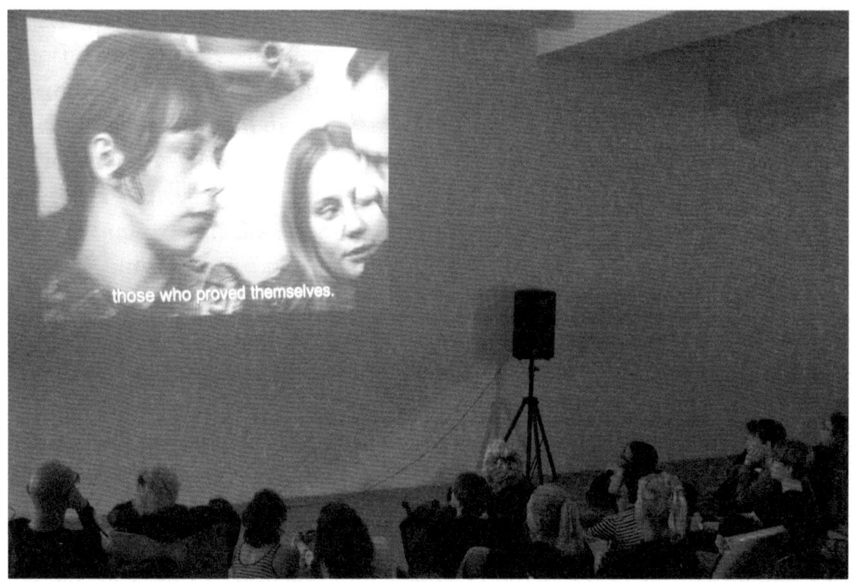

Screening of *Bambule* at "No Play—Feminist Training Camp" in 2016 at neue Gesellschaft für bildende Kunst, Berlin, photograph: No Play

with a strong emphasis on grassroots models of collective organization, knowledges based in lived experience and the handling of daily oppressions. A space for disagreement and negotiation that can create a situated public considered political" No Play—Feminist Training Camp 2016. The film raises questions like: "Where is the place (where are the places) from which society's problems can be changed; in which ways is the distinction between art and life upheld, and in which ways does it break down?" neue Gesellschaft für bildende Kunst 2017, 51.

When Meinhof left the cultural context to join the Red Army Faction, her mediums of expression were largely reduced to writing texts, manifestos, and letters, some of which were distributed by the publishing house Wagenbach. Posters were used as another form of distribution. According to a member of the *Bewegung 2. Juni*, hundreds of people showed up to meetings after seeing such posters—at least before police pressure increased. After her capture in 1972, Meinhof was put into solitary confinement. In Périots film, a judge asks her to leave the court floor after hearing her eloquent reflections on the effects of solitary confinement, which she describes as a form of torture Périot 2015. Her speech is eliminated by state power. Four years later she is found dead in Stammheim prison.

Strangely, at the end of his film, Périot focuses on the speech and representations produced by the state. In doing so, he amplifies the official narrative of history. He chooses not to concentrate on the perspective of the RAF and the militant images it produced through militant actions that then circulated in official media. One such image, produced during the kidnapping of Hanns Martin Schleyer,[30] the President of the Confederation of German Employers' Associations, is Schleyer's destroyed Mercedes. Another is the RAF's own video recording of Schleyer, which was likewise broadcast on the evening news. The group filmed Schleyer during his kidnapping and made him sit beneath a poster depicting the RAF's logo. These humiliating images attack bourgeois sensibilities as well as Schleyer's personal integrity. By broadcasting them on German television, the RAF was able to intervene in the evening news with its own militant image production. In doing so, it attacked the government's political and social environment. State-sponsored television thus inadvertently helped to distribute the RAF's logo and message.

An important part of the terrorist act is that it is seen, which highlights the role of (militant) image production itself. As Walid el-Houri states: "Showing is doing. In this sense, reality only exists through the way it is shown" Houri 2012, 126. The RAF produced its own images of Hanns Martin Schleyer. It took a while for the state news to understand that it was distributing the enemy's images through its broadcasting. Only a few days later, the RAF's images of Schleyer were replaced by a different portrait. Former RAF-member Stefan Wisniewski comments that "although the event mostly had to get by without images, it found its visual language. It was that of state institutions: there were and are no alternatives" Wisniewski 2003, 59.[31] Here Wisniewski refers not only to the visual representations of state-sponsored news programmes, but to the

30   On 5 September 1977, Schleyer was kidnapped by an RAF commando unit. His kidnappers demanded the release of eleven imprisoned RAF members. The West German government did not give in to the demands. Schleyer's family disagreed with the approach taken by the government and offered 15 million DM to the RAF; the government, however, prevented its handover. An official request made by Schleyer's son, Hanns-Eberhard Schleyer, that the government submit to the demands was also rejected. On 13 October 1977, a Lufthansa airplane was hijacked by the Popular Front for the Liberation of Palestine (PFLP). The GSG9, an elite tactical unit of the German Federal Police, stormed the "Landshut" airplane and hostages were released. That same night, three RAF members (Andreas Baader, Gudrun Ensslin, and Jan-Carl Raspe) died in Stammheim prison. When the kidnappers heard about the deaths of the imprisoned RAF members, they shot Schleyer. His corpse was found on 19 October 1977 in Mulhouse.

31   Translated by Sandra Schäfer. "Das Ereignis hatte—obwohl es weitgehend ohne Bilder auskommen mußte—zu seiner Bildersprache gefunden. Es war eine der staatlichen Ordnung: Alternativen gab und gibt es nicht" (Wisniewski 2003, 59).

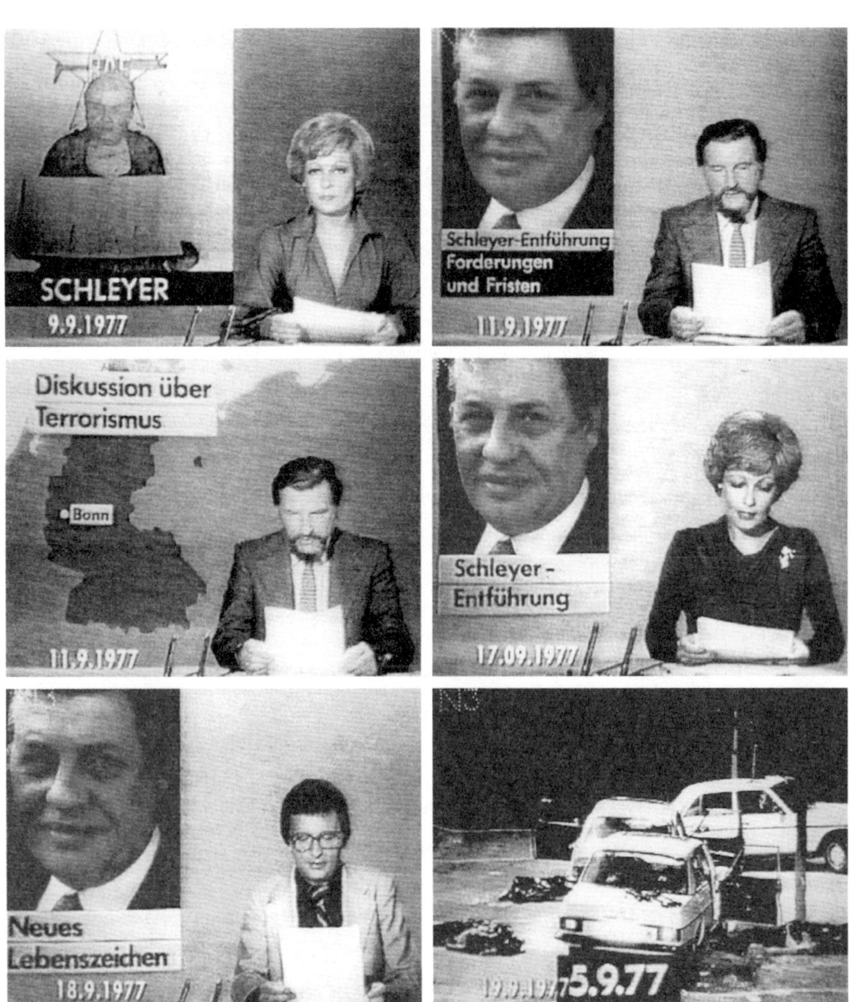

Stills from West German television, source: Wisniewski 2003

overall politics of the state. The government did not leave any space for negotiation with the RAF, even if this meant sacrificing Schleyer. It prevented videos of Schleyer from being broadcast in which he called on politicians and the general public to give in to the demands of the kidnappers in order to avoid an escalation of violence ibid., 56.[32] The government also did not allow the prisoners in Stammheim to make a public statement. According to Wisniewski, this could have changed the prisoners' public

32   Today such videos are distributed via YouTube or other online channels.

image and influenced the way the RAF dealt with Schleyer [ibid., 57]. Furthermore, Wisniewski states that the RAF would have released Schleyer if the government had allowed an international committee to examine the conditions of Stammheim prison [ibid., 56]. Interestingly, Wisniewski's interview from 2003 carries the title "Wir waren so unheimlich konsequent" (We were so incredibly resolute). The translation does not capture the ambiguous meaning of *unheimlich*, which means both "incredibly" and "uncannily".

"A working class hero is something to be" [Bruch 1977].
In contrast to Jean-Gabriel Périot's film, the video *Das Schleyer-Band* (The Schleyer Tape, 1977–78) by the artist Klaus vom Bruch was made in close temporal proximity to the events of the 1970s. Vom Bruch was based in Cologne at the time and therefore lived close to the site of the kidnapping and the government capital in Bonn. Unlike Périot, vom Bruch takes Schleyer's kidnapping as the focal point of his work. The video is a compilation of clips taken predominantly from West German television and other international stations after Schleyer's abduction in September 1977. *Das Schleyer-Band* includes official press conferences, talk show speculation, public interviews, news footage, the Eurovision song contest, advertisements, and recordings from the police radio. The video proceeds chronologically, ending with the group suicide of Andreas Baader, Gudrun Ensslin, and Jan-Carl Raspe.

Through selection, combination, and repetition of these diverse elements, Klaus vom Bruch reveals different meanings.[33] Sometimes these combinations function like parody, for example when a sequence featuring Christian Democrat politicians issuing a call for weapons is followed by an image of the weapon in the RAF logo. Vom Bruch also plays with combining symbols, for example placing "RAF" in the centre of the Eurovision song contest logo. Furthermore, vom Bruch combines moving images with different soundtracks. In one instance, he juxtaposes photographs of the wanted persons Baader, Ensslin, and Raspe with John Lennon's song *Working Class Hero*. Subtitling the lyrics in German, vom Bruch chooses a larger font for the refrain, highlighting the RAF's idolisation of the working class.[34] By playing

33   The art critic Hanne Loreck uses the terms "recycling" or "turning" to analyse the reuse of images in video works by the artist Eske Schlüters. Loreck describes how material is spun "until it is turned on its head or reveals a different side, one previously invisible" (Loreck 2006, 96). In the process of repetition, a transformation thus takes place.
34   German subtitle: "Ein Held der Arbeiter lohnt es zu sein" (Bruch 1977).

the complete song, this sequence simultaneously becomes an anthem dedicated to members of the RAF. In showing the televised message *Bitte bleiben sie am Gerät, neue Meldungen folgen* (Stay tuned, news bulletins expected), vom Bruch plays with the live broadcasting aspect of television and highlights Schleyer's kidnapping as a media event. Beyond this, he works with repetition, replaying scenes to take them out of the usual flow of news reporting. For example, footage of a Lufthansa airplane carrying members of the GSG9 (the elite tactical unit of the German Federal Police)—underscored by a celebratory soundtrack—is shown arriving in Bonn twice. The repetition emphasises the staging of the scene and encourages viewers to look at it in a different way.

Vom Bruch's video presents media expressions used by different protagonists. We encounter images of the mainstream entertainment industry, consumerism, the RAF's violent actions, and the violence used by the government. In combining these different elements, vom Bruch reveals a grotesque picture. *Das Schleyer-Band* is still challenging today because it shows the antagonism between the government and its opponents, raising the question: where did this antagonism go? The video does not

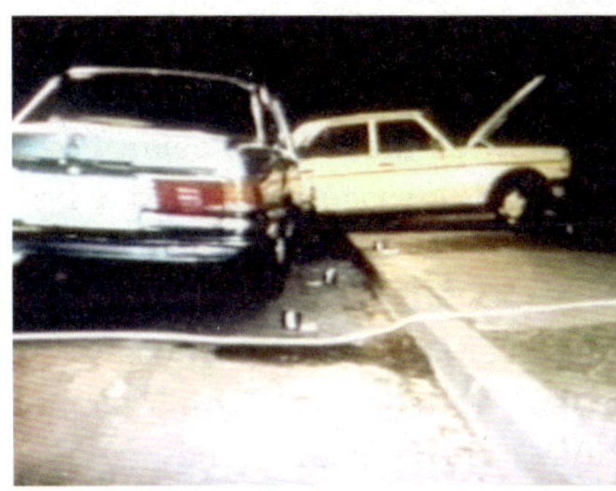

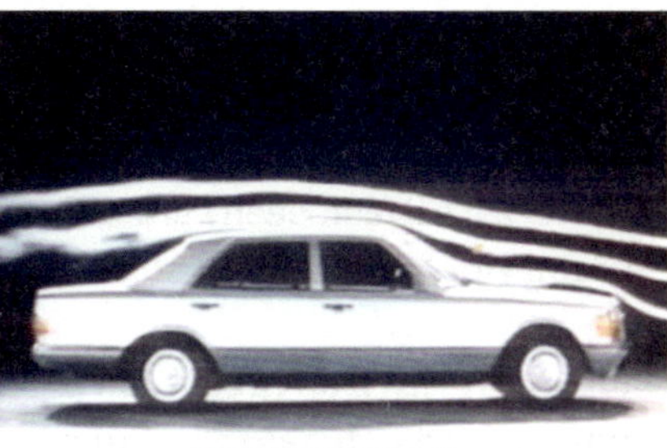

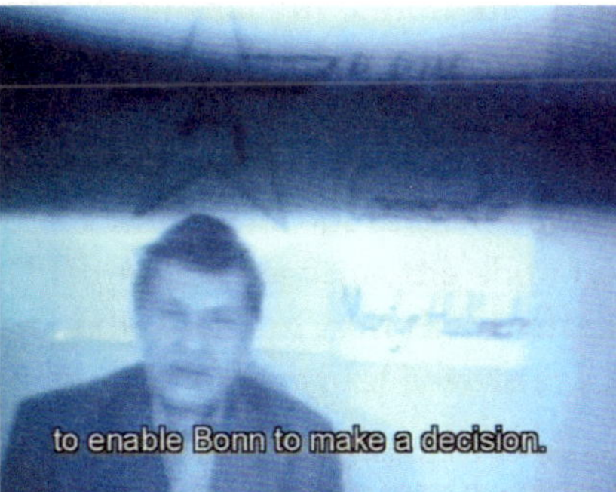

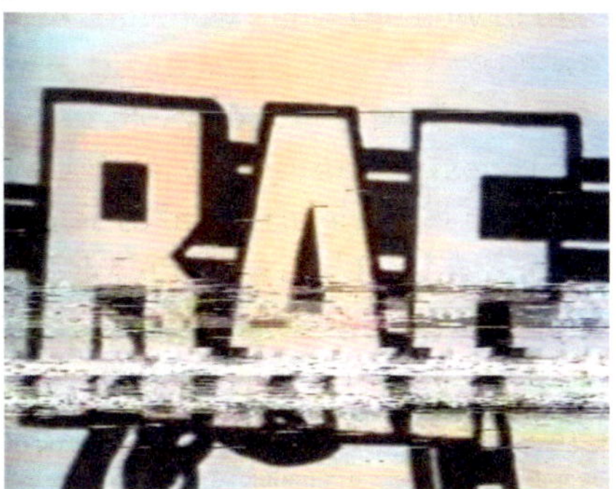

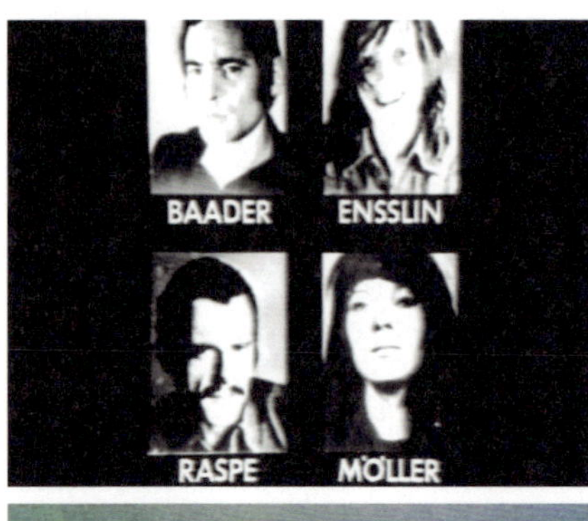

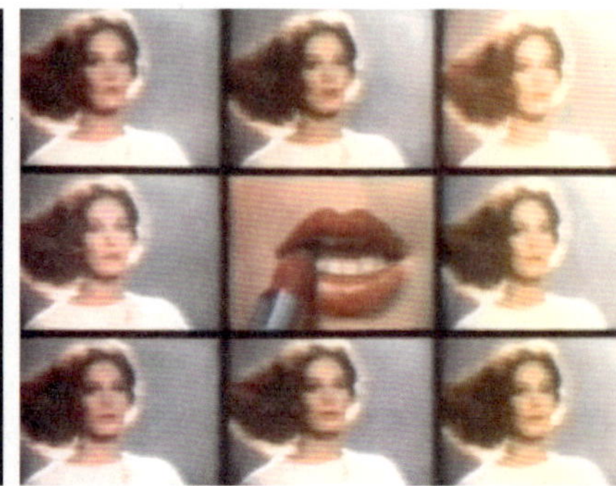

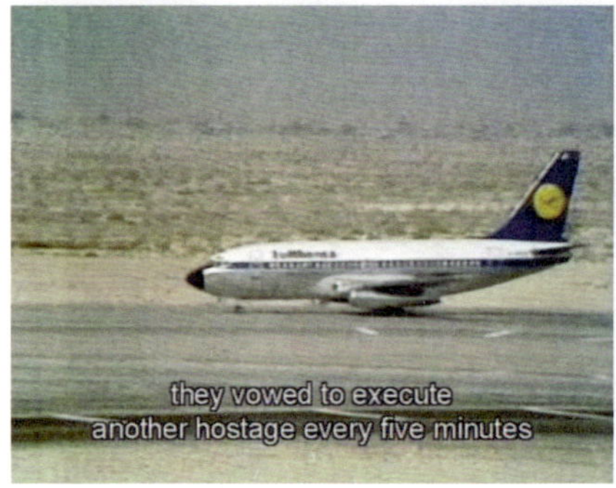

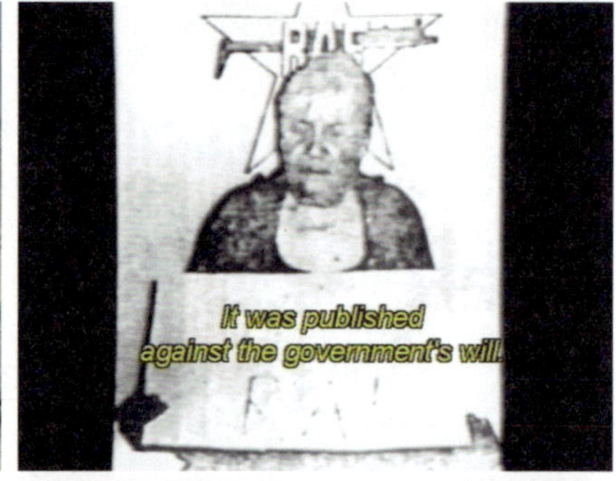

Das Umfeld
muß
eliminiert werden
"The entourage must be eliminated."

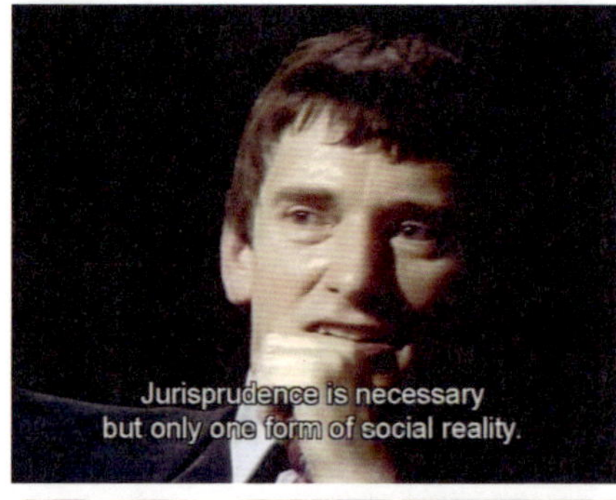

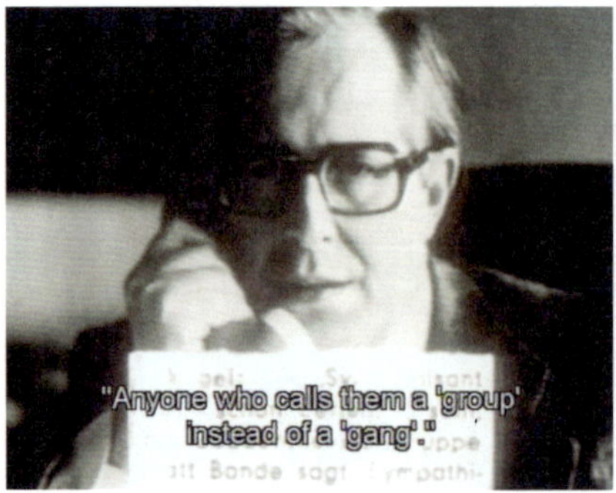

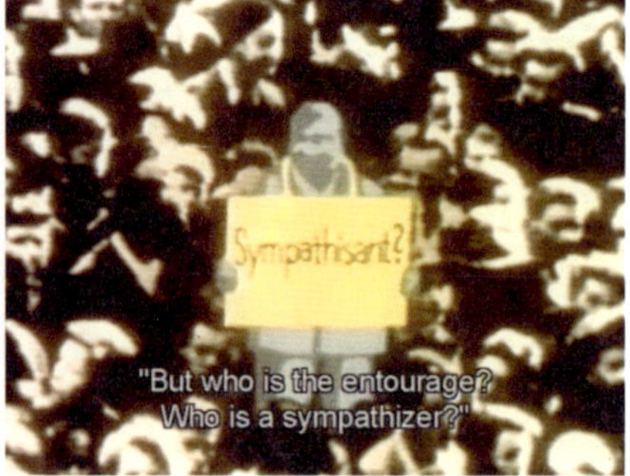

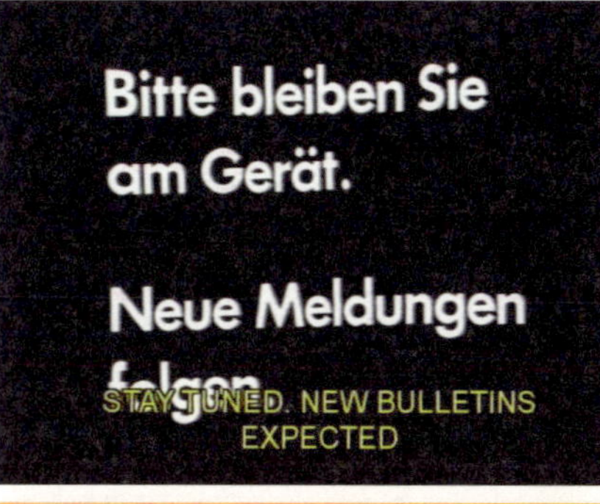

Bitte bleiben Sie
am Gerät.

Neue Meldungen
folgen
STAY TUNED. NEW BULLETINS
EXPECTED

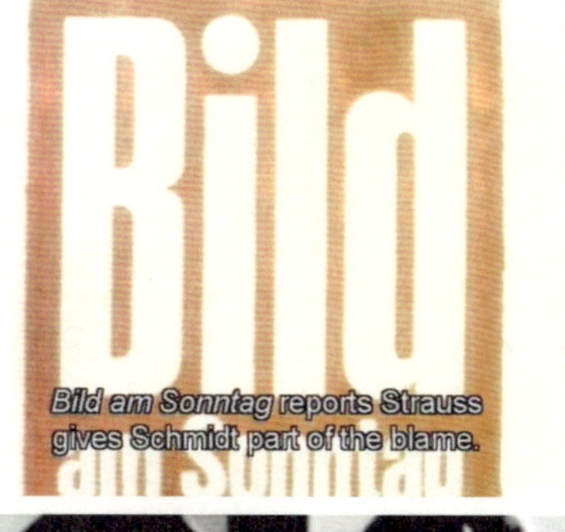

Bild
Bild am Sonntag reports Strauss
gives Schmidt part of the blame.
am Sonntag

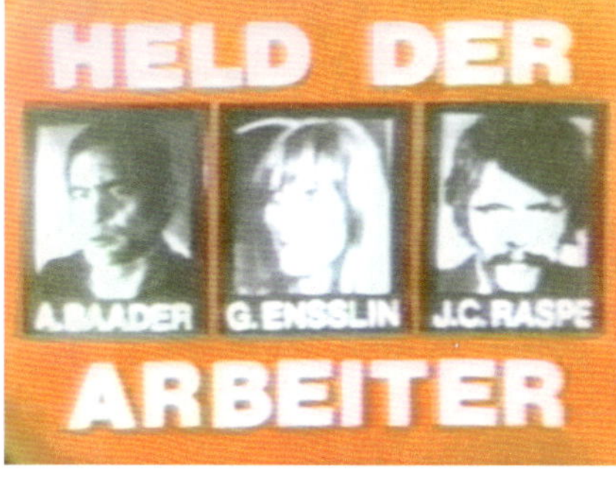

HELD DER
A. BAADER   G. ENSSLIN   J.C. RASPE
ARBEITER

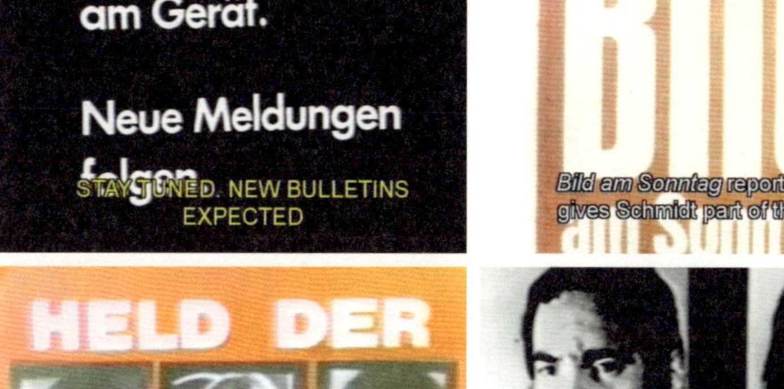

BAADER   ENSSLIN
strangled herself

BITTE BLEIBEN SIE AM

FERNSEHGERÄT
PLEASE STAY GLUED
TO YOUR TELEVISION SET
AT 3:20 P.M.
WE EXPECT TO TRANSMIT
A PRESS CONFERENCE
FROM THE PRISON
IN STUTTGART-STAMMHEIM.

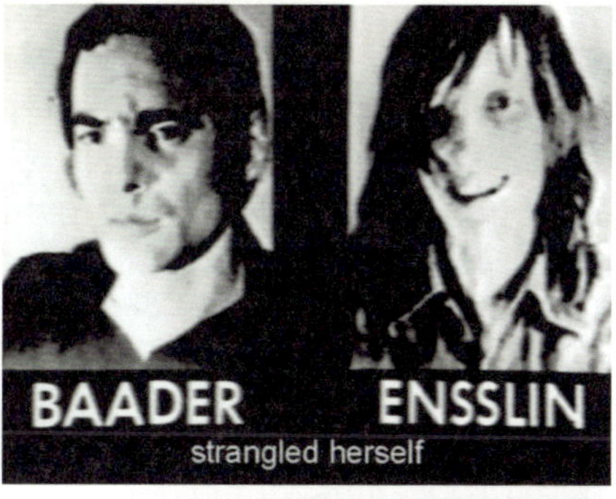

Her parents are sure
she was murdered.

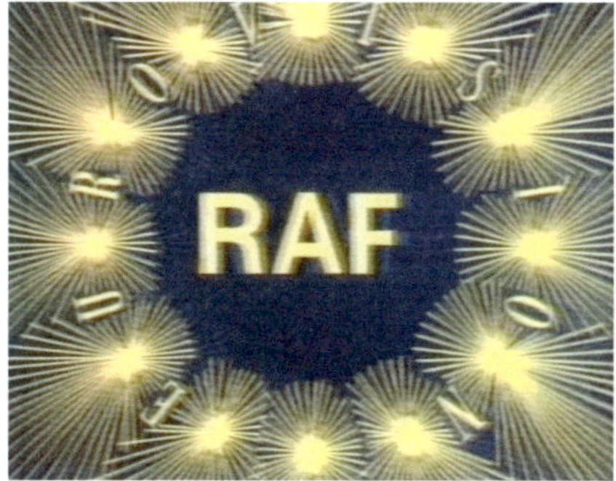

RAF

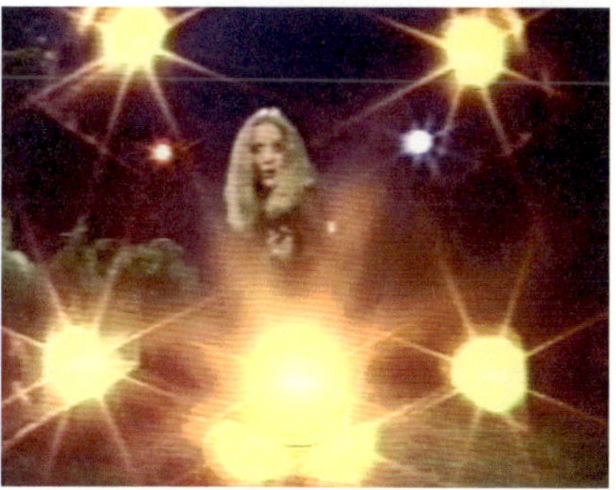
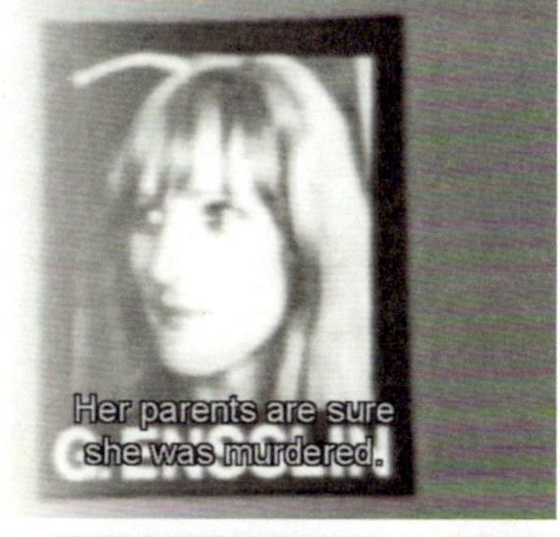

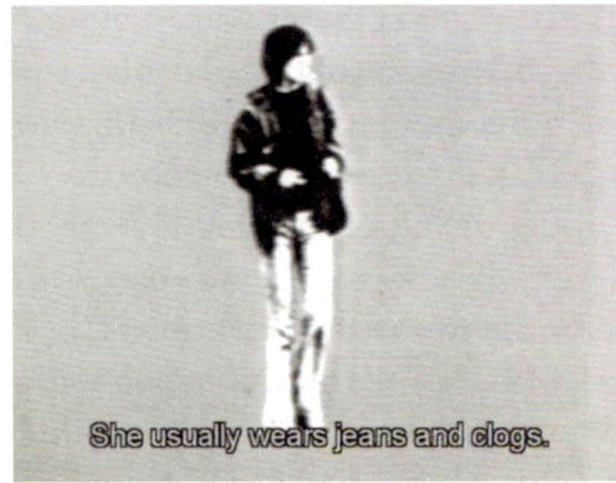

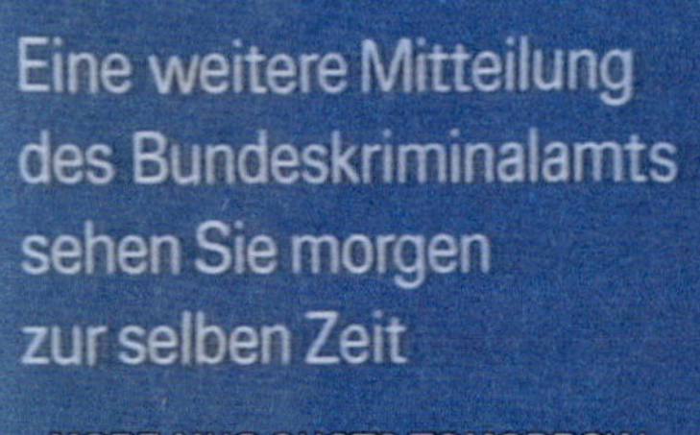

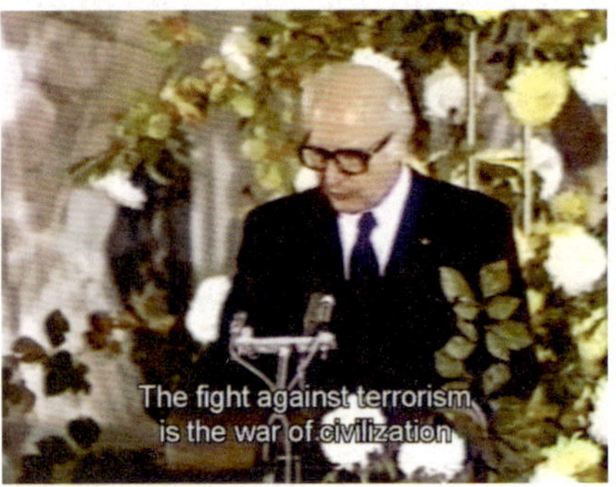

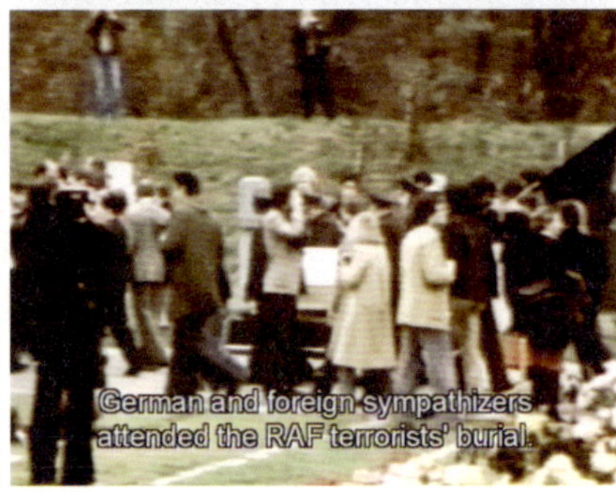

Film stills from *Das Schleyer-Band* (The Schleyer Tape) by Klaus vom Bruch, 1977–78

try to consolidate this conflict; instead, it confronts us with its different expressions, claims, and actions. Although the author is never obviously visible, he appears in the selection of film and sound clips and in the combinations of image and sound. This approach is similar to the method I use when working with found footage in the context of Hezbollah in Lebanon → see chapter 7.5.

In contrast to Klaus vom Bruch, Jean-Gabriel Périot emphasises a particular selection of material and keeps it intact. This selection includes obscure films and television contributions from the 1960s and 70s that show members of the RAF in a different light, beyond their familiar mugshot photographs. Despite the astonishing change of perspective towards the end of the film, Périot's selection of material recirculates critical articulations that have largely been forgotten. In doing so, the film interrupts the dominant narrative of history. Périot's compilation of found footage thus contains the potential to ignite a revision of our present, and this is where I locate the militant aspect of his work.

Unlike Périot's *Une Jeunesse Allemande*, vom Bruch's video was made at a polarised time, when even keeping a gun as a prop could trigger suspicion ^{Farocki 2009, 223-24}. I therefore regard *Das Schleyer-Band*—with its gestures of exposure, ridiculing of state speech, mixing of symbols, and sometimes sympathetic position towards the RAF—as a militant film.

> "The re-animation of militancy in contemporary artistic compositions and configurations, often emerging from the informal and institutional spaces of contemporary art, answers to a demand to reread the present from the perspective of a past that persists into the contemporary world and necessarily reconfigures its relation to history" ^{Demos 2015, 44}.

The "post-militant image", a term developed by the writer TJ Demos, describes the weaker role played by today's militant images, which are predominantly found in the art context ^{ibid., 41-46}. Is it true that today's militant images can only be found in this context? And if so, how effective are they? Demos addresses an important question: How are images involved in social and political reality? Meinhof left cultural production and joined the RAF precisely because she was frustrated by the limited effects of her cultural work. At a certain point, however, the activities of the RAF proved to be limited as well. Wisniewski's analysis of the visual politics of the West German news during Schleyer's kidnapping reveals how closely intertwined visual politics are with *Realpolitik*. Wisniewski brilliantly demonstrates how the news reports show the irreversibility of the government's position of non-negotiation with the RAF. Although this example does not refer to a militant image, it is evidence of the close ties between visual and state politics.

How to De/Link   2.5

The art context can, however, be a place for opposition and militancy. Often it remains one of the least controlled areas, as can be seen in Turkey's present situation. Perhaps this is proof of the art world's relatively harmless role. Yet when art institutions, artists, and curators are involved in political and social struggles, their existence becomes precarious. It therefore came as no surprise when the Turkish leftist intellectual and patron of the arts Osman Kavala was imprisoned in October 2017. After the severe conflicts in Turkey during the 1990s and the earthquake in 1999, Kavala decided to focus his work on art and culture. In 2002, he co-founded the cultural institution Anadolu Kültür, which aims to enable "the production, viewing, and sharing of arts and culture in Turkey, supporting local initiatives, emphasizing cultural diversity and rights and strengthening local and international collaborations" Free Osman Kavala n.d.. That same year, Anadolu Kültür founded Diyarbakır Sanat Merkezi (Diyarbakır Arts Centre) as its first local initiative in southeastern Turkey, the unofficial capital of Turkish Kurdistan.[35] Among other initiatives and centres, Anadolu Kültür also established Depo in Istanbul in 2008. Depo is an independent, non-commercial art space and site for critical discourse. It has taken a clear position on the Armenian Genocide[36] in several exhibition projects and was in solidarity with the Gezi Park protests.[37]

The practice of Anadolu Kültür, with its cultural centres Diyarbakır Sanat Merkezi and Depo, can be described as decolonial. The theoretician Walter D Mignolo defines decoloniality as a delinking of ties to rationality/modernity that are closely associated with colonial power. This epistemic delinking cannot be thought in the context of the universal claim of "emancipation" that is part of the project of Western modernity Mignolo 2012, 64–65. Instead, Mignolo suggests the term "liberation" as an alternative that includes emancipation ibid., 61.[38] Delinking should not be misunderstood as a complete negation of what exists. Instead, it focuses on recognising imperial and colonial techniques and using them to decolonise existing structures ibid., 88. The rhetoric of modernity creates its own "interior" that simultaneously produces an exterior. This leads to an "othering" of the "barbarian" or the "primitive" that is used to legitimise genocides ibid., 121–23. Mignolo introduces the notion of "pluriversality" as the result of a practice that decolonises modernity's concept of universality, accepting the existence of different parallel rhythms ibid., 56, 194. These differing rhythms are forms of knowledge situated in distinct bodies, spaces, and time zones ibid., 190.

Anadolu Kültür engages in an unlearning of the official narrative of Turkish history. It does so by involving the practices and knowledge

35   For more information about Diyarbakır Sanat Merkezi see: diyarbakirsanat.org/en/default.aspx.

36   Turkey still refuses to use the word "genocide" to describe the killing of 1.5 million Armenians within the Ottoman Empire in 1915.

37   The Gezi Park protests began in Turkey on 28 May 2013. Initially the civil unrest was a response to a plan to develop Istanbul's Taksim Gezi Park. This plan consisted of removing Gezi Park, one of the few remaining green spaces in the centre of the European side of Istanbul. It involved making Taksim Square into a pedestrian zone, rebuilding the Ottoman-era Taksim Military Barracks (which had been demolished in 1940), and constructing a shopping mall. The violent dispersal of a sit-in led to the development of a protest camp at the park. This was accompanied by protests and strikes across Turkey demanding freedom of the press and freedom of expression, assembly, and critique of the government's authoritarian politics. After months of heavy clashes between the riot police and protesters, the protests died down in August 2013.

38   Following the liberation philosophy of Enrique Dussel (Russel 2003).

of those who are marginalised and excluded. Furthermore, it initiates exchange and critical discourse to support diversity in civil society. Although Jean-Gabriel Périot's film *Une Jeunesse Allemande* focuses on a completely different history and context, there is a similarity in how this film unlearns the official state narrative of West Germany in the 1970s. Listening to Ulrike Meinhof speak in talk shows and interviews allows viewers to understand her critique of the authoritarian state system and its politics in the 1960s. Seeing Holger Meins's approach to filming Oskar Langenfeld shows Meins as a sensitive young man. Although this doesn't legitimise the RAF's chosen path, it doesn't perform an "othering" of radicalisation, creating an exteriority to the inner sphere of governmental rule. Given the one-dimensional narrative concerning this recent part of German history, it is not surprising that it was difficult to find funding for the film in Germany. The ignorant idea that all stories about the RAF have already been told masks a fear of facing this past.[39]

Anonymisation and Camouflage   2.6

"We saw going underground as part of building, diversifying, deepening the struggle and giving it a new aspect and element which is the capacity to live and work from a space that wasn't under attack and wasn't under the eyes of the state day to day" Antonio, Lampson, and Wexler 1976. As the case of the RAF demonstrates, going underground often leads to isolation. Other West German organisations like the *Bewegung 2. Juni*, the *Revolutionäre Zellen*, or the feminist group *Rote Zora* never went underground: they lived legally and carried out their professions alongside their militant activities. In doing so, they stayed in close contact and exchange with their political base. Their legality sometimes even served as camouflage for their militant activities.

The documentary film *Underground* (1976) by Emile de Antonio, Mary Lampson, and Haskell Wexler represents an attempt to escape

---

39   This information is based on an informal conversation with the film producer Meike Martens in 2017.

40   The Weather Underground Organisation, commonly known as the Weather Underground, was a radical leftist militant organisation active between 1969 and 1977 in the United States. Originally called the Weathermen, it grew out of the Revolutionary Youth Movement (RYM) faction of Students for a Democratic Society (SDS). Its political goal was to create a revolutionary party to overthrow American imperialism. The group conducted a campaign of bombings through the mid-1970s and took part in actions such as the jailbreak of Timothy Leary in 1970. The bombing campaign targeted government buildings and banks. Some attacks were preceded by evacuation warnings along with statements identifying what the attack was intended to protest. Although no civilians were killed, three members of the group died in an accidental Greenwich Village townhouse explosion. In its founding document, the group called for a "white fighting force" to be allied with the Black Liberation Movement and other radical struggles.

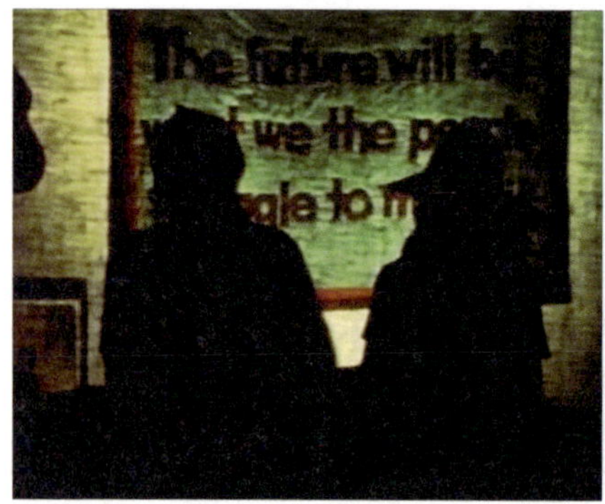

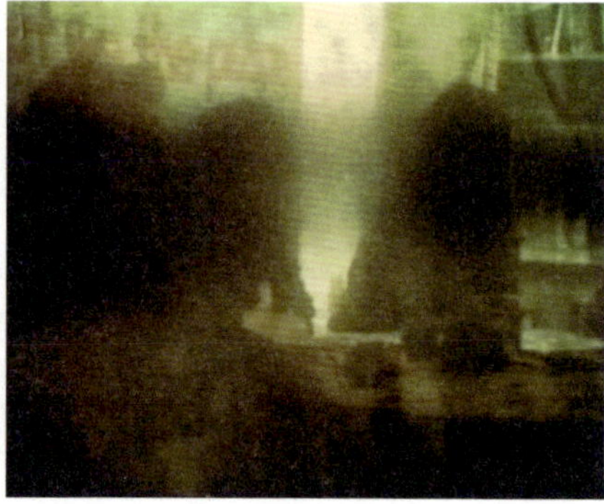

Film stills from *Underground* by Emile de Antonio, Mary Lampson, and Haskell Wexler, 1976

isolation. When the Weather Underground,[40] a militant group based in the United States, first went underground, this lifestyle opened up a space for experimentation in relationships, sexuality, friendship, and care [Green and Siegel 2002]. Yet Brian Flanagan, a former member of the group, stated in 2002 that he eventually began to feel trapped and isolated. At a certain point, he felt that the only scope of action he had left was to plant another bomb. The more violent the Weather Underground became, however, the more it suited President Richard Nixon [ibid.]. The more the Weather Underground adopted the military logic of the state, the more vulnerable they became. This development shows similarities to the failures of the RAF.

Antonio, Lampson, and Wexler filmed their documentary in 1976, one year after the Weather Underground went into hiding. At one point, a transparent material between the camera and the protagonists blurs the filmed image. During a conversation that takes place over three days, the camera often shoots from behind the group, facing the film team. A second camera only records details. This intensifies the inquisitive nature of the interview situation. The tension during filming unfolds in a conversation about the uneasy presence of the camera and the artificial situation it produces for the speaking subject. This specific way of filming succeeds in maintaining the anonymity of the group.

In the film, a female member of the Weather Underground reads a poem that she has dedicated to Assata Shakur,[41] a member of the Black Liberation Army: "For Assata Shakur: Underground is not the right word, it makes it seem too simple as if there is an easy way to disappear,

41   Shakur escaped to Cuba, where she was granted political asylum. She is the first woman to appear on the FBI's list of most-wanted terrorists. After the opening of Cuba, the United States asked the government to deliver Shakur, but Cuba—claiming its independence—refused.

a place to go. Beneath the city's streets there is no safe passage ... And during those last months they hunted you hard I was an invisible supporter walking on another front. Knowing of these tearing apart times when the days are like the flashes of a strobe-light and the earth turns with a racing rhythm forming for the guerrilla for a normal life time in a single month. And when you were captured sister I wept for all of us" Antonio, Lampson, and Wexler 1976. Written in solidarity, the poem highlights the parallel rhythms of living underground, with its particular experience of time, hiding, and day-to-day life.

In Gillo Pontecorvo's film *La battaglia di Algeri*, different cultural or religious codes are used as camouflage tactics. The chador, a religious

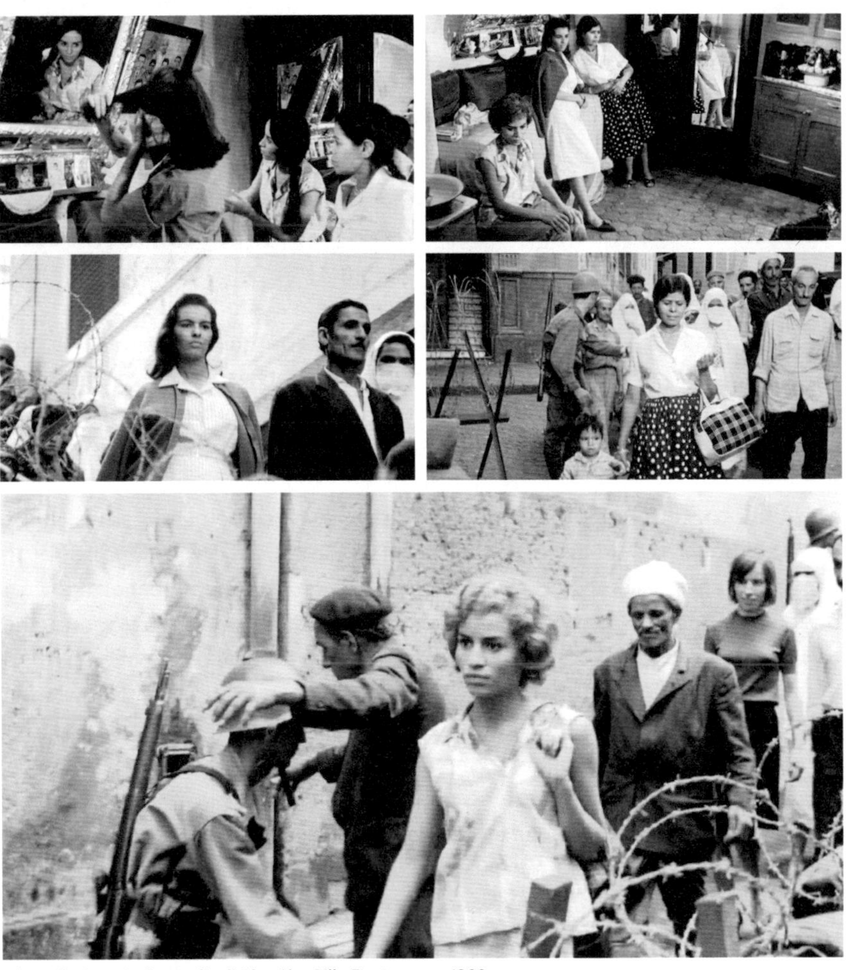

Film stills from *La battaglia di Algeri* by Gillo Pontecorvo, 1966

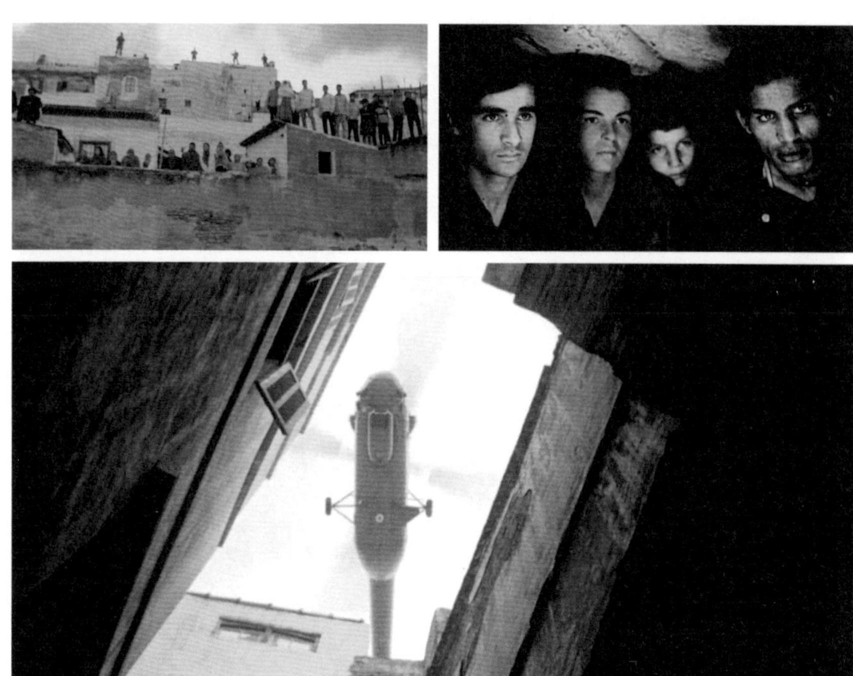

Film stills from *La battaglia di Algeri* by Gillo Pontecorvo, 1966

symbol for the protection of femininity, becomes a militant tool when an Algerian woman smuggles a pistol underneath her clothing while passing through a checkpoint. Obliged to show respect for different cultural and religious conventions, the French soldiers avoid a body check. Only a few scenes later, three westernised Algerian women smuggle bombs through the checkpoint. They use the camouflage tactic of looking similar to French women and therefore do not represent Algerian "otherness" in the colonial gaze of the French military. Unfortunately, apart from these two scenes, Pontecorvo's film pays little attention to the role of women in the Algerian struggle.

The casbah (Arabic: قصبة | citadel or fortress) constitutes another urban space of camouflage for the National Liberation Front. As an enclosure with a labyrinthine design, it becomes a refuge that protects and hides members of the FLN. At the same time, it functions like a cage that the resistance fighters cannot simply leave. This is why one FLN member in the film dreams of a romantic trip to Paris with his lover. As *La battaglia di Algeri* focuses on the developments of the militant and military struggle, the space of the rebels becomes increasingly smaller until they are caught in a tiny hideout in a house.

"Hello, citizen of the world, we are Anonymous" Anonymous 2011. Techniques of anonymisation are also used by groups like Anonymous and WikiLeaks. Their methods differ from going underground or appearing as bodies in public space to articulate protest. WikiLeaks creates an anonymous space that allows whistleblowers to share information without revealing their identity. This anonymisation enables people to act politically from within institutions such as the United States military. Political action can occur as an individual or collective act, as in the case of Anonymous. Anonymous is a group consisting of different members whose actions take place within a loose and decentralised system that follows ideas as opposed to orders. Its activities include hacking websites of organisations such as the Church of Scientology or the Islamic State (ISIS). If members of Anonymous appear in public, they wear Guy Fawkes masks to hide their identities.[42] The Anonymous logo—an ironic adaptation of the logo used by the United Nations—also plays with anonymisation. At its centre, a suited figure appears with a question mark as its head, indicating that anyone could be that person. Simultaneously, it represents the refusal to reveal an identity.

An anonymous action is recalcitrant and can be compared to "the suspension of submission" de Lagasnerie 2016, 104.[43] These political activities don't demand a political identity that is constructed and reproduced in relationships. De Lagasnerie refers to Hannah Arendt's definition of the political, which is established in a relation with others. Arendt claims that this is the moment at which the private becomes public Arendt 1958, 50–68. According to de Lagasnerie, traditional forms of protest make subjects enter into public space. He describes the condition of this political action as a submission against the other: "I address the other, I provoke its reaction … It [the subject] shows that it accepts [the enemy] as interlocutor and will negotiate with him" de Lagasnerie 2016, 106.[44]

42 Guy Fawkes tried to blow up the British Parliament in 1605. In his 1982 graphic novel *V for Vendetta*, Allan Moore developed the Guy Fawkes mask for his main character, V. V is a revolutionary who fights against a fascist regime in Great Britain. Wearing the mask allows him to stay anonymous until the end of his life. During the Occupy movement, the Guy Fawkes mask became a global symbol for resistance against the injustice of the capitalist system.

43 Translated by Sandra Schäfer. "Die Aufhebung der Unterwerfung" (de Lagasnerie 2016, 104).

44 Translated by Sandra Schäfer. "Ich spreche ihn an, ich provoziere seine Reaktion … es [das Subjekt] zeigt, daß es ihn [den Gegner] als Gesprächspartner ansieht, daß es mit ihm verhandeln wird" (Lagasnerie 2016, 106).

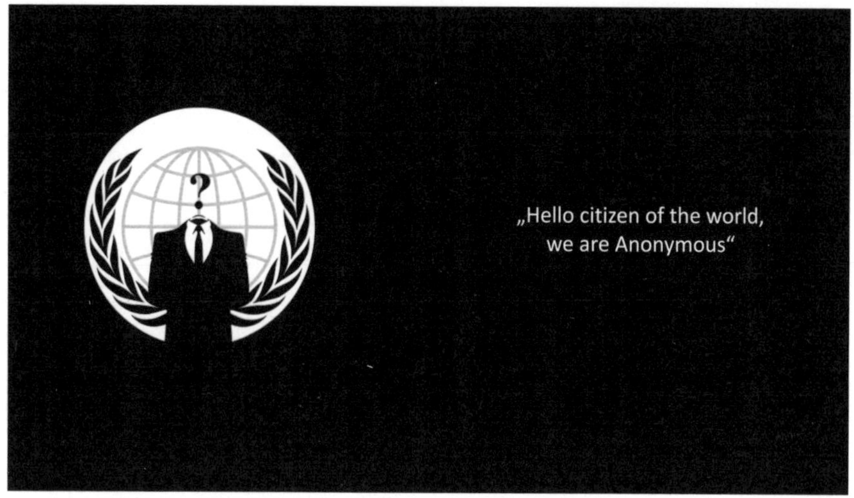

Logo and quotation from Anonymous (2011), composed by Sandra Schäfer

But "the mask, the encryption allow an intervention without establishing a relation, without knowing one's own enemies and without allowing them to answer" ibid., 108.[45] As much as I agree with de Lagasnerie that the mask can play a liberating role, someone still needs to apply the encryption or wear the mask—and, as we saw with Chelsea Manning, this person is sometimes discovered.

"Hello, citizen of the world, we are Anonymous" addresses everybody; a group that is not bound to national borders. Anonymous uses virtual space, which offers a potential alternative social world beyond family ties, friendship, nationality, and citizenship. According to de Lagasnerie, de-nationalisation would not lead to something like a global community: "On the contrary, it is a special case of the suspension of submission to forced identifications, releasing the capacity to imagine new, plural, heterogeneous, and ephemeral communities ... to have the world as a spiritual horizon and to establish never before seen, self-chosen communities" ibid., 160.[46] Again, as much as I share de Lagasnerie's euphoric idea of building different communities through the space of the

45   Translated by Sandra Schäfer. "Die Maske, die Verschlüsselung gestatten eine Intervention, ohne eine Beziehung herzustellen, ohne die eigenen Feinde zu erkennen und ohne ihnen die Möglichkeit zur Antwort zu lassen" (Lagasnerie 2016, 108).

46   Translated by Sandra Schäfer. "Ganz im Gegenteil ist sie ein Sonderfall eines Prozesses der Aufhebung der Unterwerfung mit Bezug auf erzwungene Identifikationen, um die Fähigkeit freizusetzen, sich neue, plurale, heterogene und flüchtige Gemeinschaften vorzustellen ... als geistigen Horizont die Welt zu haben, noch nie dagewesene selbstgewählte Gemeinschaften entstehen zu lassen" (Lagasnerie 2016, 105–6).

internet—leaving the ties of nation and family behind—virtual space is not an empty sphere that is equally accessible to everyone. Internet speed, control, and access vary depending on where one lives. Furthermore, struggles are diverse and local realities need to be taken into consideration. In addition, the market limits and influences the use of virtual space. Therefore, this space does not exist outside of constellations of power.

Beyond "With or Against" **2.7**

"When a common citizen commits murder, their reasons are bad or even nonexistent. Isn't the problem with the terrorists that they have reasons you might understand?" Brustellin et al. 1978.[47]

Deutschland im Herbst (Germany in Autumn, 1978), a collective film by Rainer Werner Fassbinder, Alexander Kluge, Edgar Reitz, and others, was not seen as militant by its makers. In West Germany at that time, however, you were either with or against the RAF; with or against the state. This film offers a different course of action within a polarised political climate. In this radical and courageous project, disparate filmmakers produce critical and ambivalent narratives centring on state politics and the RAF.

The filmmakers involved with *Deutschland im Herbst* develop a political approach characterised by a diversity of aesthetics and ideas. Alexander Kluge positions his camera next to the official state media for his documentary observation of Hanns Martin Schleyer's official funeral service at St Eberhard's Cathedral in Stuttgart. The preparations and enactment of the state burial are filmed in long takes, emphasising how state power is produced, edited, and staged. Kluge's reading of Schleyer's letter to his son (requesting that he give in to the kidnappers' demands in order to avoid bloodshed) exposes the harsh logic of his previous partners in politics and business, who sacrifice Schleyer for the sake of the many.[48] Their hypocrisy is revealed in their condolence wreaths and their faces. Kluge interrupts the ceremony with historical footage from the 1934 murder of the Serbian king accompanied by an off-commentary that emphasises the involvement of the German secret service. In doing so, he highlights the hypocrisy of the West German

---

47   Translated by Sandra Schäfer. "Ein normaler Bürger hat sogar nur schlechte oder gar keine Gründe für einen Mord. Ist das schlimme bei den Terroristen nicht vielleicht, dass sie vielleicht sogar Gründe haben, die du verstehen könntest?" (Brustellin et al. 1978).

48   When the Lufthansa "Landshut" airplane was hijacked in October 1977, it became clear that this calculation was a mistake.

state that positions itself as a victim but is simultaneously a perpetrator. The death of Schleyer represents the violence and military logic of both the RAF as well as the state.

Rainer Werner Fassbinder's contribution to *Deutschland im Herbst* provides a different and disturbing approach. Fassbinder explores terrorism, state violence, and paranoia within the intimacy of his relationships with his partner, Armin Meier, and his mother, Liselotte Eder. The filmmaker appears in the role of an unbearable, paranoid, and self-pitying character trying to calm himself down through the use of alcohol and cocaine. An argument with his mother resembles an interrogation that shifts between anger, desparation, tenacity, and moments of affection and gentleness. Fassbinder confronts his mother with the contradictions of her own statements. Ultimately, when he asks her to describe the ideal form of government, she admits that it would be "an authoritarian ruler, but a good one, nice and well-behaved" Brustellin et al. 1978.[49]

Fassbinder dares to articulate that although terrorists are murderers, they kill for reasons that one might share and support. He also criticises the government for treating terrorists differently from other murderers. In doing so, he points to a blind spot within democracy, revealing how state power, with its rules of exception, acts outside the legal framework. Fassbinder's segment explores the political in the depths of the personal. His willful[50] contribution represents a radical attempt to open a space for thinking that allows the spectator to experience the effects of state and police violence on the psyche, the body, and relationships.

As a collective undertaking with diverse contributions, *Deutschland im Herbst* intervenes in a hysterical and polarised atmosphere, shifting the dominant poles of articulation. The film ends with the burial of RAF members Andreas Baader, Gudrun Ensslin, and Jan-Carl Raspe at the Dornhalden cemetery in Stuttgart. It is an uncanny scene that is difficult to grasp. Hundreds of supporters and relatives are gathered. Some mask their faces, raise their fists, or hold banners. Policemen on horses survey the scene from the surrounding hills. A quotation repeats from the beginning of the film: "When cruelty reaches a certain level, it is no longer

---

49   Translated by Sandra Schäfer. "Ein autoritärer Herrscher, der ganz gut ist, ganz lieb und artig" (Brustellin et al. 1978).

50   With the use of the term "willful", I refer to Sarah Ahmed's interpretation of the will as a "name given by or in history to the possibility of deviation … the willful subject might be striking in her appearance not only because she disagrees with what has been willed by others, but because she disagrees with what has disappeared from view" (Ahmed 2014, 11, 16).

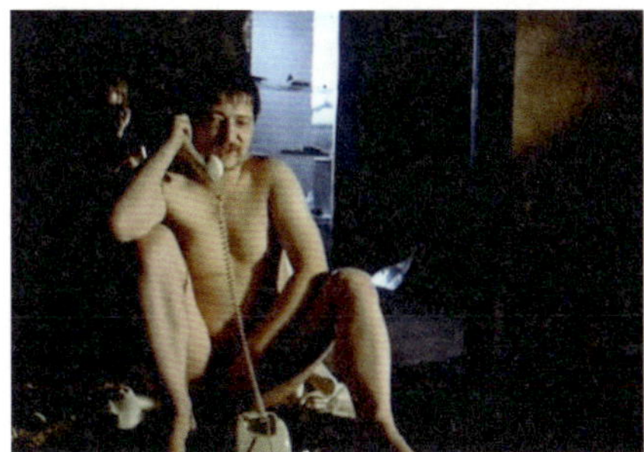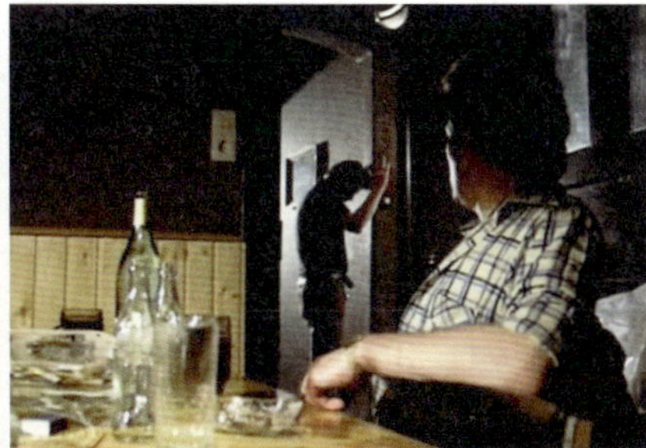
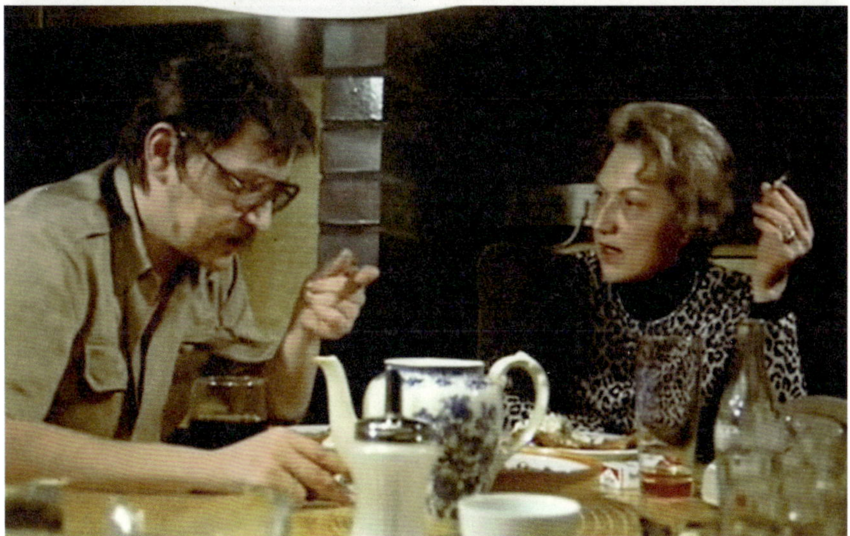

Rainer Werner Fassbinder and Liselotte Eder in *Deutschland im Herbst*, 1978

important who initiated it, only that it be stopped."[51] This quote, attributed to a mother at the end of the Second World War, seems even more out of place than it was at the outset of the film. It closes the case and offers "a redemptive image that distracts us from the contradictions of violence, the incompleteness of the events" Seeßlen 1997.[52] The statement feels like a betrayal, anticipating the atmosphere of silence in the 1980s. Nevertheless, it is not able to tame the collective effort of *Deutschland im Herbst*. The film remains a troubling and subversive undertaking that does not smooth contradictions. In this sense, it challenges polarisation and can be regarded as a militant act: diverse and irreconcilable. It does not

51   Translated by Sandra Schäfer. "An einem bestimmten Punkt der Grausamkeit angekommen, ist es schon gleich, wer sie begangen hat: sie soll nur aufhören" (Brustellin et al. 1978).

52   Translated by Sandra Schäfer. "Ein Erlösungsbild, das uns von der Widersprüchlichkeit der Gewalttätigkeit, der Unabgeschlossenheit der Ereignisse ablenkt" (Seeßlen 1997).

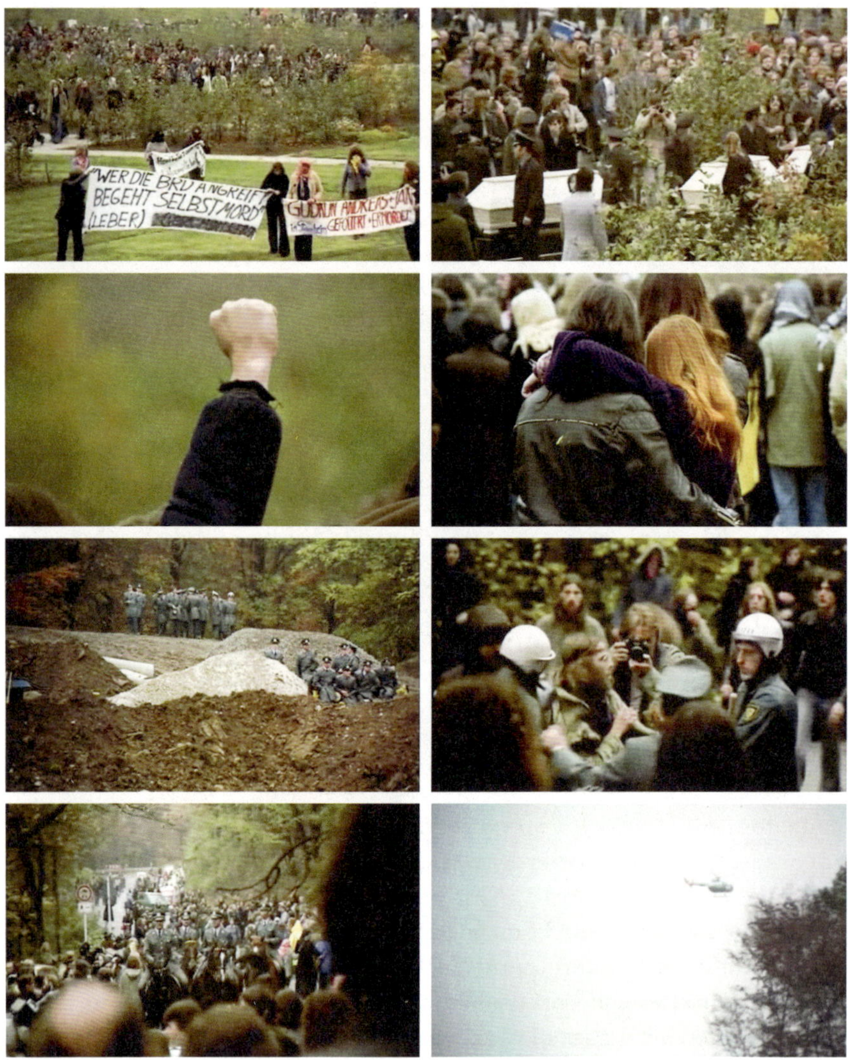

Film stills from Alexander Kluge's contribution to *Deutschland im Herbst*, 1978

assimilate to the hysteria that Fassbinder's mother, compares to the Nazi era, during which "one simply kept silent to avoid getting into hot water" Brustellin et al. 1978.[53]

53 Translated by Sandra Schäfer. "Wo man geschwiegen hat, um sich nicht in Teufels Küche zu bringen" (Seeßlen 1997).

Like the filmmakers involved with *Deutschland im Herbst*, Gillo Pontecorvo and Costa-Gavras did not categorise their films as militant. At first glance, *La battaglia di Algeri* by Pontecorvo and *État de Siège* (Stage of Siege, 1972) by Costa-Gavras appear to be classical feature films. Yet both projects derive their scripts from particular urban guerrilla struggles. *La battaglia di Algeri* was a collaboration between the former military commander of the FLN Saadi Yacef, the Italian filmmaker Gillo Pontecorvo, and the screenwriter Franco Solinas. Together with the French filmmaker René Vautier, Yacef had already developed a film treatment based on his prison memoirs. With this treatment in hand, Yacef and Vautier travelled to Italy to look for a director. Pontecorvo had also developed a script about the Algerian War of Independence called *Para*, which was supposed to feature Paul Newman as a journalist covering the war. Yacef was critical of *Para*'s Eurocentric approach whereas Pontecorvo found Yacef's script to be too celebratory of the FLN. Under these circumstances, Yacef invited Pontecorvo and Solinas to Algiers to speak with different people involved in the liberation struggle and to witness the traces of both French colonialism and the liberation. Based on these experiences, Pontecorvo and Solinas revised Yacef's script Daulatzai 2016, 25–26.

Although Pontecorvo has stated that he takes a position in *La battaglia di Algeri*, film theoretician Mike Wayne claims that this is not obvious in the film Wayne 2001, 11, 17. Wayne classifies the adoption of a neutral position as a middle-class phenomenon. He contrasts this approach with Third Cinema—and thus also Militant Cinema—which tries to show how problems are generated and attempts to take a committed stance Espinosa 1997; Wayne 2001, 13. From my point of view, Wayne does not take into account that *La battaglia di Algeri* was made as a collaboration between Yacef, Pontecorvo, and Solinas and is therefore informed by Yacef's experience as a participant in the liberation struggle. Additionally, *La battaglia di Algeri* was not filmed during the liberation struggle itself; it was produced three years after Algeria's independence from France. In this sense, it differs from Getino and Solanas's *La hora de los hornos*. *La battaglia di Algeri* reflects, instead, on the difficulties of the nation-building process in liberated Algeria. In one scene, FLN leader Ali la Pointe tells little Ali: "It is hard enough to start a revolution, even harder to sustain it, and hardest of all to win it. But it's only

afterwards, once we've won, that the real difficulties begin" ^{Pontecorvo 1966}.
At the time of its filming in 1965, President Ahmed Ben Bella had just
been overthrown and replaced by Houari Boumediene. These conflicts
reflect Frantz Fanon's suspicion towards the new elites in liberated
nations ^{Fanon 1963, 44}.

In contrast to Mike Wayne, I regard the complex lens through which
La battaglia di Algeri analyses the French colonial military regime
and the guerrilla tactics used by revolutionaries as a strength of the
film ^{Wayne 2001, 18}.[54] *La battaglia di Algeri* shows the spatial segregation
of the French colonial regime, with the casbah representing the space
of the Algerian Other. Furthermore, the Algerian fight for liberation is
represented as the struggle of a community and not of an individual. This
community is shown to have political agency. Arabic—a language that
was suppressed under colonial rule—is used to analyse the violence of
the colonial system. The opening scene addresses torture and presents
violence as the condition of the colonial regime. Rebellion against this
violence is thus introduced as a necessity from the very beginning of the
film. In doing so, *La battaglia di Algeri* makes a statement in support of
the liberation struggle.

In one scene, Colonel Mathieu, played by Jean Martin, demonstrates
the legitimisation of torture in the French colonial system: "The word
torture does not appear in our orders … Should we remain in Algeria?
If you answer yes, then you must accept all the necessary consequences"
^{Pontecorvo 1966}. Jean Martin, the only professional actor in the film, fought
in the French Resistance and was a paratrooper in the war against
colonised Indochina ^{Tunzelmann 2009}. In 1960, he signed the "Manifesto of the

54   The curator and writer Habiba Djahnine notes that "post-independence Algerian cinematographic pro-
      ductions are all marked by a uniquely national narrative, with a form of Arabic that vacillates between
      literary Arabic and vernacular Arabic. It was paramount to celebrate the people's heroism, the heroes'
      courage, and to radically denounce the abuses perpetrated under French colonization. These films do
      not necessarily dwell on the complexity of what happened during the (Algerian) War of Independence.
      Their denunciatory and accusatory tenor functioned like a catharsis for Algerians who, moved and
      astounded, discovered images of their gruesome national history that they had just lived through"
      (Djahnine 2018, 26–27). The filmmaker Sarah Maldoror, who worked as a production assistant for *La
      battaglia di Algeri*, made the short feature film *Monangambeee* in 1969. Unlike *La battaglia di Algeri*
      and other post-independence films, her work does not focus on the common heroic male narrative and
      thus does not reproduce the gender binary. Instead, it deconstructs colonial violence on several levels
      such as physical brutality, racism, and institutional dominance. Since Maldoror does not directly show
      physical violence, she was accused of producing a "woman's film" (Djahnine 2018, 29). In 1982, Assia
      Djebar made *La Zerda et les chants de l'oubli* (The Zerda and the Songs of Forgetting). For this film,
      she appropriates footage from various archives to produce a montage of North African heroes. At the
      same time, female voices can be heard singing, whispering, and screaming—mourning their lives and
      stories as well as those of the heroes. As Djahnine notes, the existence of counter-voices poetically
      destabilises and decentralises the colonial gaze (Djahnine 2018, 29–30).

121" against the Algerian War. Furthermore, Saadi Yacef, the Algerian co-producer and former military leader of the FLN, plays himself. Since only a few years had passed since Algeria's liberation, all of the lay actors in the film experienced the colonial regime. The fictionalised script is therefore informed by multiple recently lived practices within colonial and militant reality. The militant image is thus embedded in the tactical script and its circulation between the memories of real struggles and their artistic representation. This militant script is then transformed into a fictional script, circulates, and can again enter real struggles, becoming a script for further actions.

In West Berlin at the beginning of the 1970s, both *La battaglia di Algeri* and *État de Siège* were shown in small cinemas. A member of the *Bewegung 2. Juni* states that supporters of the group attended these screenings in order to study different urban guerrilla tactics.[55] One particular scene from *État de Siège* as well as a small booklet about the kidnapping of Philip Michael Santore[56] by the *Tupamaros* in Uruguay became the blueprint for the abduction of Peter Lorenz, the Chairman of the Christian Democrats in Berlin. A script from reality was reinterpreted, staged for film, and became the template for a script enacted in reality. The *Bewegung 2. Juni* attempted to adopt another method it encountered in the cinema. In *État de Siège*, a clandestine election takes place on public transportation: one member of the *Tupamaros* stays on a bus while a new member gets on at every stop to vote. When the *Bewegung 2. Juni* reenacted this method on a West Berlin subway train, the rhythm between each member's arrival and the train's departure did not match. Later it turned out that the bus election was one of the few scenes invented by Costa-Gavras.[57]

The premiere of *La battaglia di Algeri* was celebrated in Venice in 1966. Opponents of the Vietnam War identified parallels between Algeria and Southeast Asia. The film critic Andrew Sarris noted the following: "Waves of applause broke out at scenes of terrorism against the French colonials, at individual acts of murder … at times, there were cheers. 'Saigon next!' a man shouted as the Algerians blew up a crowded café in the French quarter" Jusuf 2014. What does it mean when a film sparks such reactions? Does it become militant by inciting the public to call

---

55   This information is based on a conversation with a person who prefers to stay anonymous.
56   Philip Michael Santore was an official of the United States Agency for International Development (USAID).
57   This information is based on a conversation with a person who prefers to stay anonymous.

for militant action? Or is this demand always already present in the filmic scene?[58]

The militant image only exists if people identify with it, share it, and feel affected by it. In his striking essay "Do Not Think One Has to Be Sad", the writer Jeff Derksen points out that "the militant image is always half someone else's" Derksen 2015, 16. Derksen refers to Mikhail Bakhtin's understanding of language: the appropriation of words and their meanings by a speaker with certain intentions Bakhtin 1982, 293–94. I agree with Derksen and would go even further to claim that the militant image is involved in what Sarah Ahmed calls "affective economies" that glue a community together Ahmed 2004, 119. The militant image triggers affect that can create distance or affinity. When it circulates in social media, for example, the militant image can create an affective community that goes beyond a physical locality, as could be seen in the Gezi Park protests. While these protests had a strong physical component, social media was used to connect with other localities, creating a larger international community that transcended geography.

Beyond these geographical crossings, the militant image can also travel through time. The writer and curator Sohail Daulatzai thus characterises *La battaglia di Algeri* as a nomadic text Daulatzai 2016, 38. Different groups in diverse contexts have watched *La battaglia di Algeri* and have drawn links between the Algerian fight for liberation and their own struggles. The film deeply influenced black cultural politics and was taken as a template ibid., 51. Before going underground, the Weather Underground also watched *La battaglia di Algeri* and adopted the practice of ululation for their own protests ibid., 53.

However, different (imperial) powers also watched *La battaglia di Algeri* in order to apply French colonial methods to their own warfare. Both the British military and the Irish Republican Army (IRA) screened the film during the peak of their battles in the 1960s. It was also shown in Uruguay in 1968. After one month in which 25,000 people attended screenings in Montevideo, the film was abruptly taken out of the cinema and was shown, instead, to the Uruguayan military to aid their fight against the *Tupamaros* ibid., 40. During the "War on Terror" in 2003, the Pentagon invited high-ranking military officers to a screening of the film. In their invitation, they linked the "mad fervour" of the film's Arab population to the situation in the run-up to the Iraq War ibid., XII.

---

58   Members of the *Bewegung 2. Juni* discussed the FLN's tactic of planting bombs in cafés to target civilians. However, the group agreed not to apply such methods. This information is based on a conversation with a person who prefers to stay anonymous.

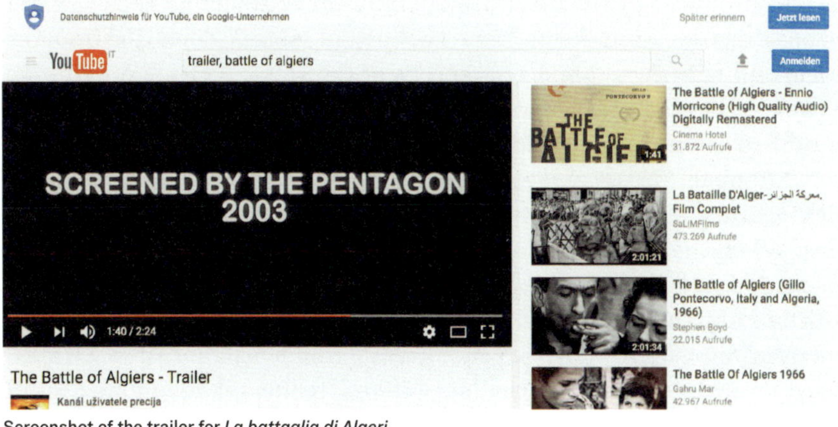

Screenshot of the trailer for *La battaglia di Algeri*

Does the fact that both sides have used this film as a teaching tool limit its militant potential? I wouldn't say so. *La battaglia di Algeri* will always haunt the imperial present with its ghosts of freedom. There is a knowledge and potential embedded in the militant script that can be activated. This is why the United States military framed the Algerian liberation struggle as "terrorism", linking it to their ideology and geopolitical divisions (the "axis of evil"). Framing the struggles in Iraq, Afghanistan, and Palestine as terrorism constructs an otherness that replaces the figure of the savage in French colonial discourse [ibid., 68]. Appropriately, the subtitle for Daulatzai's book—*Fifty Years of The Battle of Algiers: Past as Prologue*—emphasises the continuities between the decolonisation struggles of the 1960s and the struggles against imperial regimes of the present [ibid., 78].

From Militant Films to Militant Spaces 2.9

As Octavio Getino and Fernando Solanas assert, militant films are embedded in specific contexts and struggles. Their languages, methods, and tactics are developed according to the needs of these struggles. In the case of *Deutschland im Herbst*, the approach involves making space for diversity and untamed articulations within a polarised political climate. Militant techniques can also be found in the large variety of ways in which the RAF used public media in the 1960s, before its members went underground. This includes Ulrike Meinhof's journalistic work and the films Holger Meins made as a student at the DFFB. It also includes the images produced by the RAF through militant actions that then circulated on state television. All of these are militant images, deviating from the norm and fighting against the politics of the state. As time progressed, however, the RAF's actions began to approximate a military logic that exhibited certain similarities to the logic of the state.

Although *État de Siège* and *La battaglia di Algeri* appear to be classical feature films, their scripts derive from particular guerrilla struggles. When these scripts are transformed into fiction they circulate and re-enter actual struggles, becoming scripts for further tactical action. Militant film thus circulates between real struggles and fictionalised representation. *Citizenfour*, Laura Poitras's filmic collaboration with Edward Snowden and the journalists Glenn Greenwald, Ewen MacAskill, and Barton Gellman, orchestrates a distribution of secret files from the CIA. Documenting this militant act and sharing it with the public makes *Citizenfour* a militant film that attacks the surveillance system of the United States. Poitras's film *Risk* is similar. Here Poitras manages to maintain a critical stance towards the radical organisation WikiLeaks and its leader, Julian Assange, while simultaneously supporting some of WikiLeaks's ideas.

The militant image is characterised by its close relationship to action and social change. Militant films thus do not just represent militancy; they make films politically Godard 2016. There is a reciprocal relationship between real-life actions, images of these actions, and the ways in which these images again become actions. It is impossible to determine if an image will become militant, even if it relates to the activities of a militant group. Militant images are activated by spectators who become the protagonists of change. Such images and films are situated in particular struggles and are committed to those involved in both producing and receiving them. The images feed into the struggle and vice versa. This situatedness should not, however, be misread as identitarianism. As Walter D Mignolo's analysis of decolonisation highlights, militant images start from "local stories that have been marginalised due to spatial/temporal differences resulting from colonialism. Based on such stories, liberation and decolonisation are inscribed in the present; in cells of time/space within social movements of all kinds, articulated in written or oral form by intellectual activists, artist activists, etc. The negation of contemporaneity, the invention of the primitive and of underdevelopment have obscured the view that we all live in the same cosmic time and yet in different historical and temporal rhythms" Mignolo 2012, 190.[59]

Militant films engage in this process of decolonisation, undoing the neoliberal outcome of the project of modernity. Crossing temporalities—in the sense described by Walter Benjamin—is an important aspect of such images. This is why films made in the 1960s can ignite a revision of the neoliberal project in the present and enable a different understanding of contemporary struggles. "Emancipation" cannot be a criterion for militant films because of the problematic role it has played in modernity and colonisation. Can militant film be hijacked by groups like ISIS, which might also be regarded, in a broader sense, as anti-colonial? I don't believe it can. ISIS does not attempt to delink the project of modernity and open the horizon to a pluriversality of multiple histories. Instead, it is simply interested in creating a new imperium.

59   Translated by Sandra Schäfer. "Ausgehend von lokalen Geschichten, die aufgrund der kolonialen raum/zeitlichen Differenzen marginalisiert worden sind, wird die Befreiung und Dekolonialisierung gegenwärtig in raum/zeitlichen Zellen von sozialen Bewegungen aller Art, von Intellektuellen-Aktivist_innen, von Künstler_innen-Aktivist_innen, etc. schriftlich oder mündlich artikuliert. Die Verneinung der Zeitgenossenschaft, die Erfindung des Primitiven und der Unterentwicklung haben den Blick darauf verstellt, dass wir alle in derselben kosmischen Zeit und doch in unterschiedlichen historisch-zeitlichen Rhythmen leben" (Mignolo 2012, 190).

Militant Spaces

3

> "Representations of space: conceptualized space, the space of scientists, planners, urbanists, technocratic subdividers and social engineers, as of a certain type of artist with a scientific bent—all of whom identify what is lived and what is perceived with what is conceived …
> This is the dominant space in any society" Lefebvre 2007, 38–39.

On the basis of my previous analysis, I would like to extend the militant image from the two-dimensional screen into three-dimensional space: into architecture, urban space, the landscape, and the museum. How are militant spaces built? And what does it mean to inhabit them?

In 1974, the philosopher Henri Lefebvre wrote that space is not only an empty or mental sphere; it holds a multiplicity of dimensions. For Lefebvre, space is a geographical or physical location, a commodity, a political instrument, a component of property and ownership relations, and a means of creative and aesthetic expression ibid., 349. Lefebvre differentiates between spatial practices that are part of the everyday routines, networks, and pathways through which social life is reproduced ("conceptualized space, the space of scientists, planners, urbanists") and representational space, which is "directly lived through its associated images and symbols, and hence the space of 'inhabitants' and 'users'" ibid., 37–39. Furthermore, he describes the space produced by contemporary capitalism as abstract space; a space created by the imperatives of capital and managed and dominated by the state ibid., 285–91. Abstract space is defined by three tendencies: fragmentation, homogeneity, and hierarchy. According to Lefebvre, however, none of these categories can ever absolutely dominate abstract space since its social relations constantly need to be reproduced and reimposed C. Butler 2009, 18; Lefebvre 2007, 416–17. Thus, urban space is not just a product of industry and the accumulation of capital; it is also made by citizens. For this reason, citizens struggle for the right to physically occupy the space of the city with their bodies Lefebvre 1995, 194.

My research draws from Lefebvre's differentiations in order to analyse various spaces within the framework of Hezbollah. What roles do urban planning, architecture, the daily lives of citizens, and the behaviours of museum visitors play in making spaces militant? Although Lefebvre's analysis of space is predominantly a critique of capitalism, his theoretical tools are useful to examine other spatial conflicts in which national, cultural, or religious identities are at stake Houri 2012, 176. My research focuses on two spatial projects undertaken by Hezbollah in Lebanon: the rebuilding of the Haret Hreik neighbourhood in Beirut in 2006 and the construction of the Mleeta Museum of Resistance in southern Lebanon.

3.1   Two Spaces: Mleeta and Haret Hreik

The shift from the image to space reflects the difference between the two-dimensional experience of the visual and the three-dimensional experience of the environment. Are such spaces produced by their designers and architects as well as their inhabitants? Urban space, architecture, and museums produce an immersive reality from which one cannot so easily escape. Such spaces are part of daily life. We live within urban and architectural spaces and move through the spaces of museums. As Lefebvre describes in *The Production of Space*, such spaces are involved in producing actions Lefebvre 2007, 38. The notion of "inhabiting" refers to staying in a space while at the same time being internally possessed by it. Here "inhabiting" also relates to the design of space and the intentions of architects ibid., 39. Taking Lefebvre as a starting point, this text investigates how an urban or museum space can become militant.

As an organisation, Hezbollah performs multiple contradictory roles. On the one hand, it is part of the government. However, it also steps in wherever the largely absent state malfunctions. It is both a government party and an opposition. It simultaneously acts as a flexible NGO, a military unit, and a business association. It also pursues violent politics: it has supported the Assad regime in the war in Syria, maintains close and longstanding ties to the Islamic Republic of Iran, and does not acknowledge the existence of Israel.

3.1.1   The Museum of Resistance

The Mleeta theme park starts with a cinema and a propagandistic introduction film. Military equipment is exhibited all over the park, both above ground and below. An installation titled "The Abyss" (Arabic: الهاوية) — in which the earth seems to open up and swallow Israeli tanks and weaponry — invokes anti-war rhetoric under a different pretext. Authentic underground tunnels and bunkers physically immerse the visitor's body, which is placed into specific scenarios. The park has two panoramic platforms. One platform connects to a tunnel, with the hill at its back, while another is located at the highest point of the summit, offering a 360-degree view. From here visitors can see Israel to the south and Syria to the east. This is the only place in the park that provides an overview of the entire space. Military views are inscribed within both platforms. The "imagineering"[1] of the park is eclectic in its adoption of different practices that are commonly used in museums and the entertainment industry.

The park includes a small mosque and a merchandise shop that sells all kinds of souvenirs, including Hezbollah flags, mugs printed with images of the party's leader, Hassan Nasrallah (Arabic: حسن نصرالله), and a dartboard featuring Israeli politicians. A café was opened in 2016. The Museum of Resistance is one of a number of tourist attractions that Hezbollah has recently developed in southern Lebanon through its organisation *Seyai* (Arabic: سياج | Fence).[2] Plans are underway to build a cable car between Mleeta and the location where Nasrallah's son was killed. In addition, there is an Iranian park in Maroun al-Ras (Arabic: مارون الراس), a village on one of the highest mountains bordering Israel, which was the site of battles between Israeli forces and Hezbollah in 2006. The panorama windows of the teahouse overlook Israel, and a multicoloured climbing contraption in camouflage aesthetics combines playful leisure with military training. As part of its project of creating historical and political landmarks, Hezbollah has begun to turn Khiam Prison into a site for tourism. Next to the historical site in Baalbeck (Arabic: بعلبك), it has installed a small temporary exhibition tent that also sells Hezbollah souvenirs. Since 1984, when Hezbollah declared its existence as a "military Islamic resistance against the Israeli occupation" Harb 2010, 58, it has played a leading role in the liberation of southern Lebanon. The sculptures, memorials, and parks developed in this territory mark Hezbollah's presence on a symbolic level.

The Haret Hreik Neighbourhood   3.1.2

The Shia-dominated neighbourhood of Haret Hreik in Beirut houses Hezbollah's headquarters as well as several of its foundations and organisations, which are invisible to outsiders. Haret Hreik belongs to Dahiya (Arabic: الضاحية الجنوبية | the suburb), an area that has undergone many

---

1   This term is borrowed from the art historian Tom Holert, who takes it from the design context of Disneyland. It emphasises that images are made. Holert suggests that questions of visual culture cannot simply be treated with visual theory; instead, they must also be addressed through cultural studies and politics (Holert 2000).

2   Together with *Ihya'a* (Arabic: إحياء | Revival) and *Resalah* (Arabic: رسالة | Message), *Seyai* is part of Hezbollah's cultural department. *Ihya'a* focuses on memory and oral history in relation to the fight against Israel whereas *Resalah* produces theatre, music, exhibitions, films, and television (A. Daher 2015).

changes over the last decades. Foreign sociologists and urban planners first defined this district as a suburb in the 1930s when they diagnosed the ills of the city—its poor, rural, chaotic, and illegal elements—and discussed how these could be improved. At that time, however, the suburbs were not associated with a specific group. In the 1960s, leftist groups and a constituency led by Imam Musa al-Sadr started to link this space with a political identity. The suburbs thus became the space of the oppressed and the marginalised ibid., 57–58. With the outbreak of the Lebanese Civil War in 1975, this association took on a sectarian dimension and became Shiite. During forced relocations, Shiites were moved from the northern sections of Beirut to the southern parts while Maronites were relocated from Dahiya to the northern areas of the city.[3]

Hezbollah was founded in 1984 as part of an effort to fight the Israeli occupation. Its influence quickly grew, pushing the Amal party (Arabic: حركة أمل | Hope Movement) to the edges of Dahiya. The territories were divided between Hezbollah and Amal. While Hezbollah dominates the Beqaa Valley (Arabic: وادي البقاع), Amal rules parts of the south.[4] Dahiya is under the jurisdiction of both parties, with Hezbollah controlling a larger part of it.

While some regard Dahiya as just another part of the city, others see it as "Hezbollah land" ibid., 61. For Hezbollah it is a space of pride, symbolising the determination and steadfastness of the party. The way this territory is framed relates to Hezbollah's political and military involvements. After Hezbollah joined the parliament in 1992, it collaborated with Prime Minister Rafiq al-Hariri and Amal on an urban planning project called *Elyssar*, which focused on the western section of the southern suburbs. The aim of *Elyssar* was to get rid of the illegal settlements on the coast and to transform these into modern housing complexes.

The relationship between Beirut and Dahiya shifted, however, after Rafiq al-Hariri was assassinated in February 2005. It also suffered after Hezbollah's attack on an Israeli border patrol in 2006, during which three Israeli soldiers were killed and two were taken hostage. In reaction to this event, the Israeli army bombed streets, bridges, houses, and

---

3   For more on the history of Dahiya, see the research and exhibition project *"Collecting Dahiye"* by the UMAM Documentation and Research Centre in Beirut (UMAM Documentation and Research Centre 2007) or the film *Southern Suburbs* by Mohamad Soueid and Fadi Toufic (Soueid and Toufic 2006). Hezbollah's perspective is reflected in the film *My Homeland: The Story of a City and a War* (Zgeib 2007).

4   The territories are contested and the land is divided due to the influence and control of these different parties.

buildings, including structures in southern Lebanon and in Dahiya—particularly in Haret Hreik.[5] The war lasted 33 days. The Israeli government assumed that the Shiite population would turn against Hezbollah, blaming the organisation and its activities for their suffering. This did not happen. Furthermore, the international reaction—particularly in the Middle East—sympathised with Hezbollah and regarded Israel's actions as out of proportion. After the attacks, Hassan Nasrallah promised to bring Dahiya back to what it was and to make it even more beautiful. Reconstruction was overseen by Hezbollah's development foundation, *Jihad al-Bina* (Arabic: جهاد البناء | Effort for Reconstruction). The project, named *Waad* (Arabic: وعد | Promise), operated independently from the Lebanese state.[6]

The project of reconstruction belongs to a military conflict and a geopolitical system in which architecture participates in the production of space/territory. At the same time, it continues the war by other means. Here rebuilding is just as ideological as the process of destruction. Hezbollah is able to take responsibility for reconstruction work due to a weak Lebanese state structure in which different sects or parties operate in a "clientelistic" way Houri 2012, 177. Furthermore, this rebuilding project is part of Hezbollah's multiple and contradictory roles → see chapter 3.1.

Hezbollah's Use of Al-Muqawama (Resistance)   **3.1.3**
Hezbollah frames the reconstruction of Haret Hreik and the creation of the Mleeta museum as resistance. This term has been central to Hezbollah's existence since its beginning. During the Israeli occupation (1982–2000), resistance was a counter-hegemonic struggle. Since then, Hezbollah's discourse has centred on the resistance/occupation binary. "Resistance" is often used to define the party, but it can also refer to "a political and/or ideological standpoint towards the dominant West and its political, cultural, and economic influence which encompasses states and groups who are opposed to this influence as is the case in the geopolitical category 'the axis of resistance' (Arabic: محور المقاومة) or the 'the axis of

5   The war is believed to have killed between 1,191 and 1,300 Lebanese people and 165 Israelis. It severely damaged Lebanese civil infrastructure and displaced approximately one million Lebanese citizens and 300,000–500,000 Israelis. In Dahiya, 271 buildings with 4,000 apartments and 1,800 commercial units were destroyed (Waad 2006b).

6   Saudi Arabia donated 500,000 USD for the compensation programme. Qatar, Kuwait, and Iran financed both the compensation and the reconstruction (Harithy 2010, 9). The costs for reconstruction add up to 400 million USD. The first buildings were completed in 2008 and the last ones were finished in 2012 (Waad 2006b, 55–57). *Lessons in Post-War Reconstruction: Case Studies from Lebanon in the Aftermath of the 2006 War* (Harithy 2010) provides an extensive analysis of the reconstruction process.

refusal' (Arabic: محور الممانعة) that includes most notably Hezbollah, Syria, Iran, and Hamas" Houri 2012, 176. But what does it mean to build and inhabit spaces of resistance? And can one talk about Haret Hreik and the Museum of Resistance as militant spaces?

As analysed in chapters 1 and 2, militancy appears in the struggles of the oppressed, colonised, marginalised, and subaltern. Sometimes its articulations are speechless Spivak 1988 or minor expressions Deleuze and Guattari 1986. I asked several colleagues what the Arabic formulation for "militancy" and/or "militant image" would be. Although neither term exists in Arabic, my colleagues all suggested that the emphasis needs to be on the struggle and that the image-production comes from within that struggle. Yet each person I consulted proposed a different term for "struggle". The writer Adania Shibli suggests that militancy can be translated as *kifah mussallah* (Arabic: كفاح مسلّح). *Kifah* emphasises the daily struggle experienced by everybody. She would call the militant image *sora le kifah mussalah* (Arabic: صورة لكفاح مسلّح).[7] The media theoretician Walid el-Houri, however, proposes the term *nidal* (Arabic: نضال) for militancy, which emphasises a long-term struggle.[8] Shibli points out that another term for struggle, *jihad* (Arabic: جهاد)—which means mental effort—has changed tremendously since the 1990s. The political scientist Eqbal Ahmad describes this change in the way that "contemporary Muslim ideologues and militants have reduced the rich associations of *jihad* to the single meaning of engagement in warfare, entirely divested of its conditions and rules" Ahmad 2002, 2.[9] Shibli also proposes the term *iltizam* (Arabic: إلتزام), which means commitment. *Iltizam* is the stance taken by the artist/photographer who uses the medium (the camera) and the form (the image) in a process of liberation. According to Shibli, *iltizam* is closely related to *al-muqawama* (resistance), which is why *seenama al-muqawama* (Arabic: سينما المقاومة) would probably be the closest approximation to "militant image". These diverse interpretations of "militancy" and "struggle" in Arabic reveal how these terms can be defined and claimed in different ways, and how easily their meanings shift.

7   This information is based on an email exchange with Adania Shibli in 2017.

8   This information is based on email exchange with Walid el-Houri in 2017.

9   In this context, Ahmad highlights the war against the Marxist government in Afghanistan and its Soviet ally as the most famous example of *jihad* in the twentieth century. The reduction of complex religious systems and civilisations to simplistic fundamentalist systems is not unique to Muslim ideologues—it is found in fundamentalist regimes all over the world.

Could Hezbollah's spatial strategies be categorised as militant? And how do its spatial expressions relate to the criteria of the militant image, with its reciprocal relation to struggle, its situatedness, its opening to diversity, and its minor or sometimes speechless expressions? Walid el-Houri claims that Hezbollah's discourse of resistance has itself become a hegemonic project ^{Houri 2012}. How, then, do these two different forms of resistance (the counter-hegemonic and the hegemonic) manifest in space? As the curator Anselm Franke states in the context of the exhibition "Territories": "Space is a fundamental category for any form of power. It is a medium of social relations, articulated as physical and symbolic distance, proximity, position, opposition, and simultaneity. The production and control of space is thus crucial to an execution of power, representing its potency, reproducing its social order, and neutralizing and naturalizing its objectives through planning and processes that lead to a specific physical layout" ^{Franke 2003, 10}.

How is space used to change power structures and to create a memory, an identity, and a political statement within the context of a conflict based on land and occupation? And how does "inhabitation" play an intrinsic role in Hezbollah's overall discourse and strategy of resistance? My artistic research attempts to address these questions.

Before embarking on my research in Lebanon in 2014, I asked myself if and how I could work within the political framework of Hezbollah. I disagree with many of its violent political actions and attitudes, including its unconditional support of the Assad regime in Syria and its brutal attack on recent liberation movements in Beirut. I see such actions as significant contradictions to Hezbollah's discourse of resistance and its claim to side with the oppressed. After the Mubarak regime was overthrown in Egypt, Hezbollah was quick to congratulate the protesters. In the case of the Iranian Green Movement or the protests against the Assad regime in Syria, however, Hezbollah failed to support the opposition and instead made the pragmatic decision to side with its political allies.

Despite my disagreement with these fatal decisions, I decided to research the ways in which Hezbollah produces space. I surmise that its contradictory roles are inscribed within these environments. Such spaces play an important part in Hezbollah's larger framework, including the mechanisms with which it legitimises its participation in the war in Syria. In this sense, I want to decode the aesthetics of its production ^{ibid., 11}. To do so, I analyse the spatial narratives of Hezbollah's resistance in its various articulations: in daily life, architecture and urban planning, aesthetics, audiovisual representations, the landscape, and museum design. As the theorist David Harvey writes: "The first step down that road is to insist that place, in whatever guise, is, like space and time, a social construct. The only interesting question that can be asked is, by what process(es) is place constructed?" Harvey 2012, 4.

4

Territorialisation: Refrain and Assemblage

In their philosophy of the rhizome, Gilles Deleuze and Félix Guattari develop a definition of territory that is articulated through rhythm in space. According to Deleuze and Guattari, "there is a territory if the rhythm has expressiveness … It becomes expressive, on the other hand, when it acquires a temporal constancy and a spatial range that make it a territorial, or rather territorializing, mark: a signature" Deleuze and Guattari 1987, 315. In this musical understanding of territorialisation, Deleuze and Guattari introduce the refrain as an expression that manifests in space as a territorial assemblage ibid., 312. Such assemblages are in a constant process of transformation. One assemblage passes into another.[1] Deleuze and Guattari's understanding of the assemblage is not characterised by a linear development; instead, it is defined by a horizontal understanding of space formed by "densifications, intensifications, reinforcements, injections, showering" ibid., 449.[2] How can Deleuze and Guattari's definition of territorialisation as a process help us understand the role territory plays within Haret Hreik and the Museum of Resistance?

In July 2014, Hezbollah's participation in the war in Syria was visible in Haret Hreik. Barricades and checkpoints had been built to avoid further explosions by Syrian rebels. They marked the territory and served as reminders of Hezbollah's involvement in the war. Anyone who

1 In a conversation with the author in 2016, the philosopher Michaela Ott pointed out that both the English and German translations of the French term *agencement* ("assemblage" and *Gefüge*) are insufficient, as neither captures the wide variety implied in the original French. According to Deleuze and Guattari, everything can interlink with everything.

2 In her analysis of affective spaces in film, Ott refers to the process-oriented characteristic of space. "We have become accustomed to speaking about spatialisation and thinking of the spatial—with Leibniz, Cassirer, and Deleuze—as a non-substantial, heterogeneous, relational space that emerges from the occupation of places and their connections as a flexible and changing processuality" (Ott 2011, 96) (translated by Sandra Schäfer). Furthermore, Ott highlights the connection between the invention of the filmic medium and the new definitions of space developed in both the natural and cultural sciences at the beginning of the twentieth century (Ott 2011, 96). Ott argues that Deleuze does not consider the representative function of film. Instead, according to Deleuze, the world exists in an endless process of movement, time, and images. In her interpretation of Deleuze's "affection image", Ott highlights another aspect of space that is inherent to the medium of film: "Through the technically-enabled production and presentation of images that transcend or subvert human perception, Deleuze sees new spatial relations emerge with new qualities that temporarily pause the flow of filmic motion and lend film a vertical dimension of intensity" (Ott 2011) (translated by Sandra Schäfer). Deleuze exemplifies this characteristic in the close-up (Deleuze 1997, 107).

was not from Dahiya avoided going to the area. Nevertheless, the streets were crowded and the queues at the checkpoints were long. On Fridays, guns were shot into the air to celebrate the funerals of Hezbollah soldiers. These gunshots took on the quality of a refrain, as described by Deleuze and Guattari. Posters featuring the faces of martyrs were scattered along walls in the streets, forming a more obvious territorial marker.

As a visitor, I could walk through Haret Hreik or tour the Mleeta Museum of Resistance, but if I wanted to film or conduct research in these areas, I needed official permission from Hezbollah's media office. I had to pass through different thresholds to enter certain territories within Hezbollah's larger framework. Some thresholds were obvious whereas others remained invisible; some were easy to pass and others more difficult. There were some thresholds that I would never want to traverse and others that I would never be able to. In what follows, I discuss how I used myself as a detector to investigate some of the thresholds encountered during the process of filming with my team. I propose that these thresholds are markers that help define Hezbollah's territorialisation.

4.1 Thresholds in Horizontal Space

Before receiving official permission to film, I met with the mayor of Ghobeiry (Arabic: غبيري). This was possible because a member of my film team knew him from another research project. During our meeting, the mayor agreed to let us film during our next visit. Once we tried to arrange an appointment, however, this did not turn out to be the case. It became clear that we would not be able to work with anyone closely related to the party without Hezbollah's official approval. The mayor of Ghobeiry seemed to know that we still had not received permission, although we had not mentioned this. I wanted to meet the organisers, architects, and planners involved in the Museum of Resistance as well as the *Waad* reconstruction project, which meant that we would need official approval before we could start. From colleagues I learned that the usual procedure was to introduce one's project and one's team. Once the media office agreed, they would check the list of the people the filmmaker wanted to meet. If foreign film teams wanted to work in Haret Hreik, Hezbollah usually accompanied them and occasionally intervened in the filming schedule. A few days before my departure, I received filming permission. The agreement was only given verbally and I was unsure whether it would be valid upon my return.

While waiting to receive permission from the media office, I asked my colleague Nadine Khayat to join me for a walk through Haret Hreik. We visited one of the libraries and then went to the municipality, where we asked to find the *Waad* office. The office turned out to be 50 metres away. It was an unremarkable and unpretentious site; the entrance felt almost like a garage. The reception area was guarded by the same employee who would later search my team's bags when we returned to film. He was an important person who knew everyone that entered and exited the building. We asked if the director of the *Waad* project was there, but were told that he was not in the office. We could be sure, however, that he would hear about our visit. If he was indeed there, perhaps he saw us on one of the eight surveillance screens in his room.

When we came back to the *Waad* office to film five months later, we needed to pass through security with all of our film equipment. In my video installation *Constructed Futures: Haret Hreik*, this threshold is indicated by a black screen that is accompanied by an audio recording of the security check.

The Mleeta theme park also works with several thresholds. The agitprop film shown in the cinema acts like a passage that visitors have to traverse before entering other parts of the park. At the same time, it serves to frame the museum's exhibits and scenarios by telling the story of Hezbollah's resistance against the Israeli occupation. Narrated from Hezbollah's perspective, this story revolves around a guerrilla fight against the high-tech Israeli military, with Mleeta serving as an invisible outpost inside an occupied zone. Hassan Nasrallah narrates the film and serves as a guide for the viewer. At first he appears with a gentle and father-like voice; towards the end of the film, however, he angrily agitates against Israel as the enemy. Apart from Nasrallah's speech, the occupied and now liberated territory of southern Lebanon emerges as an entity loaded with affect. Nasrallah's voice functions like the refrain described by Deleuze and Guattari as an expressiveness that marks a territory Deleuze and Guattari 1987, 314. Although I was told that there was no Hezbollah flag in the theme park (which did not turn out to be true), Nasrallah's voice echoes through the space, marking it in a much more significant way than any flag could.

4.2   Appropriation and Reterritorialisation: Mleeta

In "The Abyss", the most spectacularly produced exhibition in the Mleeta
theme park, Israeli tanks plunge into a giant pit. Helmets of soldiers
symbolise Israel's defeat. One Israeli tank is captured in a netlike structure of steel cables. According to Mleeta's media officer, this tank refers
to Hassan Nasrallah's statement in the year 2000 that "Israel is more
fragile than the spider web" Mansour 2015. Usually the Israeli military either
destroyed its weapons and vehicles or took them back to Israel. Captur-
ing Israeli military vehicles is thus a gesture of appropriation. Not all
vehicles in this installation were left behind, however. The Merkava tank
is a reconstruction built by Hezbollah. It displays the group's knowledge
of Israeli war techniques and thus also appropriates the language of the
enemy. The tank's knotted barrel is an obvious gesture depriving the
phallic military symbol of its power. At the same time, this appropriation turns[3] the Israeli war tool into a tool of defeat. The symbolic gestures
within the entire space of Mleeta mark it as liberated from the occupiers.
A previously occupied space is thus reterritorialised, exposing a formerly
invisible infrastructure of resistance. Hezbollah's sculptures and architecture become concrete manifestations of Deleuze and Guattari's "refrain". In a lecture performance at the 66th Berlinale, however, the artist
Ahmad Ghossein describes this as "a new visual hegemony" Ghossein 2016.

4.3   Interventions: Playing with Refrain, Rhythm, and Sound

Mleeta is a two-channel video installation with screens that are slightly
turned towards each other. Along with the sound, the screen size[4] creates an immersive experience for the audience. In this sense, watching
Mleeta echoes the experience of visiting the Mleeta theme park. Here the
audience is likewise taken on a tour through the Museum of Resistance,
encountering a specific selection of parts, paths, and minor gestures.
In a scene depicting "The Abyss", it sounds as if stones are being
pushed back and forth. In another shot beneath evergreen trees, the
chirping of crickets engulfs the viewer. As the camera frames brown
leaves and sandbags on the ground, someone can be heard running
past. And in scenes focusing on the landscape, a pervasive siren cuts
through the panorama. These sounds intervene in the existing territory:

---

3   In the sense of Hanne Loreck's discussion of the transformative recycling of images.
4   The ideal size of each screen is 350×197cm.

they overlap, penetrate, mingle, and disturb. In this sense, audio interrupts the internal organisation of the territory ^{Deleuze and Guattari 1987, 323}. Sound is a refrain that works to de/reterritorialise the space and thus becomes visible as a tool.

In Hezbollah's films, fast-forwarding and slow motion are often used to emphasise specific scenes and gestures. This is simultaneously a way to control time, representing a gesture of power. I play with this tool at the climax of Hassan Nasrallah's speech in the film shown at Mleeta's cinema. Here the image/sound is played forwards and backwards, adopting a different rhythm. This rhythmic "scratching" technique is familiar from hip-hop. When a vinyl record is scratched on a turntable, it produces a new rhythm based on one that already exists. I use a similar method to change the existing rhythm of Hezbollah's propagandistic soundtrack and image. In this process, the closed semiotic chain is temporarily disrupted and opened.

With my counter-manipulations, I attempt to bend, turn, and intervene in the manipulative setting of the Mleeta theme park. In recognising these different manipulations, I want viewers to question and challenge their own position.[5] Viewers thus become active protagonists who are not relieved from the responsibility of questioning their own norms and values in relation to what they see and hear. The manipulations that I employ differ from Hezbollah's manipulations insofar as the latter constructs a closed semiotic chain that encourages visitors to see things in one particular way.

One screen in *Mleeta* thus shows Hezbollah's agitprop film while it is being projected in the cinema while the other screen shows an audience watching it. Through this construction, the viewer's perspective is doubled or mirrored: he or she enters into a triangular relationship with Hezbollah's film and the audience in Mleeta's cinema. At the same time, the reactions of the mirrored audience differ from those of the audience watching my video installation. Over the course of the piece, there are also moments in which both screens feature the audience, and Hezbollah's film is only present as sound. The effects of Hezbollah's film are therefore not immediate.

---

5   In his keynote lecture at the 66th Berlinale, the art critic Helmut Draxler states: "Sandra Schäfer's work *Mleeta* 'documents' a highly phantasmatic reality—a war site in the south of Lebanon becoming a propaganda museum. She also confronts the extremely manipulating scenario and the manipulating media footage with the manipulating work of her own film editing. Thus, her work forces us as viewers into a constant negotiation of our subjectivities, objectives, and norms" (Draxler 2016).

Frames and Screens

5

As a filmic term, the "frame" names the smallest unit in video: the single image. Yet framing also refers to the act of recording an image: what does the filmmaker show or leave out? The "screen" signifies the surface upon which an image is projected. The art historian and film critic Kaja Silverman uses this term based on Jacques Lacan's model for theorising the relationship between the gaze, the look, and the subject/object. "We depend upon the other not only for our meaning and our desires, but also for our very confirmation of self. To 'be' is in effect to 'be seen'" Silverman 1996, 133. Within this reciprocal relationship, Silverman defines the screen as "the site at which social and historical difference enters the field of vision" ibid., 134. Through an analysis of Harun Farocki's film *Bilder der Welt und Inschrift des Krieges* (Images of the World and the Inscription of War, 1988), Silverman outlines how the Algerian screen is replaced by the screen of French colonialism. Farocki's film describes how Algerian women were photographed for purposes of identification in 1960. These women, who would normally wear a veil, were forced to pose unveiled. The Algerian screen fades away and is replaced by a European screen "connoting 'exoticism,' 'primitivism,' 'subordinate race,' and a European notion of femininity ('woman as spectacle'). The one image, emblematized by the veil, must 'die' in order for the other to prevail" ibid., 150–51. Silverman locates another example of the screen in Farocki's film. In this case, it is the American military's inability to recognise Auschwitz in aerial photographs taken by an American soldier in April 1944. The voiceover states: "They were not under orders to look for the Auschwitz camp, thus they did not find it" Farocki 1988. The camera sees what the human eye cannot comprehend. It wasn't until 1977, when two CIA employees studied these photographs, that the concentration camp was recognised next to the IG Farben plant. The shifted historical vantage point allowed it to become legible.

"The gaze is located within desire, temporality and the body," which is why it is open to change Silverman 1996, 160. Unlike the camera, the gaze can thus be resistant and transformative. There is a similarity here to Judith Butler's thought, which argues that our affective responses are mediated through normative frames that restrict what is perceivable. Butler, however, highlights the disobedient act of seeing that steps out of these normative frames and allows a seeing in the non-seeing J. Butler 2009, 31, 72, 75.

5.1 Hezbollah's Frames

How, then, does Hezbollah create its frames and screens in the Mleeta Museum of Resistance and the neighbourhood of Haret Hreik? In the following, I introduce some of the frames and screens that I encountered during my work in this context.

In the Mleeta theme park, the exhibition titled "The Abyss" echoes a common anti-war rhetoric. As part of the dramaturgy of the space, however, visitors must first pass through a cinema. Here film acts like a filter that makes viewers look differently at the installations that follow. Rather than depriving the Israeli enemy of its military power, these scenarios are read through a militarised logic of war. The film serves as a threshold that is simultaneously a frame or screen.

In a conversation with the director of the *Waad* project, Mr el-Jeshi, he asked me how I would position myself towards the party. Was I with or against Hezbollah? How would the party be represented in the film? I explained that my approach was different: being with or against the party is not an option for me. Instead, I was investigating how space is produced within the framework of Hezbollah. It was only when I joked about being grilled (referring to the hot air of the air conditioner) that he accepted my position, categorising it as a philosophical approach. The challenge of this conversation was not to accept the screen/frame that Mr el-Jeshi proposed and to insist on a space that allowed for reflection and criticism.

5.2 Our Bodies Are Political

I am often told that my perspective is that of an outsider. In a way this is true, as I neither belong to the community of Hezbollah nor to the national framework of Lebanon. I speak very little Arabic and am not Shiite. I can't and don't try to blend in and pretend to be part of these communities. As soon as I start working within a specific context, however, I get entangled. I have to position myself within Hezbollah's particular framework because certain claims are made about my body, my identity, and my thinking. I face the challenge of either being with or against the party. For this reason, I have to assert that I am in principle neither. This perspective may be more easily granted to me than to someone from Lebanon and reflects a privilege that I enjoy as an outsider.

My Lebanese colleagues and I were approached in very different ways. For example, they were always asked which sect they belonged to. If their name didn't immediately indicate it, they were questioned about their neighbourhood or which part of Lebanon their family came from. My colleagues dealt with these situations differently, depending on who was asking and whether they wanted to be identified or not.

In his short text "If You Can't Walk on Water I Never Get Out of the Boat", the architect Joseph Rustom transcribes a phone conversation with a Sheikh from a mosque in Beirut Rustom 2012. To introduce himself, Rustom uses the religiously neutral first name Yusuf instead of Joseph. For this reason, the Sheikh initially assumes that he is Shiite or Sunni. Sensing Rustom's hesitation, the Sheikh asks further questions that allow him to identify Rustom's religious and family background. Touching on sensitivities having to do with the mosque's history (the land it was built on was bought from the Syrian Catholic Church) as well as the Sheikh's own religious and family background, the Sheikh refers to the common history of Maronites and Shiites,

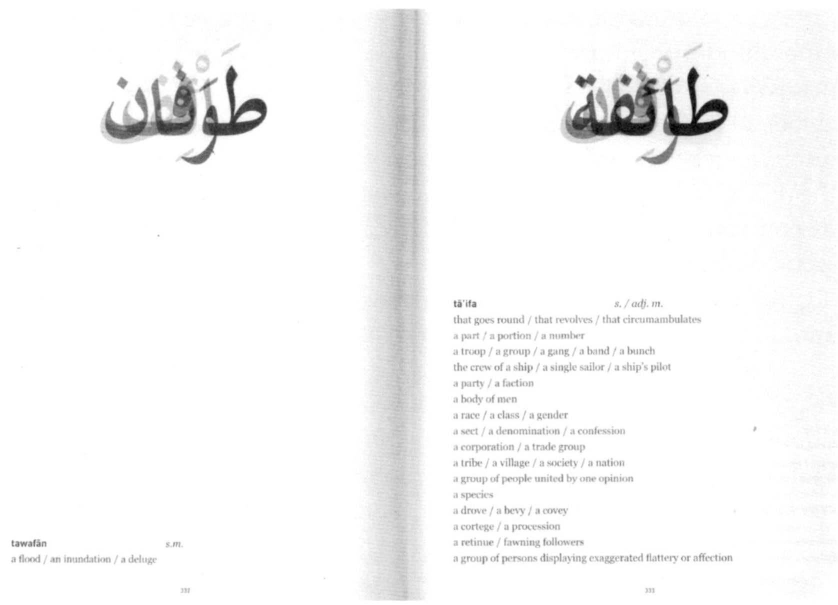

Ta'ifa by Joseph Rustom, 2014, calligraphy by Guy Asmar

highlighting that they were always "in the same boat" ibid., 39.[1] Rustom points out in a footnote that in Ottoman Turkish, *tai'ifa* meant the crew of a boat or people together on a boat ibid., 39. Today the Arabic term *ta'ifa* (Arabic: طائفة) is used to designate a religious community in Lebanon. According to Rustom, the Arabic word *ta'ifiyya* (Arabic: طائفية) stems from *ta'ifa* and denotes "the name given to the Lebanese system of government that proportionally allocated political power among the different religious groups according to a system of representation based on predefined ratios. These religious groups therefore possess an immense power over the organization of the political, economic, social, and cultural life of the Lebanese" Rustom 2014, 328. Rustom collects a compilation of obsolete, seldomly used, and current definitions of different forms of the word *ta'ifa* taken from Ottoman, Persian, and Arabic dictionaries published between 1860 and 2010. In this process, a temporal space opens in which different images related to the word resonate. It oscillates between the image of territory, community, the individual, the circle, and the line.

While filming *Constructed Futures: Haret Hreik*, a protagonist tried to create conflict within my team by emphasising our different backgrounds. He pointed out that a certain colleague would have to stay in Lebanon after the film was finished whereas I would leave the country and be out of reach. In making this comment, he highlighted the different vulnerabilities of our bodies according to territorial influence. In another situation, he gave us a taste of what this looked like, using his mobile phone to call my colleague's boss while we were sitting in front of him. Though it was meant as a joke, this gesture of domination showed the reach of his influence. It also revealed that our bodies are not neutral: as political entities, they are part of a constant process of negotiation, territorialisation, and domination.

Although there is a geographical distance between where I live and, in this case, where I work, these contexts are entangled. The secretary of another protagonist studied in Hamburg, lived there for many years, and spoke fluent German. In this encounter, I could not maintain an outside position. Something similar happened after I learned that another protagonist's brother is based in Berlin's Kreuzberg district, the same neighbourhood that I used to live in. He insisted that I

---

1   In this framework, the Sheikh also highlights the Memorandum of Understanding between the Christian Free Patriotic Movement and the Shiite-Muslim Hezbollah Party in February 2006 and the successful project of *al-'aysh al-mushtarak* (Arabic: العيش المشترك | living together) (Rustom 2012, 39).

get to know his brother, his brother's wife, and their children while we were all in Beirut.

My film team is made up entirely of women. This played a significant role in the patriarchal contexts within which we worked. At times it gave us more freedom, as we were taken less seriously. At other times, however, not being taken seriously was frustrating and limited our possibilities. However, having an all-women team also enabled us to film protagonists that we would not have been able to work with as male filmmakers. Furthermore, this team was very diverse: our backgrounds ranged from German to Lebanese, Shiite to Sunni, Christian to Druze, religious to atheist. This created conversations and exchange within the group itself as a small social community. It also influenced how we were perceived from the outside. Due to this constellation, the team could not easily be framed. In some situations we made strategic use of staying unidentifiable whereas in other cases we made tactical use of essentialist classification. The category of "woman" was sometimes helpful but not always a voluntary choice. In any case, the refusal of determined positions became an important political strategy throughout the making of both *Mleeta* and *Constructed Futures: Haret Hreik*.

Intimate Relations and the Sovereign Order   5.3

"Honestly, when we sacrifice our children, we don't mourn for houses.
Nor furniture or anything else" ^{Malak 2015}.

Posters of martyrs line the entrance to the building where Ms Ibtissam —an employee of the rebuilding project *Waad*—lives. They indicate the deaths of Hezbollah soldiers who used to live here. When we enter Ms Ibtissam's living room, we learn that one of these soldiers was her son, who died in the war in Syria. Although he is dead, his body is present all over the room. On a folding screen, sixteen photographs depict Ms Ibtissam's son in relaxing and domestic contexts, smiling into the camera. In a photographic series above the sofa, he poses in military clothes. In one image he hugs his mother, who smiles confidently. On her mobile phone, Ms Ibtissam shows us the last photograph she took together with her son in a grocery shop; it is particularly special for her. A portrait of Ms Ibtissam's husband hangs on the wall above the table. The military dress of both father and son demonstrates the intergenerational link between men within the military context of

Hezbollah. The party is also present in a letter of honour dedicated to Ms Ibtissam's son. This document is shown in a display case together with his military boots and a personal letter he wrote to his family. The intimate familial relationship is placed into close proximity with the sovereign order of Hezbollah. These are inseparable and closely intertwined, as Ms Ibtissam's living room demonstrates. On two sliding doors, the young man appears as a life-sized soldier. Ms Ibtissam notes that this door fulfils her son's wish to protect the female family members from the gaze of male visitors in the hallway. Her daughter, a professional graphic designer, created the composition. It was only after the death of Ms Ibtissam's son that his wish was realised.

More posters lean on the wall surrounding the television. A logo in the corner of each image indicates that these have been produced by Hezbollah. They depict Ms Ibtissam's son wearing military garb at war. The text accompanying each image praises him as a martyr. These posters stand in contrast to the lascivious Bollywood-dancing scenes on the TV. Hezbollah's letter of honour, the organisation's logo, and the military clothes indicate the presence of the sovereign order in the private context of the home. Part of Hezbollah's widespread civil activities include honouring the deaths of martyrs. The Martyr's Institute (Arabic: مؤسسة الشهيد | Al-Shahid Social Association) provides support (financial and otherwise) to families that have lost loved ones in the war. Furthermore, the party officially engages in the memorial process and assists the families of martyrs, for example, by maintaining tombs. The Memories of the Martyrs Centre attempts to enhance and preserve the legacy of martyrs involved in the Islamic resistance J. Daher 2016, 112. Such official services take care of the economic needs of families and attempt to integrate individual mourning into an official mourning practice and narrative. Controlling the commemoration of Hezbollah soldiers is just one of the organisation's efforts. As the theoretician Joseph Daher states: "In all these activities, it is evident that Hezbollah expends a conscious and considerable effort in shaping how the wider Shi'a population perceives the historical narrative of resistance and the party's role in it. This narrative is heavily linked to—and reinforced by—the religious symbolism associated with Shi'a faith" ibid., 112.

In Hezbollah's poster designs, the soldier appears confident, powerful, and determined, posing on the front line with a missile or against a blurred background. In an odd way, Hezbollah's logo on these posters recalls the practice of body branding. By means of this logo, the party lays claim to its soldiers. Ms Ibtissam's visual mourning practice can thus be regarded as a way to recover the body of her dead son. As the film scholar and curator Laliv Melamed notes in her research on homemade commemorative videos of Israeli soldiers: "In the process of mourning, the sovereign political order meets individual love" Melamed 2018.[2]

In Ms Ibtissam's living room, this "individual love" appears in an illuminated glass display case that holds her son's last possessions. The case has a mechanism that makes its four platforms spin. It carries banal objects like his half-used shower gel, perfume, watch, house keys, and Iranian bank notes. Desiring to stay in touch with her son through these objects, Ms Ibtissam ordered the case after seeing it in a mobile phone shop. A display that usually presents commodities for sale now gives visibility to commodities that are loaded with meaning. The case turned out to be too small for all of the items, so a carpenter made it bigger. A squeaking sound hints that the motor is overloaded. Presented in a shrine, these objects allow Ms Ibtissam to maintain contact with her son's present-absent body.[3] I notice how irritated I am that this relation takes place through these objects. As Melamed writes: "The notion of being connected has to go through the medium, and the medium not only recovers a body of sorts, but reciprocity and the being in-relations" Melamed 2018. In the case of Ms Ibtissam's living room, the medium is both photography and the commodified presentation of things. This memorial practice shows how closely the private sphere is linked with Hezbollah's institutionalised power. Hezbollah's language is inseparable from Ms Ibtissam's own commemoration practice. Her arrangements demonstrate the attachments, affinities, dependencies, and intimacies that persist between the family and the organisation in memory and mourning.[4] Recalling Kaja Silverman's use of the "screen"—which is established

2 In her research, Melamed focuses on commemorative videos and, among other things, the precarious role of the girlfriend in Israel. In the context of Hezbollah's hegemony, the clear division of gender plays a central role within the heteronormative family. The woman as sister and mother is best represented in the Shiite role model Zaynab, "a pious individual whose voluntarism in health, education or welfare serves as her contribution to the community development" (J. Daher 2016, 124). The male role model, on the other hand, is Husayn, the grandson of the prophet Muhammad, who is chivalrous and strong. Commemorative videos also exist within the context of Hezbollah and display some similarities to those discussed by Melamed in her analysis.

3 These private photographs and possessions recall Melamed's discussion of the tension between the banal and the uncanny in the "ordinariness" of the home movie: "Characterized as 'ordinary,' the home movie is a singular, non-authoritative utterance that hinges on the tension between the banal and the uncanny, in trying to find a way to make sense of something individual on its own, distinct, without erasing its individuality, its oneness, its distinction." (Melamed 2018).

4 Melamed draws a similar conclusion from her analysis of commemorative home videos made in Israel (Melamed 2018).

between the subject and the object, influencing the gaze →see chapter 5—
Hezbollah's expansive and holistic approach[5] intervenes in the processes of subjectivisation. In this case, it enters the intimate relationship to the dead in the practice of mourning. This becomes apparent in some of Ms Ibtissam's statements, which repeat Hezbollah's official narrative of resistance. At other moments, however, her speech becomes more uncertain and it seems harder to legitimise the official narrative that her son was fighting to defend honour and protect his female family members Malak 2015.

5.4   Staging Minor Gestures

In certain scenes of *Mleeta*, I work with a performative figure: a man dressed in king's blue. It was hard to choose a colour that didn't represent a specific political party or group. I chose this particular blue to differentiate it from Rafiq al-Hariri's light blue and because it stands out against the palette of the landscape. The colour maintains an ambiguity between leisure, the military, and corporate belonging. Together with the performer, I developed poses and gestures that are not so easily identifiable within this setting of "Are you with us or against us?" Jeshi 2015. While sitting in the cinema, the performer turns his gaze away from the screen as if to look at his phone. At the panorama, he holds the handrail overlooking the landscape. In the last scene, he walks down the staircase of the viewing platform and stands at a circular fountain, looking at the water. The performer could be a park employee, a former fighter, or a tourist. His role and his gestures remain uncertain. Kaja Silverman describes the relationship between the pose and the subject as follows: "The pose inscribes the subject that makes use of it into the image" Silverman 1997. Through the pose one becomes a subject. Although these staged minor gestures differ from the obvious poses Silverman refers to in her text, they retain this possibility of inscription. In *Mleeta*, the ambiguity of these gestures multiplies or blurs the subject. For this reason, the camera is not able to verify who this performative figure is.

5   Hezbollah's institutions and religious, social, and political practices constitute an important part of its hegemonic apparatus. Audiovisual productions play an essential role in these multifaceted activities.

Hezbollah's media office works with a system that my team was not familiar with. We did not know the criteria, for example, for receiving filming permission. We sent the office a description of our project and a list of people related to the party that we wanted to speak with. I wasn't sure if the verbal permission I received shortly before my departure would be valid once I returned. This uncertainty lingered until I came back to Lebanon in 2015 and started to film. The process continued in a similar way. For example, the media office provided my team with the protagonists' phone numbers. We then called to arrange meetings. One meeting turned out to be very tense and tough. We later found out that apart from this person's hardline position, which we were already aware of, the media office had not informed him that we would be getting in touch, which was why he was highly suspicious of us. This "mistake" helped us recognise the workings of the system and the invisible boundaries we faced.

At the same time, we also had scripts—some of which were less visible than others. For example, we had an official list of people we wanted to meet: figures who were related to Hezbollah or to the organisation's projects. In addition, we kept an unofficial list of people who were not related to the party; names that were not necessarily mentioned. Despite the invisible boundaries imposed on our team, we attempted to maintain a space to think and work within these clearly defined territories.

The Camera's Perspective in Horizontal Space 5.6

As a tourist site, the Mleeta Museum of Resistance is a public image created by Hezbollah. Although the museum claims to celebrate the liberation of all Lebanese people, it is a territory marked by Hezbollah's perspective. This is why some people would refuse to visit. Nevertheless, anyone can access the site. Visitors are allowed to make photographs and videos—professional film crews must, however, receive permission from the museum's media department. Once permission is given, the crew can move and film freely throughout the site. This changes, however, as soon as you leave the park. When I tried to film the museum from the surrounding mountains and valleys, I was immediately stopped. It was strange because I could have filmed these same landscapes from inside the park, only from a different angle. As soon as the tourist site is left behind, the gaze of the camera becomes a problem. My eyes, however, are allowed to frame this perspective. What is the difference? Does the territory work according to other rules? Or is it the perspective? Or the recording? Or is it my body and its relation to the camera that makes this framing problematic? All these aspects matter. In this territory, there seems to be a struggle about who is allowed to produce images and how these images can be framed. Furthermore, my body—as a political entity—carries an uncertainty as to how and where these images will circulate. They might even become a tool for foreign intelligence. Thus, controlling image production—with all its frames and screens—means dominating and controlling the territory. At the same time, the manner in which the gaze of the camera and the gaze of the military frame (and thus control) the territory is somehow superimposed.[6]

For similar reasons, the camera's gaze is not allowed in Haret Hreik. Although it is officially a public space, Haret Hreik is tightly controlled by Hezbollah and its community. If you don't belong to this community, you are not allowed to film or take photographs and will immediately be stopped. Foreign film teams are usually accompanied by a security guard who makes decisions about what to film, for how long, and from which perspective. The guard thus attempts to control the frame or screen. Yet, as can be seen in numerous films produced by foreign media, there are still many ways to create frames or screens in the editing process. It remains difficult to control post-production, which often takes place outside of Hezbollah's territory. In any case, Hezbollah's tight control of the framing in Haret Hreik is one reason why I decided not to film urban space under these conditions.

5.7   How to Frame the Intimate and the Sovereign Order

Each of the four video channels in *Constructed Futures: Haret Hreik* introduces a protagonist or place that is relevant to the project of reconstruction. These include the architectural engineer and director of the *Waad* project, Hassan el-Jeshi, in his office in Haret Hreik; the leading architect, Rahif Fayad, in his office in Tallet el-Khayat (Arabic: تلة الخياط); an employee of the *Waad* project, Ms Ibtissam, in her living room in Haret Hreik; and a group of Hezbollah's followers listening to Hassan Nasrallah in the assembly hall Mujama al-Shouhada (Arabic: مجمّع الشهداء) in Haret Hreik.

6   I go into more detail about this superimposition in my discussion of panoramic space (→ see chapter 6).

The videos depict the rooms in which these people were interviewed, but I do not show them talking.[7] This technique emphasises interior space, the voice, and the spoken narrative. The philosopher Maurice Halbwachs suggests that the architecture surrounding us embodies a language that carries the imprint of the other Halbwachs 1980, 128–29. In this sense, I regard space as an area of inquiry. Ms Ibtissam's living room is filmed in long takes, allowing the gaze to rest and move through each image, investigating its details. The duration also invites viewers to become immersed in this space. The dramaturgy starts with images of Ms Ibtissam's son on a folding screen next to an armchair. Gradually the photographs shift from a civilian to a military context. The images are clearly framed and filmed with a tripod, positioning the viewer at a distance. The sequence ends with a shot of objects spinning in a glass display case. Thus, a circle is made through the space of Ms Ibtissam's living room. In this movement, her speech shifts from discussing her involvement in the reconstruction, to making official statements about the project, to speaking about the loss of her son. At this point, the uncertainty in her voice mingles with statements familiar from the party context. The gaze of the camera leaves space for the spectator to look around. Pauses between Ms Ibtissam's statements also allow the viewer to experience this space through its sounds. Kaja Silverman's idea of the screen appears in photographs, posters, objects, the arrangements of objects, and Ms Ibtissam's speech. When I showed Ms Ibtissam a first cut of the video, she was initially irritated by the long pauses. From the television station al-Manar (Arabic: المنار), she was used to pauses that are filled with music. When she asked about the silence in my film, I explained that I wanted to leave room for the spectator to experience the space and to think about what she says. She added that the long pauses make the viewer curious to hear what she will say next.[8]

7   The sequence filmed at Mujama al-Shouhada is an exception.
8   This conversation took place in September 2016 in Beirut when I showed Ms Ibtissam an edited sequence from our long conversation.

6

Vertical vs Panoramic Space

The Israeli architect and researcher Eyal Weizman uses verticality to describe the occupation, control, and division of space in Israel and Palestine. Israel's control of the air plays a particular role in monitoring electromagnetic signals or operating unmanned aerial vehicles (UAVs) or spy satellites. Unmanned aerial vehicles, commonly known as drones, are used for surgical killings. Vertical space is also adopted as an occupying force when Israelis rent or buy flats in multi-storey houses in Jerusalem Weizman 2007, 13; 2002. Ever since the Gaza barrier was built, "people and explosives are routinely smuggled in tunnels dug beneath the walls of Gaza, while home-made rockets are launched through the airspace above them" Weizman 2007, 13. Territory is divided and organised into multiple layers in order to find design solutions for a conflict of two states Weizman 2003, 117.

In his project *Fish Story*, the photographer Allan Sekula describes the new role of panoramic space in the nineteenth century. He begins with Friedrich Engels's idea that the spatial and aesthetic contrast between the ugly city and the beautiful harbour lost its significance when seas and rivers became part of the landscape of industrial capitalism. Sekula recognises the integration of maritime space in Dutch marine paintings of the seventeenth century, which depict the systematic relationship between ships and cities. He describes the paradox of the panorama, which is "topographically 'complete' while still signalling an acknowledgement of and desire for a greater extension beyond the frame" Sekula 1995, 43. This is particularly apparent in marine panoramas: the sea always goes beyond the frame.

The new panoramic perspective first appeared when steam trains crossed the landscape and it moved out to sea with the development of the steamboat ibid., 44. Sekula analyses Willem van de Velde the Elder's drawing *The English Fleet at Anchor off Den Helder* (1653). English battleships line up on the horizon at the strategic port between the island of Texel and the Dutch mainland. Sekula points out that "expansive panoramic space is always haunted by the threat of collapse or counter-expansion. Thus, the panorama is always implicitly or explicitly militarized" ibid., 47. The horizon marks this possible threat of counter-expansion.

In van de Velde the Elder's drawing, the line of English battleships mirrors of Dutch perspective: "The blockade matches and implicitly 'contains' the otherwise expansive view from the Dutch coast" ibid., 47.

6.1   The Vertical and the Panoramic in Mleeta

The vertical and the panoramic are central to Mleeta both as a concept and as a space. The summit of Mleeta, now home to the Museum of Resistance, was formerly used as a hideout for the resistance. During the war, Hezbollah fighters built a tunnel and bunker system as a form of protection from aerial strikes. Evergreen trees hid the men from the thermal cameras of Israeli military planes flying overhead. Today, the guerrilla techniques of hiding and invisibility are exposed.[1] In this state, they also "contain" the previously expansive Israeli view: the gaze from the air.

The aerial view plays a central role in Mleeta's symbolic installation "The Abyss", which stages Israel's defeat in the year 2000. Large Hebrew letters scattered throughout the installation explicitly address the Israeli gaze from the air. According to Mleeta's media officer, Ahmad Mansour, they spell out the names of the seven Israeli generals who were in charge during the battle Mansour 2015. Three letters also refer to the abbreviation of the Israel Defense Forces (IDF). In addition, the letters spell out *Habotz Halebanoni* (Hebrew: הבוץ הלבנוני | Lebanese mud), an expression used by critical Israeli citizens to question Israel's involvement in the war in Lebanon. Since the Hebrew is not translated it remains hidden from those who don't read the language or aren't familiar with the discourse. Instead, it is intentionally directed towards the sky to remind the Israeli military of the critical voices in Israel's own society. In using this tactic, Hezbollah demonstrates that it knows the internal discourse in Israel. It employs the language of Israel's critical voices and turns this speech against its enemy. This is a symbolic act of using, showing, and "turning" that plays with—and at the same time communicates to—the aerial view of the Israeli military, whose presence in the sky is still an act of symbolic control over the territories below.

1   In her text "How to Fabricate Heroes", the artist Paola Yacoub focuses on the exhibition of death in the context of Lebanon. She analyses the difference between the invisibility of Hezbollah's military chief Imad Mughniyeh during his lifetime and his visibility after death, when his face adorned buildings. During his lifetime, "Mughniyeh's invisibility and elusiveness were legendary. He never gave interviews. And the one and only circulating portrait of him was thought to be someone else. Press reports claimed that Mughniyeh had had plastic surgery in order to disguise his facial features" (Paola Yacoub 2013, 322).

Panoramic space is exposed and staged at Mleeta's two panorama platforms. With Syria to the east and the mountains of Israel to the south, the view relates to Sekula's idea that expansive panoramic space is haunted by collapse or counter-expansion. The military aspect of the panorama is inscribed in this view. When the landscape is seen from this elevated (sublime) position, the gaze of tourism collides with the gaze of the military. A Lebanese friend highlights a very different way of seeing this landscape. For him, it holds memories from the time before the occupation. Simultaneously, it contains the tension of peacefulness just before the next bombing. Due to his memories, he perceives the landscape outside of Hezbollah's propagandistic framing → see chapter 8.2. This shows how our perspectives differ according to our contexts, histories, and recollections.

Interventions into Vertical and Panoramic Space 6.2

Mleeta addresses the aerial view right from the start. A Google-animated nosedive from space lands directly into the brownish pixels next to the car park at the Museum of Resistance. This nosedive produced by Google Earth exemplifies the verticality of space and the military surveillance gaze of satellite cameras. Google Earth is the "poor" consumer version of "real" military technology. This tool has certain similarities to Charles and Ray Eames's film *Powers of Ten* (1977). Sponsored by IBM, the Eames Office developed this animation to familiarise viewers with computer technology.[2] Today, anyone can download Google Earth and dive into low-resolution images anywhere on the planet. As the writer Vera Tollmann states: "From a contemporary perspective, one could say that Google Earth is a way of familiarizing users with surveillance, with the feeling of being observed from above, of being watched by state-operated technology" Tollmann 2014. Since I only have access to the consumer version of this technology, I address the satellite view through this "poor" animation.

In my video, I shift from this gaze of aerial surveillance to Hezbollah's computer-animated flight through the Mleeta theme park. This immersive shot in the museum's introductory film recalls the aesthetics of video games or drone camera footage. The animation is seen projected on the screen in the museum's cinema. Filmed from an off-centre angle, the experience is disrupted and distorted. An audience is

---

2   Fifty-two years later, Google produced a computer-animated remake. The film begins with a young smiling woman on the grass at Google headquarters.

seen watching this animation on the second screen of the two-channel video installation.

In the sequence focusing on "The Abyss", I address the gaze from the air. The sky first appears on the left screen. Then there are two skies, with a moon on each screen. If these shots are combined to form a continuous image of the sky, the second moon becomes a stumbling block. Slightly shifted, the doubled image loses its illusionary quality of representing space; instead, it points to the image as a frame. In contrast to the doubling of the image, a continuous space is established at the level of sound. An airplane can be heard moving through space from left to right, suggesting the aerial view of the military. This airplane is not, however, present in the image.

This scene is followed by another shot of the sky, screened through the leaves of evergreen trees. Images of these trees spread to both screens, accompanied by the artificial sound of crickets. The sound engulfs the viewer. The camera's gaze turns to the ground, which is covered with brown leaves and sandbags, as someone is heard running past. A far-away and close-up shot focus on a camouflaged net hiding something underneath the trees. This sequence traverses the space while only framing specific fragments of it and sometimes adding staged sounds. The duration of each shot encourages the viewer to pause while looking and listening. I play with the immersive qualities of image and sound. Sometimes these work against each other, revealing an illusion, and sometimes one completes the other.

The video installation continues with a point-of-view shot through the tunnel and bunker system. Two different paths appear, like mirrored images/spaces. On one screen, the camera stays underground and enters into a small room with a weapon and an embrasure. *Wama Rameyta Ith Rameyta Walakenna Allaha Rama* (Arabic: وَمَا رَمَيْتَ إِذْ رَمَيْتَ وَلَكِنَّ اللَّهَ رَمَى | And you threw not, when you threw, but Allah did) is written on the wall. This underground message from the past—addressing fellow fighters— remains hidden from aerial view.

After the camera exits the long tunnel, it reaches one of Mleeta's panoramic platforms. An image of the landscape blocked by a handrail appears on the right screen. It is followed by an image on the left that shows the torso of the figure in blue. He stands on the platform holding the handrail and looking out over the landscape. These shots avoid a direct image of the space; instead, the spectator looks at someone else looking at the landscape. This is a mediated space, imagined through the figure's gaze. The landscape itself remains hidden. The image jumps to the screen on the right, which shows three young girls posing in front of the panorama while a fourth girl photographs them. Here, again, the gaze of the military and the gaze of tourism collide. The image jumps again, and the landscape is finally seen without interference. The artificial sound of a siren rips through the panorama. A cut takes the viewer to the 360-degree viewing platform located at the summit of the mountain. From this platform, the viewer sees a continuous panorama with Syria on the left screen and the mountains of Israel on the right. The sound of the siren fades away. Jumping from left to right and leaving one screen black underscores my fragmentary understanding of the space. It also allows me to jump geographically while traversing the park. Through my framing and editing, I create a tour that differs from the course set by Hezbollah.

Coding/Decoding vs Propaganda

In previous chapters, I have called the Museum of Resistance "propagandistic" to emphasise the manipulative nature of its staging. In propaganda, the instrumentality of information is central, highlighting techniques that induce the receiver to believe certain ideas. The truth has become a contested terrain in today's era of fake news. What kind of truth is performed, by whom and for whom? The distribution of (fake) news is enmeshed in a wider network of discourses, power constellations, and systems of domination. As the sociologist Stuart Hall points out in his concept of media, the process of communication is not as mechanical as the term propaganda implies—and the audience is not passive Hall 1980, 118. For this reason, the writer Zeina Maasri does not regard "propaganda" as a particularly helpful term in analysing the political posters made by different groups during the Lebanese Civil War Maasri 2008, 5–15. Nor does she find the distinction between propaganda and activism helpful, since propaganda is found in both hegemonic and counter-hegemonic contexts ibid., 5. Instead, Maasri refers to Hall's concept of media communication. According to Hall, the content of media is not transparent and the communication process is not linear. Hall describes the encoding and decoding of media as complex processes within relations of dominance. In these processes, encoding and decoding are not symmetrical Hall 1980, 128. A code is used to produce a message that enters social practice, where it is decoded. This implies the possibility of oppositional readings, in which a receiver decodes a message in a way that counters its encoding ibid., 127.

Although Stuart Hall developed his media theory in the 1970s, his concept is relevant in analysing Hezbollah's productions. Hezbollah is aware of the (emotional) effectiveness of images, architecture, (urban) design, and sculpture. The encoding of messages and values is part of its multiple (media) productions. This process is embedded in the group's much wider system and its holistic approach → see chapter 5.3.

According to Henri Lefebvre, architects and planners are involved in encoding representations of space Lefebvre 2007, 37–39. The rebuilding of Haret Hreik is thus both a real manifestation in space[1] and an encoded sign that is represented in architecture and discourse.

Hezbollah regards the reconstruction of Haret Hreik as an act of resistance and Hassan Nasrallah has referred to it as a "second victory" Waad 2006a. Nasrallah's rhetoric continues the logic of war in civic space. At the same time, this second victory is not complete without people. In this sense, the bodies and architecture in Haret Hreik become signs of the party's perseverance. These signs are addressed to both Israel as well as Hezbollah's own community. The notion of sacrifice is central to the inhabitants of Haret Hreik. Ms Ibtissam, who lives in the neighbourhood and works for the *Waad* rebuilding project, highlights her willingness to sacrifice not only buildings and furniture, but also her life or the lives of her family members for what she calls "the culture of Hassan Nasrallah" Malak 2015. Walid el-Houri and Dima Saber analyse Hezbollah's willingness to sacrifice: "Ashura is not simply a ritual enacting the tragedy around which the Shiite identity is constructed but also represents the fundamental system of values that Hezbollah keeps reasserting in its media discourse" Houri and Saber 2010, 80.

The decision to rebuild Haret Hreik's architecture in the same way it appeared before the war emphasises how reconstruction impacts the collective memory of the neighbourhood and its community. Referring to Auguste Comte, Maurice Halbwachs argues that "the physical objects of our daily contact change little or not at all, providing us with an image of permanence and stability. They give us a feeling of order and tranquility, like a silent and immobile society unconcerned with our own restlessness and changes of mood" Halbwachs 1980, 128. Halbwachs states that "every collective memory unfolds within a spatial framework" ibid., 139. The architectural concept of sameness thus plays an important role in creating and maintaining a community among Hezbollah's supporters.

According to Hassan el-Jeshi, the director of the *Waad* project, this architectural approach intends to "keep the environment whole, not to disrupt the people's memory" Jeshi 2015. Painting the facades of both the

---

1   Hezbollah's diversity of practices comprises "military, social and political institutions (hospitals, schools, universities, scouts, parliamentary bloc, services, media, research centers …) alongside the discursive elements present in media and other productions (music videos, songs, posters, political statements" (Houri and Saber 2010, 78).

damaged and newly reconstructed buildings beige and white creates an impression of homogeneity ibid.. The project's leading architect, Rahif Fayad, emphasises the small size of the area that was rebuilt. He points out that this area belongs to the surrounding neighbourhoods and should blend in with these spaces. Furthermore, Fayad highlights the necessity of rebuilding the social sphere: the emotional, practical, and religious intelligence that supported the resistance Fayad 2015. According to Fayad, there is a close relationship between creating architecture similar to buildings that existed before the war and preserving the social fabric.[2]

Fayad argues that individual memories of the war and its destruction are inscribed in the bodies of Haret Hreik's inhabitants. This is why there is no need to maintain a visible memorial site. Furthermore, due to the short intervals of warlessness, these bodies will not have forgotten the war before the next one takes place ibid.. For this reason, there will always be a gap between the subjective memory of destruction and the visual and physical "wholeness" of a space that doesn't leave any discernible ruptures between the old and the new. The code inscribed in the sameness of this architecture devoid of ruptures, the speed of reconstruction, and the return of Haret Hreik's residents represent the invulnerability of this community.

The Past Infuses the Signal in the Present 7.2

In the architectural approach to Haret Hreik's reconstruction, the role of the past relates to the creation of a "wholeness", with all the different meanings described above. The past is likewise exhibited at Mleeta. The previously hidden architecture of the landscape is exposed and put on display. The past is present in the visibility of Mleeta's strategic location as well as its underground infrastructure. Graffiti meant for the gaze of fellow Hezbollah fighters during the occupation has now become public. Tunnels and bunkers appear as authentic signs of the resistance; at the same time, however, they are spaces designed for the use of tourists. Their staging is only complete with the visitor's presence. The "realness" from the past infuses the signal and its encoding.

According to Stuart Hall, an "oppositional code" is produced when a receiver decodes a message contrary to its encoding Hall 1980, 127. In

---

2   By this he means bringing people back to the same houses with the same neighbours. A neighbourhood is, however, never homogeneous. For a variety of reasons, not all of Haret Hreik's previous inhabitants have moved back (UMAM Documentation and Research Centre 2007).

"The Abyss", Hezbollah appropriates an oppositional code used by Israeli citizens critical of Israel's occupation of southern Lebanon. Hebrew terms from this critical discourse are incorporated into Hezbollah's own discourse of resistance → see chapter 6.1. Through Hezbollah's use of this oppositional code it becomes part of a discursive battle of domination and power. At the same time, this code is part of a discourse of resistance that has become a dominant project.

Walid el-Houri analyses Hezbollah's hegemonic discourse of resistance as an empty signifier. Citing the theorists Ernesto Laclau and Chantal Mouffe, el-Houri argues that in order for a discourse to become hegemonic, it needs to work as an empty signifier that operates as an inscription surface and is open for a wide variety of demands Houri 2012, 184–85. According to el-Houri, an empty signifier does not offer any political programme. Instead, it works with various demands that are based on a moral ground ibid., 180–83. In this sense, a hegemonic discourse will, according to Laclau and Mouffe, "suppress its literal content—its specific demands, its specific origins as a single issue movement—in favor of its metaphorical dimension—its self-representation as the principle of order itself" Smith 1998, 167. To become a hegemonic discourse, Hezbollah had to represent its discourse as the principle of order while also incorporating different struggles beyond its main cause of the Lebanese-Israeli war. Hezbollah claimed to end corruption, institute economic and political reform, and fill the gap after the withdrawal of the Syrian troops Houri 2012, 185. However, it did not support the uprisings in Iran or Syria. As a consequence, Hezbollah's image was damaged—particularly in the Arab world. Instead, "[Hezbollah] decided to rely on the geopolitical dimension of resistance, perhaps forgetting that the two [resistance against corrupt leadership and support of the poor] are inseparable in the minds of many of their supporters who identify with those demonstrating against corruption and poverty" ibid., 206.

The Mleeta Museum of Resistance and the rebuilding of Haret Hreik are empty signifiers in the discourse of resistance. Both projects work as territorial markers in space. In this sense, the discourse of resistance inhabits this space and the bodies within it.

7.3 My Encodings, Their Encodings

My audiovisual work intervenes in Hezbollah's spatial and audiovisual encodings. I am simultaneously attracted and irritated by Hezbollah's way of working; there is both a closeness and a difference. When I work in the context of Hezbollah, I have to endure these contradictions that cannot be solved. Instead, they become part of the process. Furthermore, maintaining an ambiguous attitude allows my team to reposition itself during the working process. As already discussed, Hezbollah's own narrative includes critique expressed by Israeli citizens. Large environmental installations incorporate landscape and architecture, often addressing the aerial view and the Israeli Other. In "The Abyss", anti-war aesthetics are turned into a militarised war narrative. Hezbollah's encodings do not leave much space to think along different lines. Instead, certain framings attempt to dictate how to feel and think.

My role as an observer/decoder does not free me from encoding in my own video work. My approach to encoding reacts to Hezbollah's way of working, which wants visitors to become participants and attempts to narrow their view. I do not want to completely release my audience from this experience. Instead, I try to challenge viewers to reflect on their own positions. To do so, I employ some of Hezbollah's methods, but I use them differently. Furthermore, I intervene in Hezbollah's encodings through distancing techniques that reflect on the role and gaze of the participant/spectator. The Mleeta theme park is a public image in which all of the perspectives have been designed, defined, and controlled. For this reason, I am allowed to film from any angle and for as long as I want, and can even work with a performer → see chapter 5.4.

Constructed Futures: Haret Hreik requires a different way of working. First of all, Haret Hreik is not a public image and not everybody is allowed to film there. Due to the controlled framing of this space, I decide not to film the streets. The only images of exterior space are shot from a window, if I am granted permission to do so. At the level of the images I produce there is thus an absence of the outside architecture/neighbourhood. Instead, the video includes sketches, models, and visual representations from Hezbollah's agitprop films. I also film the interiors of the rooms in which I meet with interlocutors. At the level of sound, the individual voices of architects, planners, and others involved in the reconstruction project describe Haret Hreik. In using this technique, the image of the neighbourhood remains a blank space at the level of my own visual production. Instead, it is envisioned and sketched—emphasising the imaginary meaning of the architecture and the neighbourhood. Through filming interiors, architectural space is inverted, exposing the private and intimate sphere.

As discussed in chapter 5, Kaja Silverman bases her analysis of the screen on Jacques Lacan's theory of the relationship between the gaze, the look, and the subject/object. Silverman highlights that subjectivation is dependent on the gaze of the other Silverman 1996, 133. The screen appears between the subject and the other as the place where social and historical difference enter the visual field ibid., 134. What does this mean in the context of Hezbollah's media productions related to Haret Hreik? What narratives are developed and how do these relate to resistance? Whose gaze—which audience—is addressed?

Media produced by Hezbollah accompanies the rebuilding of Haret Hreik and participates in distributing a certain set of values. Two films about the *Waad* project begin with images of destruction, ruins, and victims who turn into successful actors. One film shows ruins illuminated by artificial light and accompanied by dramatic music.[3] This scene is followed by a tracking shot that reveals a wedding in this space, highlighting how life goes on. Construction workers, craftsmen, and the director of the *Waad* project are depicted at construction sites in Haret Hreik. These scenes establish certainty concerning the rebuilding project. They introduce Hezbollah's social and financial support network and demonstrate how the organisation takes care of its community.

After an extended sequence of destruction and warfare, the second film highlights a huge gathering in a public square in Haret Hreik, with crowds surrounding and celebrating Hezbollah's party leader Hassan Nasrallah. Here the victims are again turned into agents. The film then follows a typical convention of promotional videos within the construction sector, presenting the planning and rebuilding of the district in fast-forward. This technique suggests that all is under control. At the end, fireworks celebrate the completion of the reconstruction. Strangely, these explosions resemble bombings. The footage runs forwards and backwards, accentuating the cycle of destruction and reconstruction.

These films address different gazes: their meanings change depending on who is watching. One audience is Hezbollah's community,

---

3   In their lecture performance and publication *O Syria*, Joseph Rustom and Paola Yacoub analyse the romantic images of war ruins in video clips filmed during the war in Syria (Yacoub, Rustom, and Wildner 2013). Rustom's text *Drunk on Ruins* elaborates various definitions of ruins. He focuses on pre-Islamic Arabic poetry, examining how the traces left behind by Bedouins trigger a sense of mourning. The philosopher Georg Simmel elaborates a definition that highlights the sudden and intentional ruin and differs from the timeless view popular during Romanticism (Yacoub, Rustom, and Wildner 2013, 19–54).

whose members see themselves represented simultaneously as victims and powerful actors. This paradox is often found in movements facing large and powerful military enemies Houri and Saber 2010, 80. Another gaze belongs to Lebanese and Arab audiences who see themselves as victims in the Arab–Israeli conflict and are in favour of the party. The Museum of Resistance, the urban rebuilding of Haret Hreik, and Hezbollah's films serve to articulate a similar narrative and values.[4] The third gaze belongs to an Israeli audience that can be divided into three groups: the public, the military, and the media. The Israeli public sees Hezbollah's films, museum exhibitions, and urban scenarios after these have been incorporated into specific media narratives. Whereas the Israeli military and secret service are interested in studying the effects of military and psychological warfare, the Israeli media incorporates Hezbollah's filmic material to create specific media events on Israeli television.

Hezbollah's (media) productions are part of what it calls psychological warfare (al-Harbe al-Nafsia | Arabic: الحرب النفسية) or media war (al-Harb el-E'lamia | Arabic: الحرب الإعلامية) ibid., 79. This specific strategy addresses the Israeli audience in particular and is based on the power of the gaze and the spectacle of power. In this context, urban and museum scenarios are meant to offer a warning and to reflect a public exercise of punitive justice.

Hezbollah's social self-assurance—as a community—plays another important role. Public gatherings at the multipurpose hall Mujama al-Shouhada serve as a place for the community to meet and be seen. Simultaneously, images of these gatherings circulate and represent the community to a larger audience. Inside the hall, large screens mirror the audience before the actual programme starts. The crowd is reflected and watches itself. This mirrored image reveals the social importance of the audience's role. An all-male VIP area in the front of the hall faces the rest of the audience. These VIPs gaze at the crowd and the audience is able to see who is present. The audience is separated into two further parts: another all-male VIP area facing the stage and the general (gender segregated) audience. Camera cranes float above the crowd. A camera owned by Hezbollah's television station al-Manar is positioned on a pedestal at the highest point overlooking the room. Other journalists are allowed to film from a corner.

4   This perception has shifted since Hezbollah's support of the Assad regime in Syria.

Hassan Nasrallah usually appears in a live broadcast; he very rarely appears in person. On the screen he is an oversized fatherly figure in religious clothes. Although these events create a bond between the community and its leader, Hezbollah also disseminates Nasrallah's messages via radio, television, and the internet. Through these mediums, his voice and image reach a wider audience that includes the diverse groups mentioned above. In doing so, Nasrallah simultaneously takes the role of a political and religious leader.

7.5   Dis- and Re-Location

At Mujama al-Shouhada, I film an event in a public space that is simultaneously a media event. My camera is located next to other journalists' cameras, but it is not in the privileged position of the cameras operated by Hezbollah. I observe both how the event is staged and how other cameras film it. The mirrored image of the audience immediately catches my attention and I film it in long takes. Later, during the editing process, I notice that it is impossible to use any of my other recordings: the video either becomes a stereotypical representation of this community as an agitated crowd and/or slides into reproducing and amplifying Hezbollah's narrative and staging. Instead, I decide to use two single shots of the stage, filmed from the same position. The first shot is a close up and the second is filmed with a wide angle. This approach emphasises my body, the camera's position, and the framing of the image. I shoot the mirrored image of the audience and an announcer praising Hassan Nasrallah before he appears on the screen. Just before Nasrallah starts his speech, I cut the image. In showing this edit, I give visibility to what is left out. Cutting Nasrallah's contribution also serves as a critical gesture towards his omnipresence in this context. Instead, the video highlights the margins of the event, its staging, and the excitement of the crowd. When the video installation is shown in an exhibition, the audience is placed into proximity with another audience and another space. This forced proximity is experienced differently depending on the situated knowledge of each individual viewer.

Haret Hreik only appears on an imaginary level in *Constructed Futures: Haret Hreik*. The video thus incorporates Hezbollah's own audiovisual narratives. As already analysed in my discussion of the agitprop film screened at the Museum of Resistance →chapter 4.3, I do not simply include Hezbollah's filmic material inside the frame of my audiovisual narratives. Instead, I use several methods to reframe, distance, and deterritorialise these images. I project Hezbollah's films about Haret Hreik in the conference room of the *Waad* office and shoot the projection from an off-centre angle. This makes it more difficult for my audience to position itself. Furthermore, the projection is affected by changes in sunlight. This conference room—the actual room where the architects met to discuss the project—also appears in Hezbollah's films. Locating Hezbollah's audiovisual images of Haret Hreik's reconstruction in the space where the planning for this project took place is a gesture of distancing and reframing. Simultaneously, it allows my audience to see the audiovisual narratives that Hezbollah has produced to frame this endeavour.

How My Work Speaks Back, or "The Eye Is Nothing but Desire"

In reflecting on the relationship between the gaze, the subject/object, and the intermediary role of the screen, I find it important to question how my work is perceived by different people in different contexts. How do my videos resonate and what feedback do I receive? The reactions to the videos I made in Lebanon have been particularly strong and diverse, touching different sensitivities. The following selection of responses represents only a small sample. These examples are fragments of a much broader feedback loop. Here I include different reactions, comments, and discussions. These responses take the form of remembered conversations, emails, screenshots of texts in revision mode, and transcriptions of conversations.

Katja Schroeder, Curator of Kunsthaus Hamburg   8.1

In August 2016, while working on my dissertation at a friend's house in the Swiss Alps, Katja Schroeder contacts me. We have plans to show *Mleeta* and *Constructed Futures: Haret Hreik* at Kunsthaus Hamburg in autumn. Katja has just watched the videos on Vimeo. She sees the Museum of Resistance as propaganda that presents war and violence in a heroic way and creates a memorial to it. She is irritated by Hezbollah's use of the term "resistance". She thinks of resistance as an act of emancipation, but feels this concept is lacking in Hezbollah's museum. She wonders how I position myself to Hezbollah and why I became interested in this subject. I explain that I share her concerns and irritation about the use of this term in Hezbollah's discourse. I point out that the organisation has changed since its foundation in the 1980s. The concept of resistance also changed from real resistance (for example, in the fight against the occupation of southern Lebanon) to a discourse of resistance that has become a hegemonic project. At the same time, this project has become questionable due to Hezbollah's unconditional support of the Assad regime in Syria. I explain that my work aims to examine how this

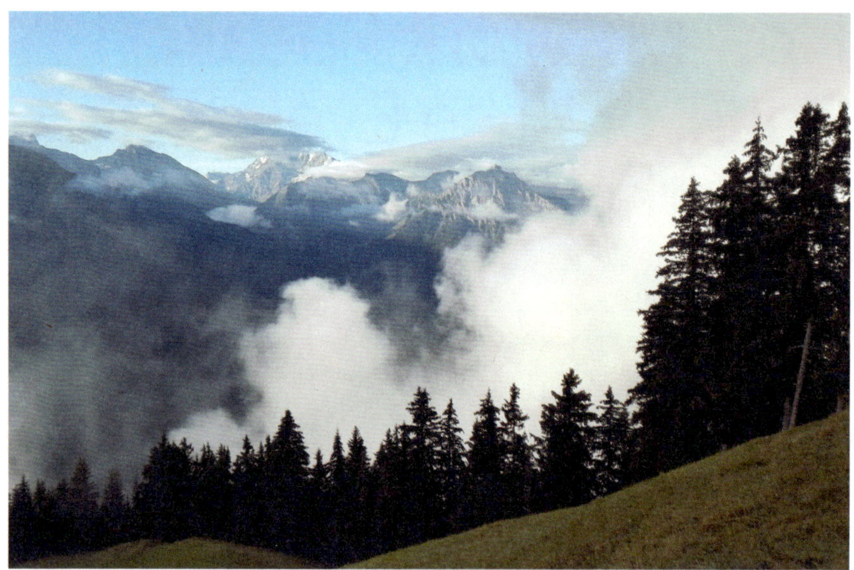

View from Riederalp, Switzerland, photograph: Sandra Schäfer, 2016

narrative of resistance manifests in the aesthetics of space, focusing on the Museum of Resistance and the rebuilding of Haret Hreik. I tell her that I don't see my video installations as a simple repetition of propaganda; instead, I deconstruct these settings in a way that does not release viewers from the uncomfortable challenge of positioning themselves in relation to what they encounter.

During the presentation of my videos at Kunsthaus Hamburg in November 2017, the media theorist Walid el-Houri provocatively comments on a remark from the audience that the Museum of Resistance is propaganda. He argues that while Hezbollah's museum is indeed propagandistic in the sense that its purpose is to advance a particular narrative imbued with particular values and ideas related to the movement, it is important to point out that museums, as institutions, have always advanced particular official or dominant narratives. In this sense, museums are equally propagandistic anywhere in the world, to varying degrees of subtlety. In other words, the Mleeta Museum of Resistance is not so different from the museums and cultural sites we find all over Europe.

10.11.16

Dear Sandra,

It has been such a long time since our last meeting, so long that I cannot recall anymore if it was in Berlin or Beirut, winter or summer.

I arrive in Berlin only a few hours after your talk on the 16th, missing (again!) your work on Lebanon.

I saw the movie about the museum and wanted to write to you. Non-Lebanese spectators might be intrigued by the architecture, the artefacts, and the discourses. I was touched by the way you filmed the nature. It reminded me of certain summer days during the war when the sun shone and all was quiet and serene, before a bomb suddenly exploded. At the same time, these scenes recall the state of the site before its occupation. They thus seemed peaceful and threatening, imminent and timeless.

I wish you all the best for the 16th. I'll be in Berlin until November 30 in case you have time for a coffee or a drink.

Very best,

Joseph

Joseph draws a distinction between the gaze from outside and inside. These two gazes seem to see and experience differently. Although the discourse, architecture, and artefacts might interest the gaze from outside, Joseph highlights the superimposition of different temporalities within his memory of the landscape. He recalls the time before the occupation, the possibility of another bomb explosion interrupting the silence. He thus perceives the landscape outside of the narrative of propaganda. The landscape claims its own temporality and space, resisting Hezbollah's framing. Kaja Silverman describes memory as a complex conglomeration of images and values that are temporal and changing Silverman 1996, 157. In this sense, "the flow of perceptions across the psyche leaves behind 'traces' or imprints. These memory traces are far away from providing a registration of the 'real'" ibid., 158. The traces in Joseph's memory intersect with the images of the landscape. This differs from my perception of the landscape due to my particular experiences and memories. Here it is helpful to distinguish between the "visual" and the "look". The latter is located within desire, the body, and temporality, and can thus change what the camera/gaze records. Silverman quotes Sally Potter's 1983 film

The Gold Diggers: "I know that even as I look and even as I see, I am changing what is there" ibid., 161.

8.3   Conversation with the Writer Adania Shibli[1]

Adania: When she [Ms Ibtissam] is speaking, her speech makes something else invisible: that she's borrowing discourse from Hezbollah, or maybe even a historical discourse going back further in time. It could also be a contemporary discourse related to when someone goes off to war and might get killed. There is an acceptance of that outcome. You get the feeling that she's concealing something. It raises the question of whether she's able to say what she really wants or thinks. In my view, her borrowing of ready-made words is a form of denial. In this way, one can form a narrative that is also cheating or hiding something.

Sandra: I think that it shifts in the conversation. You can notice how the speed of her speech changes. When she talks about her son, it's not that easy anymore—she's hesitant.

Adania: Towards the end she becomes more hesitant. It suddenly shifts from a political argument to a social one. Maybe this didn't come across in the translation, but she says that her son went to Syria and was ready to be killed in order to protect honour.[2] So if it's a question of honour—and not of occupation and resistance—it becomes a social conversation. I think that as a party, Hezbollah isn't able to address and justify this war in a convincing way as "resistance". So it's not about resistance, it's about protection and about the female; protecting "our women"—mainly—and not "our houses". I'd like to connect this issue with the Israeli act of destruction. Ms Ibtissam mentions "what a house means for us, if our sons are lost". What she says here is interesting in light of how, in the 1980s, Ariel Sharon told the Israeli army to deal with Palestinians.

---

1   This conversation took place on 16 November 2016 at Kunstraum Kreuzberg, Berlin. This transcription is largely unedited to stay true to its original character.

2   Since I speak very little Arabic, I am dependent on translation. Before the first screening of *Constructed Futures: Haret Hreik*, Adania worked all night to check the translations of the dialogues, finding important subtleties that had been lost. For example, when Ms Ibtissam describes Hezbollah's participation in the war in Syria, she says "the war against Syria". She explains that Hezbollah participated in the war to protect the country's honour and its women. Thanks to Adania's help, Mr el-Jeshi's dominant tone becomes apparent when he asks: "What does she want from me? Where does she want me to sit? Do I sit here or there? What is her programme?" (Jeshi 2015). His comments mark how we intervene—through film and recording—into his territory.

Sharon—whose nickname is "the Bulldozer" (Arabic: البلدوزر)—believed in destruction. He said something to the effect of "we should not kill Palestinians, because they do not care about the deaths of their children. They will have more children. But if you destroy their houses, they will care." So it's very interesting to hear this kind of shift from her (what a house means for us, if our sons are lost). Sharon said that "we should destroy the first house, and then the first row of houses, and then ten whole rows of houses, until they stop." This is an ideology of destruction. So there is both an ideology of reconstruction and an ideology of destruction—and it extends beyond war. This is an interesting shift in perspective between a woman who loses her house or her son and an Israeli army officer who is responsible for this destruction.

Catalogue Text for the Diagonale Film Festival in Graz 8.4

In February 2017, I receive the first draft of a catalogue text about *Constructed Futures: Haret Hreik* for the Diagonale film festival in Graz. When I read the text, I am irritated by its tone. The author uses

Sandra
Schäfer

DE 2017, 27 min
DCP, Farbe

Spektrum

Österr. Erstaufführung
Diagonale'17

Constructed Futures: Haret Hreik

Förderungen
Akademie der Künste
der Welt, Köln (DE),
ifa Stuttgart (DE),
Rosa Luxemburg Stiftung, Berlin (DE)

The Haret Hreik neighborhood in Beirut is a stronghold of Shi'ite Lebanese. The Hezbollah headquarters, hidden from the outside, are also found there. *Constructed Futures* offers insight into the propagandistically motivated rebuilding after the bombing in the 2006 Lebanon War and in four chapters follows the path of an ideology that considers architecture as a theater of war where decisions are made about the construction of space, landscape, and memory.

Die Erinnerung an den Hisbollah-Kämpfer Hassan hat sich in die Wohnung seiner Familie eingeschrieben: Überlebensgroße Poster des Mannes in Militärkluft zieren die Räume, persönliche Utensilien werden in einem Schrein aufbewahrt. Hassan ist als Märtyrer einer barbarischen Ideologie in Syrien gestorben, seine Mutter ist stolz auf ihn. Wie sehr Krieg und Widerstand das Leben und Denken der schiitischen Libanes/innen in Beirut prägen, zeigt sich in dem Viertel Haret Hreik, das nach außen hin unsichtbar das Hauptquartier sowie die Unterstützerbasis der Hisbollah beherbergt. *Constructed Futures* gibt Einblicke in den propagandistisch motivierten Wiederaufbau nach der Bombardierung des Viertels im Libanonkrieg 2006 und spürt in vier Kapiteln einer Ideologie nach, die Architektur als einen Kriegsschauplatz denkt, auf dem über die Konstruktion von Raum, Landschaft und Erinnerung entschieden wird.

ast

Screenshot of the Diagonale catalogue, 2017

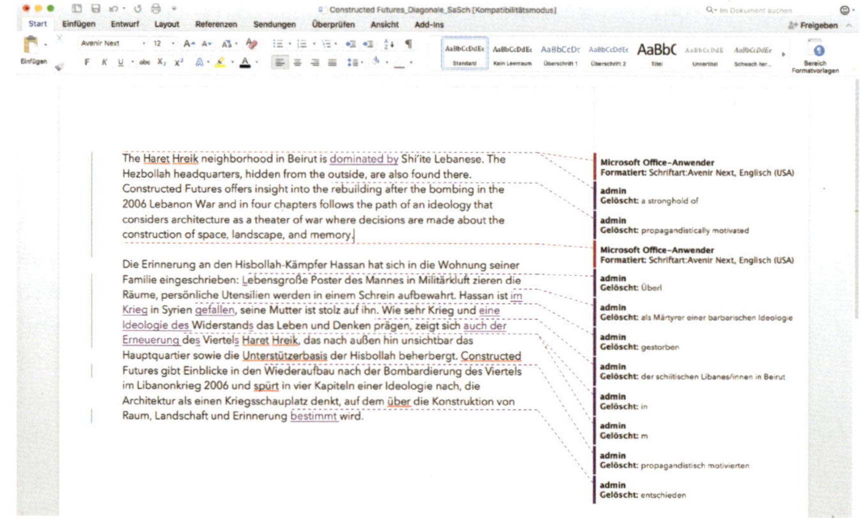

Screenshot of Microsoft Word document, 2017

military terms like "stronghold" to describe the neighbourhood of Haret Hreik and its inhabitants. The reconstruction is compared to a "theater of war" and Hezbollah's participation in the war in Syria is described as part of its barbaric ideology. An "othering" takes place that narrows and simplifies the contradictions of Hezbollah's rebuilding project. I am irritated that my video triggers this way of seeing/reading. I correct the text and ask to include these changes when it is published.

8.5 Exhibition and Discussion at the Contemporary Image Collective (CIC) in Cairo[3]

Ahmed Refaat, one of the curators of the Contemporary Image Collective (CIC | Arabic: مركز الصورة المعاصرة) in Cairo, sees *Constructed Futures: Haret Hreik* at the 67th Berlinale in February 2017. He asks for a Vimeo link to watch the video again and share it with his colleagues. In March 2017, I receive an email from the curator Andrea Thal, who tells me that the CIC intends to show the piece in a project focusing on liberation struggles, ideology, neoliberalism, and security regimes. I am pleased because I appreciate the CIC's programme and would like to share my work with an Egyptian audience. Just one week later,

---

3   The exhibition project "If Not for that Wall: Imagined Life in a Museum Vitrine" took place at the CIC in May 2017.

I receive an email from Andrea that expresses hesitation about showing the piece. These doubts have been triggered by discussions about the risk of showing another artist's film. In the first chapter of the exhibition project "If Not for That Wall", a work by this filmmaker was confiscated during a raid, leading to accusations and detentions. Now there are concerns about possible reactions to my work. Although Andrea and I both have European passports, the other members of the team are more vulnerable, including the participating artists from the region. We arrange a Skype conversation while I am in Graz for the Diagonale film festival. In the meantime, Ahmed is suddenly called up for military service. For this reason, the show will probably need to be postponed.

During our Skype conversation, Andrea explains that she and Ahmed have watched the film again with a different group of people. Everyone agrees that showing the work as part of an exhibition would be a big risk. The exhibition is a format that is open from 12 to 9pm and is easily visited by informants. Compared to other formats like screenings or discussions, exhibitions are particularly exposed. Andrea tells me that some people were concerned about the film's positioning towards the war in Syria. Others were interested in the approach I took. Everyone thinks that the work requires a conversation, but they are unsure if this will be a yelling match or a situation in which people are too cautious to talk. Apart from possible difficulties with the government, a second risk relates to the negative attitude towards Shiites in Egypt. Someone could start a Facebook campaign bashing Shia people and the CIC as an institution. Both risks are higher if the work is shown in an exhibition. With a screening, however, the CIC can react to the current political situation. If, for example, house searches have taken place just before the event, they can organise the screening as a private event with registration. We also discuss presenting the work as an installation that only exists for a couple of hours, accompanied by a discussion. Andrea mentions her sensitivity to the presence of propaganda in the third and fourth sections of the video. The narrative of the mother and her martyr son reminds her of the overall presence of such images after the revolution in Egypt.

We ultimately decide to show the installation on monitors in a temporary extension of the exhibition space set up in the library. This will be accompanied by a discussion in the evening. My presence is possible because the curator Berit Schuck has invited me to hold a workshop for former MASS Alexandria students in the framework of

"Farocki Now: A Temporary Academy". The Goethe Institute Alexandria funds my trip.

The temporary exhibition at the CIC was packed. In the following transcript, I have chosen a few largely unedited sequences from the discussion. Unfortunately, the tape recorder stopped after the first hour. The entire discussion lasted approximately two hours.

Audience: Is it the case that with those examples—of Germany in the Second World War, Lebanon, Bosnia, or wherever else—architecture cannot impose a new reality even though, at least in Germany, the aim was to wipe out the memory of the war? In the case of Beirut, they tried to rebuild the architecture without losing the experience of the war. But does this experience relate to objects or is it actually maintained in people's psyches? After the rebuilding of West Germany, the Germans still retained the experience of the Second World War; they didn't just lose it. So it's not just the architecture. Is it the relationship between the architectural object and people's actual lived experience? How does architecture affect people's psyches?

Sandra: From my point of view, it isn't necessarily that one to one, in the sense that a form has an immediate effect on people's psyches. But it isn't completely unrelated either. In the case of the reconstruction of Haret Hreik, the formal choice of architecture has several meanings and impacts. Rebuilding the blocks as they were closely relates to bringing people back into the same neighbourhood constellations and rebuilding the social fabric. Painting both the destroyed and intact buildings the same colours is an attempt to make the ruptures invisible. There is an attempt to conceal the actual destruction—not to leave any visible wounds—and to make the present match the past. This approach also speeds up the rebuilding process, which is important for Hezbollah at the level of providing for the needs of its support base and making the destruction look undone as quickly as possible. This, again, shows strength. There is another aspect to rebuilding the neighbourhood as it was. The philosopher Maurice Halbwachs states that collective memory constitutes itself in space in relation to the silent objects surrounding us. This helps explain the importance of the sameness of the architectural form and the urban fabric from before the destruction. Yet individual memory can't be controlled and smoothed so easily.

Experiences leave traces on the psyche, which is why personal memories are moving and uncontrollable. We know this from our individual experiences and attempts to create a balance. The rebuilding of Haret Hreik is part of a power struggle that manifests in space. Its residents become part of this struggle because they live in a territory that is marked and dominated by Hezbollah. This doesn't mean that everybody in the neighbourhood is a party member. A district like Haret Hreik is still diverse, although segregation has taken place since the civil war. Haret Hreik is Shiite dominated now, and Hezbollah's headquarters are located there.

Audience: I'd like to take the discussion away from the distance of the Second World War and move it to two other instances of reconstruction. Besides Dahiya, there are two further important cases: one is the city centre in Beirut and another is Gaza. I think these comparisons are very important and relevant in terms of the narrative of resistance and *Jihad al-Bina*. Especially the comparison with what Hariri did [in the city centre of Beirut] with the reconstruction. Here the focus was on neoliberal lifestyle; upscale, decontextualised, franchised. It [the reconstruction of Haret Hreik] is an attempt to offer an alternative. But unlike Gaza and Jenin, where the form itself is relevant because of urban warfare, the reconstruction in Lebanon was an attempt to create and open up ways for tenants ... From what I see from the reconstruction model and thinking [in Haret Hreik], there isn't necessarily resistance in the form. The principle is to rebuild as fast as possible and to go backwards in time. The physicality of the object is not very relevant, in my view, as opposed to the social and political space.

Sandra: I absolutely agree with what you say about the aspect of time in relation to Hezbollah's rebuilding project. And I also see the difference between Hariri's project in the city centre and Hezbollah's project in Haret Hreik. The latter aims to bring the same people back to the neighbourhood whereas Hariri's project threw the old shopkeepers out of the *souks*. Although in the case of Haret Hreik, some tenants decided not to come back because they no longer wanted to become targets due to Hezbollah's politics. For this reason, the war and the rebuilding project had a further homogenising effect on the neighbourhood. Nevertheless, in both projects, the form of the architecture correlates with the social. As the architect Rahif Fayad explains, Hezbollah wanted to rebuild the social fabric, which is why the project also considered the larger framework of Dahiya. This is also why they rebuilt the structures as they were. There were other reconstruction plans from the Urban Design Department of the American University of Beirut (AUB), which included more greenery, wider sidewalks, and different kinds of buildings. But this would have brought many changes to the neighbourhood. Haret Hreik would have looked very different from the rest of Dahiya and the project would have taken longer to realise. Instead, the *Waad* reconstruction project even rebuilt "mistakes" resulting from the density of the neighbourhood and the close proximity between building blocks. This demonstrates that the social has to do with the physical: they cannot be isolated. Rebuilding the destroyed houses as fast as possible, in the same form, and without any rupture between the past and present is a gesture of resistance. It is, however, very different from the destruction in the urban warfare of Gaza and Jenin, where space is fragmented in terms of how the land and air are occupied and controlled. The Israeli architect Eyal Weizman describes this fragmentation as the "verticality of space". For this reason, urban warfare in Gaza and Jenin triggers particular tactical forms of resistance in that specific territory. These necessarily take different shapes than Hezbollah's project in Lebanon.

Audience: But that makes the architectural decision a political decision. It's not an architectural decision to build a house in the "wrong" way. An architect only builds a house "wrong" if a politician tells him or her to build it exactly the way it used to be. So it's not architectural, but political.

Sandra: I think it's difficult to distinguish the two. It's a political decision, but a politician doesn't necessarily need to make this decision. I think an architect can also make this decision because the architectural concept is embedded in an urban, social, and political reality. Furthermore, the architect's work is usually assigned by a client. In this case, the client is—first of all—the party. The flat's tenants/owners come second. Haret Hreik is a very dense neighbourhood; there's not much space. The social aspect—the rebuilding of the social fabric and the aim for the community to locate itself in space—has a lot to do with architectural form. Even though this form may conceal the actual pain and destruction of the war, which is inscribed in the psyches and memories of the people.

Audience: I wanted to ask about the idea of the artist who remakes something. I'm curious about the psychological state. As we've seen here [in Egypt], it's the graffiti that gets erased, not a whole building. When a building is remade, is there a loss of hope; does it leave behind desperation? Or do people feel that they have to get over this stage and reconcile with it? That's my first question. The second question relates to the buildings themselves. Artistically—or in terms of form and material—do they take these issues into consideration and is there an awareness of the possibility that they might be destroyed again?

Sandra: Regarding your second question: yes, everybody is fully aware that another war could happen in Lebanon in the near future. This war has left behind many traces. It has definitely been an economic loss but it simultaneously aimed to weaken Hezbollah through targeting its civil environment. According to these aims, however, the war wasn't very successful. I remember the architect Rahif Fayad's angry statement that the rebuilding project doesn't require a monument to remember the war because the intervals of warlessness are so short. Ms Ibtissam also emphasises that she doesn't mourn the loss of houses if she's willing to sacrifice her sons and her husband in the war. Nevertheless, everybody has to come to terms with the experience of war and violence. This is, however, treated very differently on an individual level. Hezbollah's official narrative of resistance—which is repeated by Ms Ibtissam—no longer works when she has to legitimise her son's death in Syria. I think this has two reasons: firstly, the war in Syria doesn't fit into Hezbollah's narrative of resistance, and secondly, Ms Ibtissam suffers from her son's death but tries to appear strong and invulnerable. I already partly answered your first question. Just to add to what I've already said, I think that the form and speed of rebuilding has a lot to do with the anticipation of another possible war in the near future.

Audience: This feeling of remaking something and knowing that it will be destroyed: how can you do that if it's not a picture, but a building? All of this will be destroyed: what emotions does that bring up? What are the ruptures and the feelings? What does it do to the mind of the artist? It's very harmful and very bad for art if I know that after a while, nothing will be left. So, you met him [the architect]?

Sandra: Yes.

Audience: Here [in Egypt] we're trying do something with art—for social change. But the regime refuses this. We need to know, as it's very similar to some situations here, how did they do it in Lebanon?

Sandra: If you mean, what can be learned from the rebuilding of Haret Hreik, you've seen the videos and we've discussed it. It's up to you to make comparisons. If you mean, how were these questions approached in a wider Lebanese art context, I can't answer that question right now. It feels too big and broad for me to answer, I'm afraid. Nevertheless, I'm not sure if the specific case of Hezbollah can so easily be transferred to the context and situation here in Egypt.

Audience: I was interested in the idea that Hezbollah is a non-state organisation, NGO, or party, and their role in the reconstruction, their involvement in Syria, and how people living in Lebanon accept these proposed sites. I want to compare this to Egypt: the role of religious groups in informal settlements, for example—how they have a very powerful impact and can propose an authoritative model for urban reconstruction or development in these spaces. My question has two parts: first, since you're interested in the idea of the Iranian Revolution, Hezbollah, and religious groups, have you considered making a piece about the religious groups in informal settlements here in Cairo? Second, from your perspective, how can this model of Hezbollah's reconstruction in Beirut inspire us to create other models of reconstruction or urban development for informal settlements in Cairo? It seems that people are more likely to accept the role from Hezbollah or groups coming from them than from a state organisation.

Sandra: Concerning the first part of your question, I don't have any plans to make a film about the influence and role of religious groups in the informal settlements in Cairo. And I'm not very familiar with the situation here in Egypt. Related to that—and concerning your second question—I think that you can probably answer this better than I can. Nevertheless, I think that Hezbollah's position in Lebanon is a very particular one that relates to its multiple and contradicting roles as a government party, an opposition, an NGO, a military unit, etc. The weak Lebanese state structure with its "clientielism" of different sects and political groups—and the attempt to represent them equally in the government—needs to be taken into consideration as well. The Arabic term *ta'ifiyya* is used in relation to this. But what you say about informal settlements is generally true:

usually the state, if there is a strong state, is the common enemy shared by informal settlements all over the world. However, Haret Hreik is not an informal settlement. It's part of Dahiya, where some informal settlements exist. Hezbollah's urban-planning organisation *Jihad al-Bina* is involved in a cleansing of informal settlements in southwest Beirut as part of the *Elyssar* project—an urban transformation programme following a neoliberal approach. I think the writing and thought of the sociologist Asef Bayat could be helpful in regard to your second question. He has lived in Cairo for many years, which is why he is familiar with the situation here, and he has written about informal settlements, the role of religion, and the state.

Conclusion

As my work elaborates, Hezbollah's resistance cannot simply be understood as the revolt of the marginalised against a hegemonic force. This is largely due to the organisation's present role in the government and the region. Therefore, Hezbollah's recently built and inhabited spaces of resistance differ from the militant images produced during the decolonisation and liberation struggles of the 1960s and 70s. They also differ from the methodologies of the militant image introduced in chapter 2. As I have demonstrated, Hezbollah's "resistance" has become an empty signifier that incorporates different struggles and contradictions → see chapter 7.2. My video installations *Mleeta* and *Constructed Futures: Haret Hreik* show how these contradictions are subsumed under this term.

My filmic work traverses these contradictory spaces. I do not recreate the architecture of Haret Hreik, the space of the museum, or the landscape; instead, I work to dislocate their elements by means of filming, framing, editing, and sound. As elaborated in the previous chapters, my work intervenes in Hezbollah's context in different ways. For example, I use artificial sounds or "scratch" existing sounds to develop a rhythm. In doing so, different expressions compete with one another. The audience is exposed to these and has to position itself in relation to what it sees and hears. Each video runs in an endless loop. The audiovisual narrative of the installation is thus a continuous repetition of rhythms and competing expressions in space, echoing the circular path through the landscape of Mleeta.

In Hezbollah's projects, space is used to create a memory, an identity, and a political statement within a struggle related to issues around land and occupation. In this regard, the strategy of "inhabitation" is an intrinsic part of Hezbollah's overall discourse of resistance. In his work on memory, the philosopher Maurice Halbwachs states that collective memory is produced in relation to the silent objects that surround us in space Halbwachs 1980. This clarifies the idea behind Hezbollah's project to rebuild the architecture and urban fabric that existed prior to Haret Hreik's destruction. However, individual memory is not so easily erased. Traumatic experiences leave traces in the psyche, which is why subjective memories are moving and uncontrollable. For this reason, Hezbollah's oral narratives play an equally important role in the Shiite belief system.[1] Mujama al-Shouhada, the multipurpose hall in Haret Hreik, contributes to building and stabilising the ideology of resistance. As a space for Hezbollah's followers, it helps members affirm themselves as a group while connecting with high-ranking figures and Hezbollah's religious and political leader, Hassan Nasrallah.

Violence

As analysed in chapter 1, violence can take many forms and is inseparably tied to the system of democratic law Benjamin 1999. Violence is an intrinsic part of Hezbollah's spaces of resistance. It is inscribed in the buildings of Haret Hreik due to the destruction that preceded the rebuilding project. The violence of a possible future war also informs the architecture on a physical level. In a conversation with an architect from Hezbollah's reconstruction team, the architect and artist Mohamed Safa learned that during the July War in 2006, the Israeli army used a vacuum bomb that pulverised concrete. If the concrete of a building was 50cm thick, however, its lower floors remained undamaged. This knowledge was used to improve the construction of new buildings. In a description of his sound installation *50cm Slab*, Safa writes: "The 50cm thick slab is no longer limited to its basic role of supporting the upper levels but gains a protective quality and turns into a shield for the lower ones. Apart from the practical nature and utility of the shelter, it represents the inevitable coming war—be it with Israel or some other foe—and affirms its devastating results. And so, this operation restarts the normalization of the 'state of exception' by invoking the idea of war in the very foundation of structure. Hence the exception becomes the norm" Safa 2018. Furthermore, the "sameness" of the architecture does not leave space for ruins or scars.[2] Memories of violence and destruction are thus kept in the individual bodies of inhabitants. At the same time, returning to Hezbollah's territory exposes residents to possible future violence depending on the organisation's political involvements. For this reason, past and future violence collide in the architecture as

1   One example is the story of Karbala, which helps sustain the Shia narrative of resistance. The Battle of Karbala was fought in the desert between Husain Ibn Ali's troops and the Umayyads in 680. After Husain refused caliph Yazid I's demand for allegiance to his caliphate, the Kufan governor sent thousands of soldiers to fight against Husain's small group of supporters. Despite the hopelessness of winning, Husain and his troops did not give in and lost the battle.

2   Whereas the "Yellow House", built in neo-Ottoman style in 1924 by the architect Youssef Afandi Aftimos and extended by two further floors in 1932 by the architect Fouad Kozah, is kept as a ruin. Located on the former "Green Line", it was used by snipers during the Lebanese Civil War. Today it houses an urban planning office and an exhibition related to the city of Beirut (Beit Beirut n.d.).

a repeating rhythm of wars in which it is expected that the future will repeat the past.

The Mleeta Museum of Resistance and its surrounding landscape used to be a space of real struggle and violence. As a museum, it now acts on the level of symbolic violence. Within this public memorial to the resistance against Israel's occupation of southern Lebanon, visitors become live protagonists. The museum is embedded in ongoing geopolitical conflicts due to its position near the border to Syria in the east and Israel's mountains in the south. The violence inscribed in its staging addresses the different gazes of a diverse set of visitors as well as the drones and satellites flying overhead. For visitors, the museum offers a playful form of training that is meant to clarify the ongoing threat of the enemy. As part of Hezbollah's wider programme for culture and tourism in southern Lebanon, it belongs to Hezbollah's discourse of resistance as a dominant project. And like the organisation's other projects, it contributes to stabilising and consolidating Hezbollah's power.

Showing and Sharing

When *Constructed Futures: Haret Hreik* is shown in an exhibition space, each screen is a different size and is positioned at a different height and angle. The viewer can never see all of the screens at the same time. Depending on the angle, however, he or she can make connections between two or three screens. The screens are installed in an interrupted line, emphasising the installation's fragmentary character.

In both *Mleeta* and *Constructed Futures: Haret Hreik*, different bodies negotiate space. These include the visitors who roam through the museum, the inhabitants who live Haret Hreik, and the architects who plan urban space in their offices. The last two remain visually absent in *Constructed Futures: Haret Hreik*. In *Mleeta*, an ambiguous male figure performs minimal gestures within the museum park. On both a physical and symbolic level, my body also travels through the space of the museum and the city. It is briefly marked by my voice at the beginning of *Constructed Futures: Haret Hreik*, when I refer to my German nationality. Finally, the bodies of viewers traverse the virtual and physical spaces of my video installations.

In my installations, these concrete spaces—which are embedded in specific territorial frameworks—are transferred to other geopolitical contexts. During a conversation with curators in Berlin about *Mleeta*, the Museum of Resistance was discussed as an "event architecture"

(*Erlebnisarchitektur*) that is increasingly found in other museum contexts.[3] In contrast to many such museums, however, the Museum of Resistance is part of an ongoing geopolitical conflict that manifests in space. The different elements of this space are infused with meaning: the landscape with its demarcations, the commemorative stones for soldiers, the underground tunnels used by resistance fighters, and the evergreen trees that camouflaged fighters from the thermal cameras of the Israeli military. Mediated by the museum, visitors can experience this past. The call for resistant subjects in the conflict with Israel is inscribed in the landscape. Due to the way in which the Museum of Resistance contextualises this conflict, Mleeta is seen as an ideological and propagandistic project.

Often my installations are shown in white cubes that are turned into black boxes. However, the seemingly neutral white cube that has dominated the exhibition context since the beginning of the twentieth century is just as ideological as the aesthetics of the Museum of Resistance.[4] In 1976, the artist and critic Brian O'Doherty provocatively proposed that the white cube had become an aesthetic in which the artwork merely functioned as a frame O'Doherty 1976, 15.[5] According to the art critic Simon Sheikh, the social and the political are expelled from the white cube in order to establish the lasting value of the art inside Sheikh 2009. Dorothea von Hantelmann and Carolin Meister go so far as to say that the autonomy of art cannot be upheld, as it is always put to use within a socio-economic structure Hantelmann and Meister 2010, 16.

Unlike the modernist white cube, the social and the political are not left out at the Museum of Resistance. They are the subjects of the museum and simultaneously expand beyond it, to the surrounding landscape. Observation platforms allow visitors to view the landscape and

3 For example, the Rhine-Ruhr region in Germany advertises "event museums" (*Erlebnismuseen*) on topics including science, religion, and art (https://erlebnismuseen.de/museen/museumkunstpalast, last accessed 20.03.2018). In the desert of Negev in southern Israel, there is a plan to build a huge leisure park focusing on the Old Testament and Jewish traditions (apr/dpa 2018).

4 The white cube has been an emblem of modernity since the twentieth century. The colour white—which often remains an unnoticed aspect of exhibition design—represents civilisation and morality and distances itself from the "Other" (Steyerl 2008). Since the end of the eighteenth century, the museum has been an ideological construction within the Western project of modernity. In this context, museums have participated in producing a bourgeois subject with a sovereign gaze and a new understanding of history (Hantelmann and Meister 2010). The art historians Dorothea von Hantelmann and Carolin Meister compare exhibitions with the politics of rituals that explicitly address individuals who need to be civilised (Hantelmann and Meister 2010, 10–11). For more on the ideological use of the term "modernity", please see the research of art historian Kerstin Stakemeier. Stakemeier dissolves the term "autonomy" through a discussion of artistic forms of derivation (Stakemeier 2018).

5 Furthermore, O'Doherty points out that galleries are points-of-sale that serve to produce a surplus value that lends the work a sense of timelessness (O'Doherty 1976, 79).

its demarcations. The border between inside and outside doesn't delineate the boundaries of the museum; instead, it refers to geopolitical borders. Apart from the contextualisation provided through the film shown in the museum's cinema, the visitor has an immediate experience of the landscape. He or she moves through the underground passages, stands behind a weapon at an embrasure, or walks under the leafy canopy of evergreen trees. Visitors thus experience the space while simultaneously performing it. The exhibitions and the landscape are, however, experienced differently depending on each visitor's history and memory. In terms of a social economy, the Museum of Resistance represents a territorial mark that aspires to consolidate power.

Simon Sheikh proposes extending Brian O'Doherty's analysis of gallery space—and the ways in which certain artistic methods challenged the space and politics of the modernist white cube—to other spaces, such as territories, states, and institutions. In this process, the inclusionary and exclusionary mechanisms of such spaces can be examined Sheikh 2009. In considering the design and role of Hezbollah's spaces within the extended geopolitical framework of Beirut, Lebanon, and the neighbouring territories of Israel/Palestine and Syria, it is exactly these mechanisms that I am interested in. I thus see my work as traversing Hezbollah's territorial, aesthetic, and political frameworks and allowing the spectator to enter. Furthermore, my video installations shift Hezbollah's spaces into other territorial contexts.[6]

How, then, is my work shown in an exhibition context? At the Berlinale in 2016 and 2017, *Mleeta* and *Constructed Futures: Haret Hreik* were exhibited in black boxes alongside other films and installations. The audience was exposed to an amount of video that was impossible to watch in its complete duration. The exhibition visitor thus could not establish a sovereign point of view in the sense of an overview. Instead, he or she received a fragmented perspective that varied according to his or her own choices and navigation through the space. Hito Steyerl notes: "Today, cinematic politics are post-representational. They do not educate the crowd, but produce it. They articulate the crowd in space and in time. They submerge it in partial invisibility and then orchestrate their dispersion, movement, and reconfiguration. They organize the crowd without preaching to it. They replace the gaze of the bourgeois sovereign spectator of the white cube with the incomplete,

6   In showing my work, I discovered that Hezbollah's spaces were sometimes regarded as "other"—that is, situated far away in their specific locality.

obscured, fractured, and overwhelmed vision of the spectator-as-laborer" Steyerl 2009. According to Steyerl, the museum has become a social factory that everyone contributes to producing. This includes the reproductive labour of the cleaning personnel, the unpaid interns, etc. Visual politics has shifted from the field of representation to the production of a crowd as a multitude. Steyerl argues that in its fragmentation and rupture of the paradigm of productivity, the museum-as-social-factory addresses the missing, multiple subject: "But by displaying its absence and its lack, they [the museum-as-factory and cinematic politics] simultaneously activate a desire for this subject" ibid.. According to Steyerl, the image is missing so that this subject can appear.

Militant images or spaces are never just found in museums. In the context of Hezbollah's visual and spatial politics, the screen isn't always necessary. Hezbollah's image of resistance can also turn into architecture that is produced and inhabited through numerous everyday actions. The Museum of Resistance is part of a territorial framework that needs to be occupied at both a symbolic and real level in order to consolidate the power and reach of Hezbollah's community, party, and military. According to Walter D Mignolo, Hezbollah's followers are neither a multitude nor a pluriversality Mignolo 2012, 56, 194. Instead, they are a stringently organised apparatus. In contrast to this organised apparatus, the neighbourhood of Haret Hreik is much less homogeneous. To create cohesion, Hezbollah continually refers to outside danger and thus establishes a state of exception as a permanent condition meant to bind the national body. The Mleeta Museum of Resistance normalises this state of exception to the same degree as the rebuilding of Haret Hreik.

If a viewer who is involved in the political context of Lebanon sees my video work, the separation of image and reality cannot be upheld.[7] After a screening of *Constructed Futures: Haret Hreik* in Beirut, someone commented that the work would encounter as many different ways of seeing as there are contexts. For some viewers—particularly those in Lebanon and Syria who have directly experienced the repercussions of Hezbollah's politics—it will be more difficult to watch. Likewise, the neutrality of the black box cannot be maintained in political contexts that are restricted by or in conflict with Hezbollah's politics. As described in the previous chapter, the team at the Contemporary Image Collective in

---

7   This separation also cannot be maintained as soon as a viewer feels that his or her values or norms have been challenged. This became apparent during a screening at B-Movie cinema in Hamburg, when *Constructed Futures: Haret Hreik* was shown as part of the Arab Film Club. One viewer felt irritated by Hezbollah's use of the term "resistance" and the hatred with which Israel was encountered.

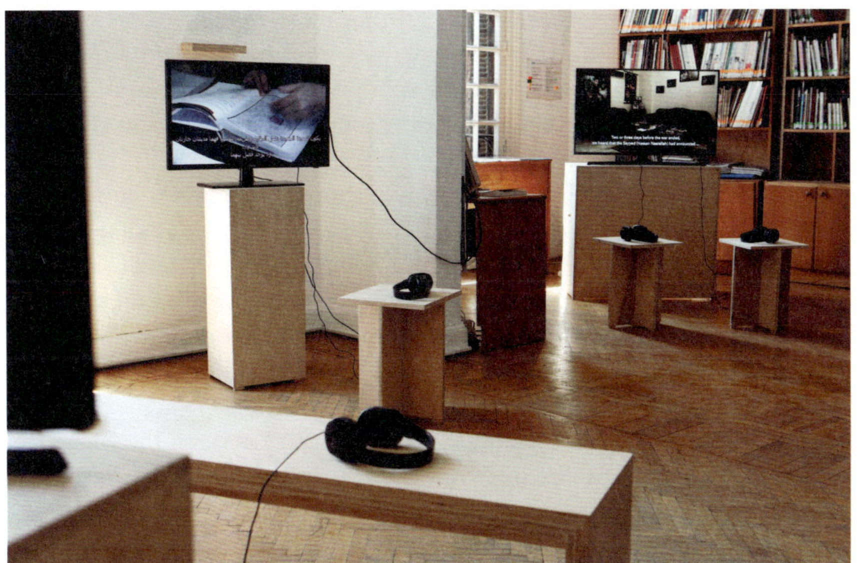

Installation view of *Constructed Futures: Haret Hreik*, Contemporary Image Collective, Cairo, 2017

Cairo had to find inventive ways to bypass the restrictions and control of the present regime. For this reason, we briefly installed *Constructed Futures: Haret Hreik* in the library rather than exhibiting it in the white cube gallery space. This approach of adapting the screening situation to the context also suggests the different vulnerabilities of those involved in showing the work.

My research on the politics of Hezbollah departs from the common comfort zone of the art context. Within the art field, some see this as a no-go topic. Discussions with curators indicate these discomforts and difficulties. It seems that Hezbollah's images and spaces—otherwise positioned within a specific political and aesthetic context—are inherently problematic as soon as they start to circulate in other spaces. My decision to work within this context and to show my video installations and films will therefore always be affected by the various contradictory roles Hezbollah plays in the overall political framework of Lebanon and its international involvements. These roles affect how my work is perceived and how (and if) I can show it in specific contexts. At the same time, the work triggers reactions in viewers whose memories, norms, or values are—consciously or unconsciously—challenged.

Apart from exhibiting these works in the black box, I sometimes show them as single-screen projections accompanied by discussions in cinemas or other spaces. In May 2018, *Constructed Futures: Haret Hreik* was shown in a programme on architecture hosted by the Arab Film Club at B-Movie cinema in Hamburg. This programme was developed together with refugees, some of whom came from Syria. Here the geopolitical space of film and reality intersected.

From the start of this project, a particularly important question revolved around how to show the work in Lebanon. I began by sharing and discussing edited sequences with the protagonists I filmed. However, showing the work publicly in Lebanon turned out to be difficult and took some time. I was thus delighted when the artist Helene Kazan invited me to show *Constructed Futures: Haret Hreik* within the framework of her project "Points of Contact" in Beirut in 2018.[8] My screening was part of an experimental roundtable titled "Built Between the Slow, the Structural and the Spectacular". Artists, architects, urban planners, and activists screened films, presented performances, and participated in a conversation about "heritage", environmental pollution, and different ways of intervening through activist work. Contributions by the artists Rania Stephan and Mohamed Safa closely overlapped with my research. Stephan's work includes several short films that were made in Haret Hreik and the town of Bint Jbeil during and shortly after the July War in 2006 Stephane 2006. Due to the state of exception at that time, the streets were accessible and anybody could film. In this situation, Stephan focused on details from everyday life. Safa, on the other hand, presented an abstract sound installation titled *50cm Slab*. This work centres on a process of learning from the July War, using the state of exception to improve the rebuilt architecture.

Constructed Futures: Haret Hreik was also shown as a single-screen projection at the Arab Centre for Architecture (Arabic: المركز العربي للعمارة).[9] The audience for this screening included urban planners, architects, and artists. The discussion that followed touched on

---

8   I first met Kazan at the conference *Middle of Where, East of What? New Geographies of Conflict* at the Institute for Cultural Inquiry in Berlin in 2016. At the conference, she presented a paper on the role of risk in Lebanon during the First World War. Her paper discussed the unequal understanding of the value of human life within colonialism and analysed its continuities in the geopolitics of the present. Since then, we have been in an exchange about the anticipation of future wars—and, in the case of Kazan's work, other risks, including those related to the environment—produce the conditions for architecture and domestic space.

9   The Arab Centre for Architecture is a non-profit organisation that aims to preserve and disseminate the modern architectural heritage of the Arab world. It wishes to raise awareness about the cultural value of architecture and urbanism, including its social impact. The centre focuses on recent architecture. This raises questions around what is included in the canon. Before the screening, I spoke with an architect who pointed out that the collection is largely composed of work by famous architects from influential families.

how the film is seen differently in Lebanon. One audience member emphasised that a Lebanese or Syrian audience would find it unbearable to listen to Hassan Nasrallah. Another audience member contradicted this statement, pointing out that the "Lebanese audience" does not exist as such, and that the film is probably seen in even more diverse ways inside of Lebanon than in the so-called West.

While in Beirut, the filmmaker Monika Borgmann and the publisher and activist Lokman Slim invited me to show both video installations at their exhibition space THE HANGAR in Haret Hreik/Ghobeiry.[10] THE HANGAR is part of the UMAM Documentation and Research Centre, where I did a lot of work while in Beirut. Borgmann and Slim offered to let me use the archive to research documents related to the rebuilding project after the July War. THE HANGAR is geographically close to Hezbollah's territory, where *Constructed Futures: Haret Hreik* was filmed. For many of the film's protagonists, the exhibition space is only a ten to fifteen minute walk away. However, UMAM's outlook is very critical of Hezbollah's politics. The Slim family villa, which houses UMAM, was built in the mid-nineteenth century, long before the segregation that took place during and after the civil war. THE HANGAR is thus simultaneously both outside and inside of Hezbollah's territory. For this reason, I was curious to see if the film's protagonists and other neighbours from Dahiya would attend the exhibition in addition to visitors from Beirut's art scene. The latter had other obstacles to face, since going to Haret Hreik or Dahiya meant overcoming mental boundaries as well as crossing the physical checkpoints that mark the territorial Other.

My Role

Although I am an outsider working in the context of Hezbollah, I am also a social actor. It is impossible to maintain a neutral position while working in this context since I bring projections and specific experiences along with me: what Donna Haraway calls "situated knowledges" Haraway 1988. As soon as I am entangled in a specific situation, I start to act and react to what I encounter and to how I am approached and questioned. Yet it obviously makes a difference whether or not I am involved in a certain community on a daily basis. The privilege of coming and going and living my daily life elsewhere brings with it a particular responsibility—one that needs to be addressed. Some of the questions I asked myself throughout the working process were: Why do I work in this context? What is the

10   The exhibition opened on 26 September 2019.

aim of my work? How do I represent this struggle? Who do I share the work with? And what does this "showing" do?

I engaged in this work because I am convinced that what is seemingly far away is more closely entangled with my own local context than appears at first sight. Hezbollah's involvement in the war in Syria is only one aspect. The effects of these politics show that geographical distance can no longer be upheld. In Berlin's Neukölln district, my neighbours include people from Palestine, Lebanon, and, recently, a new generation from Syria. My interlocutors in *Constructed Futures: Haret Hreik* have family and friends who live in my neighbourhood or have studied at the same university I attended in Germany. Another entanglement goes back to the First World War, when Germany—together with its ally, the Ottoman Empire—made strategic use of Islam in the fight against France, England, and Russia.[11] Philip Scheffner's film *The Halfmoon Files* (2007) explores this history based on recordings made by scientists who documented the voices of Muslims detained in German camps. In Scheffner's film, these voices are like ghosts that pass through space and time to repeat the past in the present.

While working in the context of Hezbollah, I maintained an ambiguous relationship to Hezbollah's spatial politics. I struggled to hold a space to listen, understand, question, disagree, and distance myself. In my video editing, I focus on how this ideological framework is built without using overt commentary. At the beginning of *Constructed Futures: Haret Hreik*, for example, I briefly introduce myself, highlighting one of the many thresholds that needed to be passed during filming. Some viewers have commented that my position doesn't become visible in the work. It's true that I don't take an obvious role in commenting or speaking. At first sight, my films might therefore seem distant and my position might seem invisible and neutral. This judgement is, however, based on a superficial understanding of documentary filmmaking. Choices were made about who to meet, how to film, and how to edit: such decisions are never neutral. Working with a predominantly female team is, for example, a political decision. Within this team, my colleagues and

11   In 1914—as a war strategy implemented by Germany and the Ottoman Empire—*jihad* was announced in Constantinople. Muslim soldiers in the British, French, and Russian armies were encouraged to change sides. In Germany, Muslim soldiers were kept in special camps with North African and Indian soldiers captured from the French and British armies, in order to prevent them from engineering a revolt against their colonial "masters". Beginning in 1915, the newspaper *Al-Djihad* was published every other week in Arabic, Turco-Tartar, Georgian, Hindi, and Urdu. It was distributed in the camps as a propaganda tool to convince soldiers to fight a religious war against Russia, England, and France, who were accused of destroying the Islamic caliphate (Tieke 2014).

I were able to position ourselves in strategic ways during the filmmaking process. This, too, is a political method. We thus worked with a political attitude that didn't indicate a fixed position from which to act. Furthermore, my approach to editing leaves space for viewers to construct their own experiences and challenges them to position themselves in relation to what they see.

I am aware that my films open a potential minefield. The Islamophobia in Europe, Hezbollah's non-acknowledgement of the existence of Israel, the reactions of the *Antideutschen*[12] to Hezbollah's politics around Israel, Hezbollah's support of the Assad regime in Syria, its designation as a terrorist organisation in some countries, and the clientelistic context of Lebanon are just some of the conflicts my work touches upon. This is, however, also why I made these films. To the same extent that I regard my work as a social act within a specific framework, the exhibition of this work also becomes a social act. In this sense, I come back to the idea that "showing is doing" →see chapter 2.4 and extend it—in relation to my artistic practice—to "sharing is doing". This raises questions around whom the work is shared with and where it is shown →see chapter 8. My motivation to make these films is thus fundamentally connected to sharing them. It also relates to entering a political context without a fixed position; traversing it with an attitude that tolerates contradictions without giving up my own values.

Both works will continue to circulate and raise controversy and questions. In terms of my larger question about militant images and spaces, Hezbollah's practice demonstrates that the architecture a community builds cannot be separated from its politics. Hezbollah's spaces of resistance differ from the diverse practices of militant-image-making described in chapters 1 and 2. Here, instead, resistance has become a dominant project. I regard my artistic work as a contribution that enters this political minefield. Through showing, manipulating, and questioning Hezbollah's spaces of resistance, I want viewers to reflect on geopolitical framing as well as their own norms, values, and certainties. Working in this context certainly made me reflect on mine. Hezbollah's identitarian politics are not a singular case; they can be found in the framework of any audience, both inside and outside of Lebanon. I thus hope that although this work is localised and specific, it will raise questions beyond that context.

12   The *Antideutschen* (Anti-Germans) are a radical leftist group in Germany and Austria that criticises German nationalism; antisemitism, which is seen as deeply rooted in German cultural history; as well as mainstream anti-capitalist views on the left, which are seen as simplistic and structurally antisemitic.

Constructed Futures: Haret Hreik

Four-channel video installation, 2017

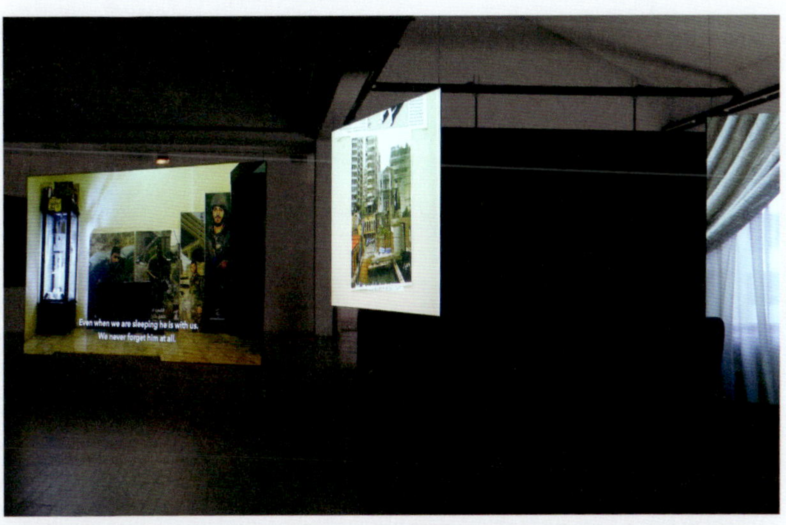

Constructed Futures: Haret Hreik at the 67th Berlinale, Forum Expanded, "The Stars Down to Earth", Akademie der Künste, Berlin, 2017

Waad Office, Haret Hreik

Hassan el-Jeshi, Architectural Engineer and Director of the Waad Project,
Resident of Haret Hreik

Sequence C

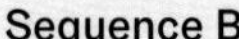

Sequence B

Sequence D

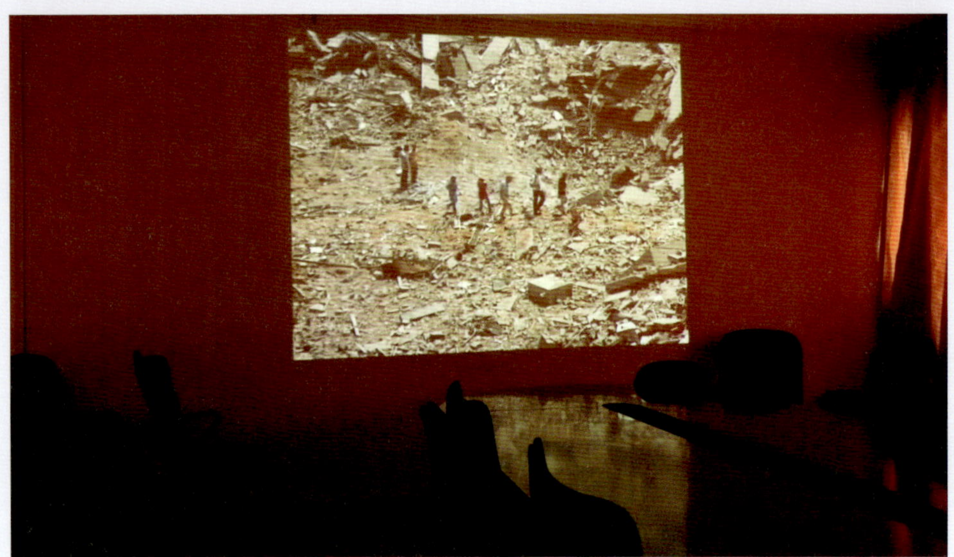

[Dramatic musical score]

Sequence C

Sequence B

**Sequence D

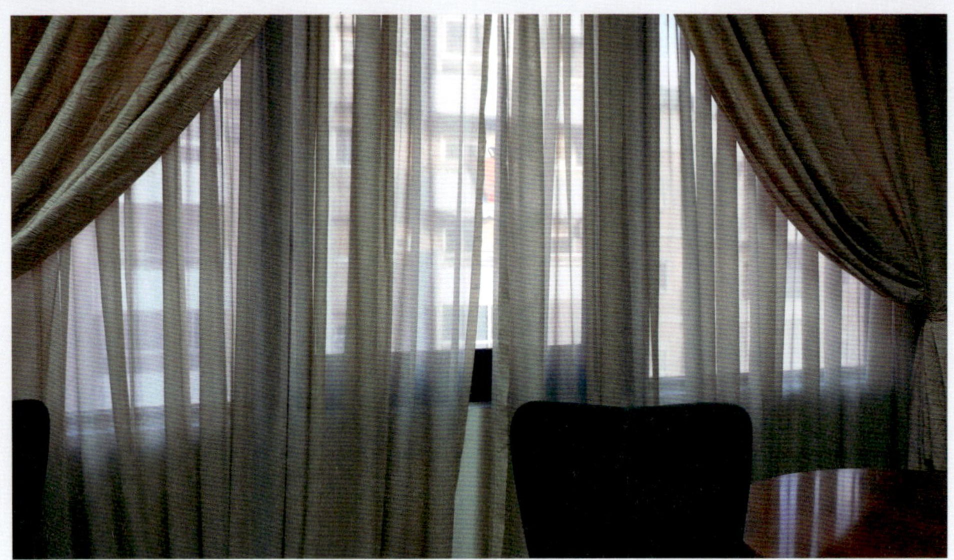

Hassan el-Jeshi: "Of course, as we know, this is an exemplary residential area. Of course it has some of the party's institutions—civil institutions—as well as some of Hezbollah's party offices. It also has residences for some party members."

Sequence C

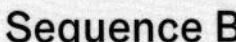

Sequence B

Sequence D

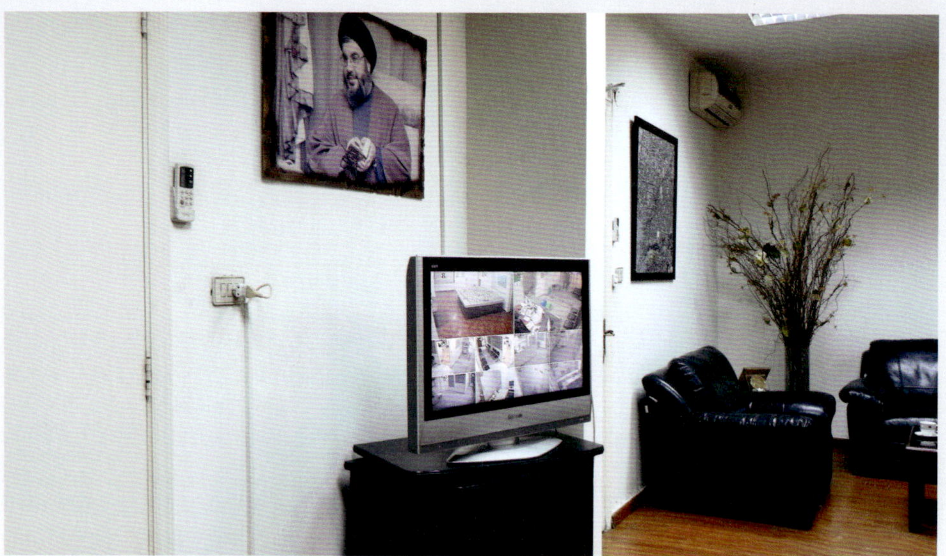

Hassan el-Jeshi: "We say that we embrace people. The Israeli wants to push people away from you, and you are embracing those people. When the attack was over, our first project was to give people money to rent apartments and buy furniture. We called it the Ewa project. This was the first project."

Sequence C

Office, Tallet el-Khayat

Rahif Fayad, Architect and Professor,
Resident of Tallet el-Khayat

Sequence D

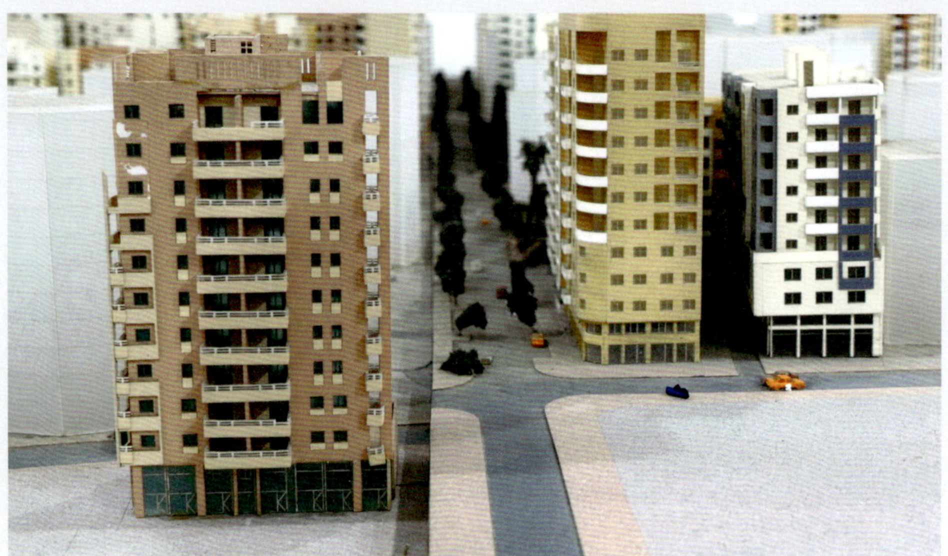

Hassan el-Jeshi: "We were very careful not to disrupt people's memory. We relied on the buildings that were damaged but not destroyed. We fixed their facades to match those which were rebuilt, to preserve a homogeneous environment."

Sequence C

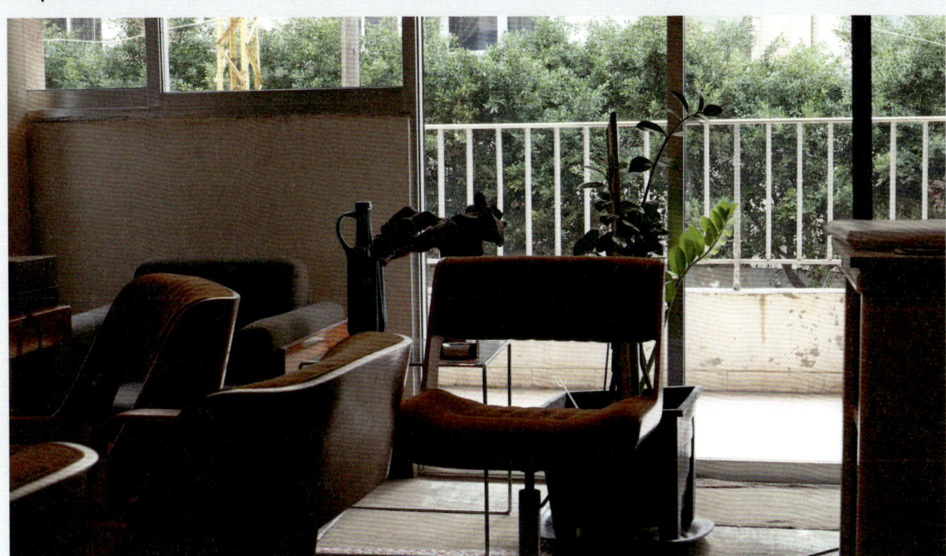

Rahif Fayad: "I am a resistant architect. And I present that to have a change, to refuse to produce the same thing, to conserve some local identity. And this has to be done exactly according to the objectives: climate, topography, material, way of life, the sea, the sun."

Sequence D

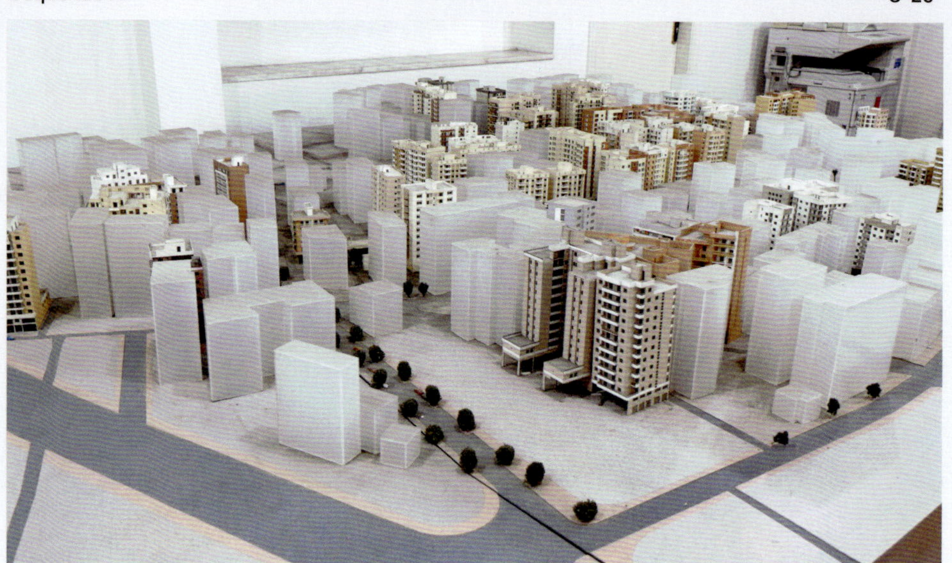

Hassan el-Jeshi: "We painted the new buildings beige and white. We used the same colour
    of mortar and paint on the damaged buildings. This way the environment remained whole:
    its character and the sight of it as well."

Sequence C

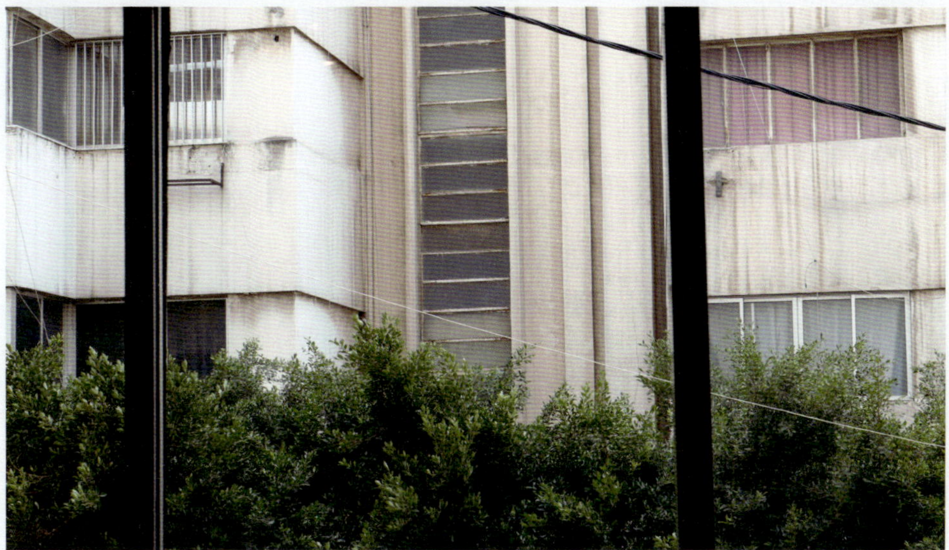

Rahif Fayad: "If we are going to proceed with the same brilliant glass cubes ... we are not able to produce anything in human progress, in human civilisation."

Sequence D

Sequence C

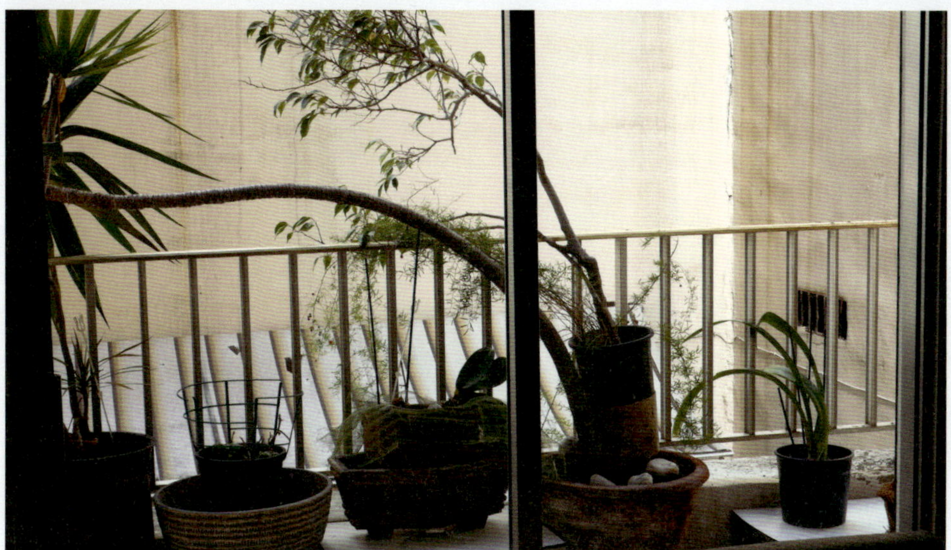

Rahif Fayad: "What we have done here is also a direct resistance. Not a general resistance on the basis of a philosophical approach … but a direct resistance. Because it's a direct answer to a destruction problem done by Israel."

Sequence D

Sequence A

Sequence C

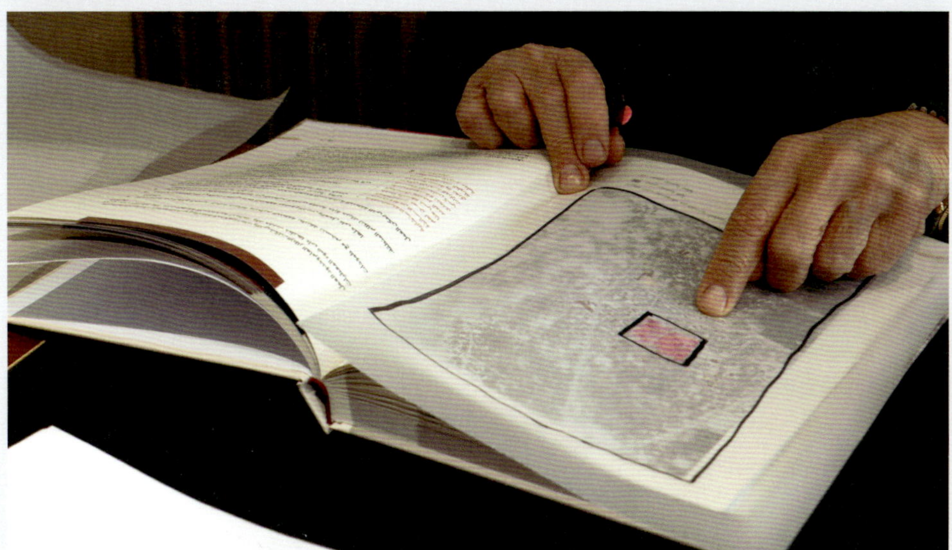

Rahif Fayad: "The spirit of the reconstruction has to respect the existing spirit of the whole area. We cannot parachute in a small new town. The new town or part of town that we are going to build has to be familiar to the existing fabric, to the existing inhabitants. To have the same theme, the same mentality. They are neighbourhoods and there is no cut between this one and that one."

Sequence D

 0'00"

Sequence A

Private Home, Haret Hreik
Ibtissam Malak, Architect and Employee of the Waad Project,
Resident of Haret Hreik

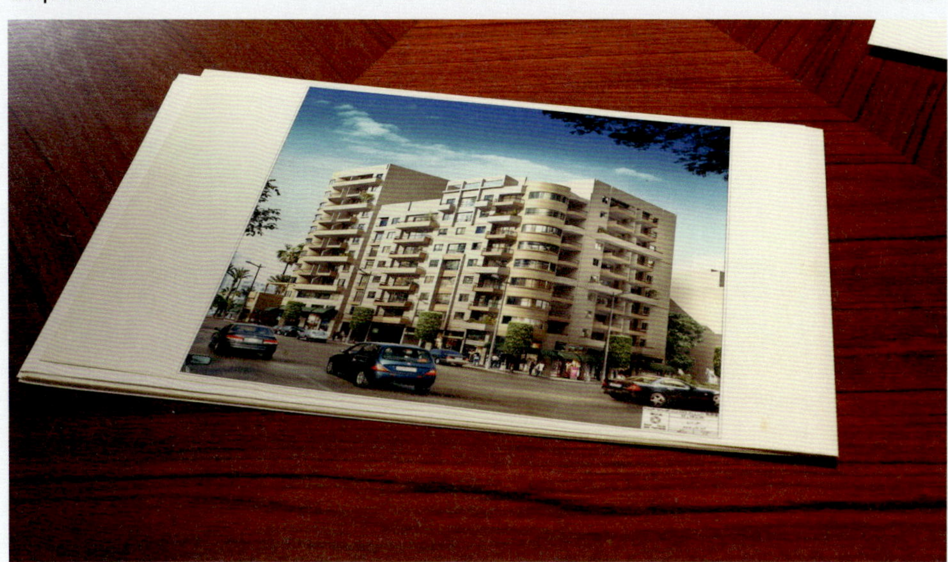

Rahif Fayad: "And if somebody said he has to destroy this because they were with the resistance, I said we have to reconstruct this social fabric particularly because they were with the resistance."

Sequence D

 0' 40"

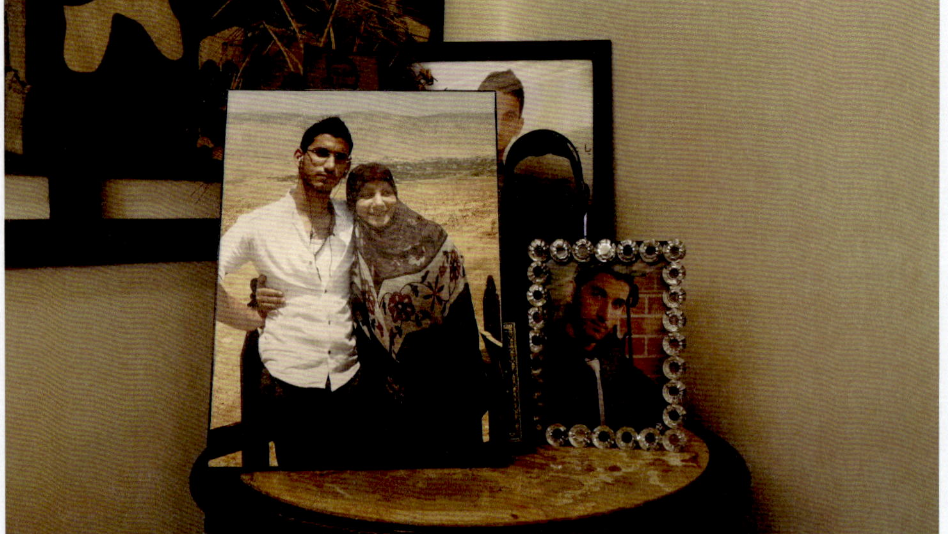

Ibtissam Malek: "I have been an employee at the Waad project since the beginning."

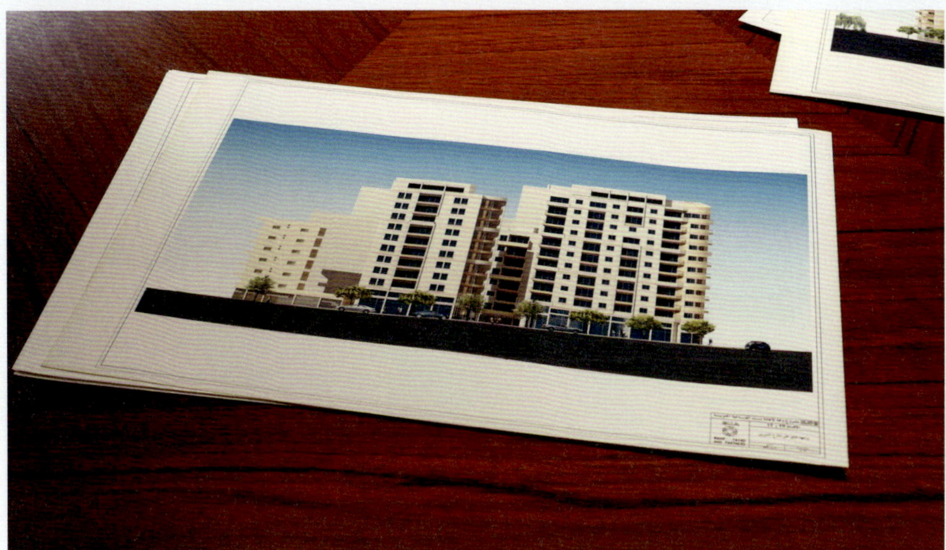

Rahif Fayad: "Another one says that we have to conserve inside this part two or three buildings, as they were destroyed … to remember the war. And I answer very strongly: 'We don't have to remember the war, because the war is coming again.'"

Assembly Hall, Haret Hreik
Mujama al-Shouhada

                                                            1'59"

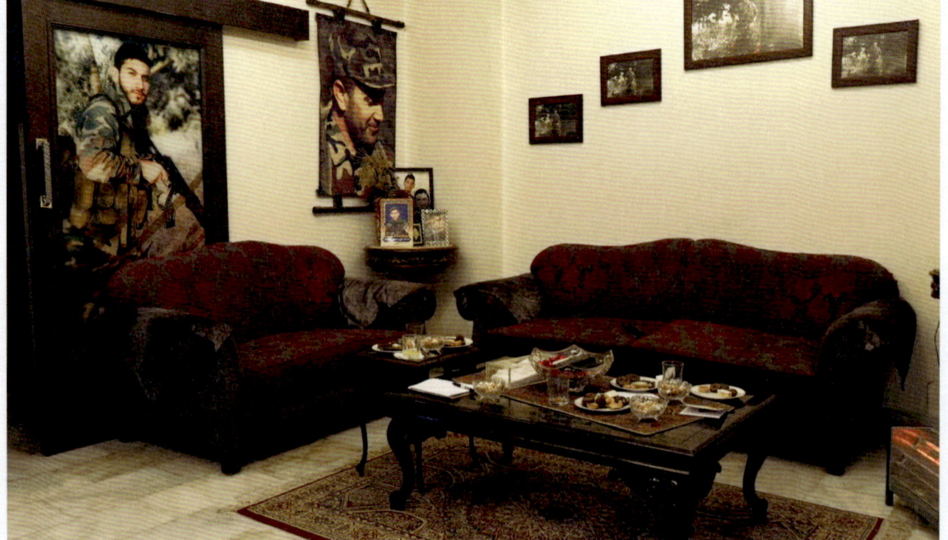

Ibtissam Malak: "Two or three days before the war ended, we heard that the Sayyed [Hassan Nasrallah] had announced that he would rebuild the flats that had been destroyed. This image was in our heads. Because of this, people felt relieved psychologically."

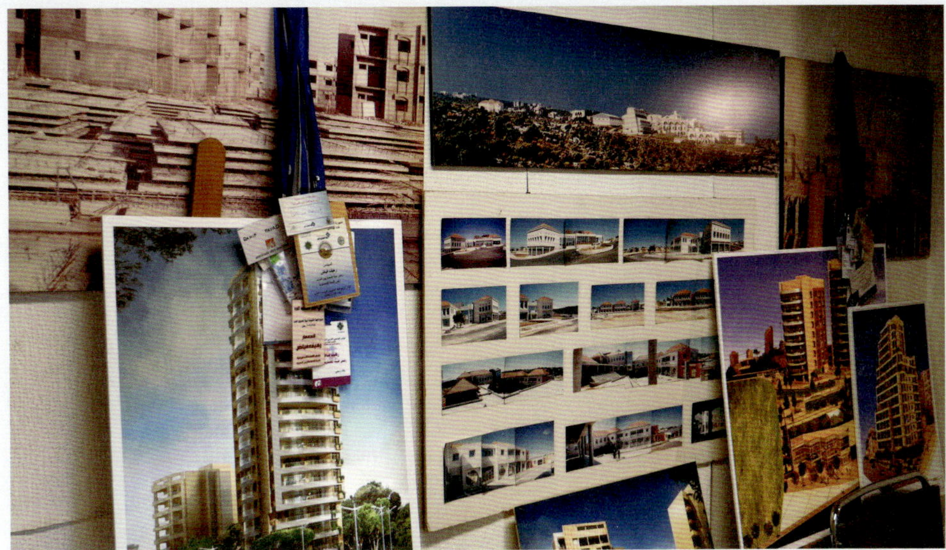

[Silence]

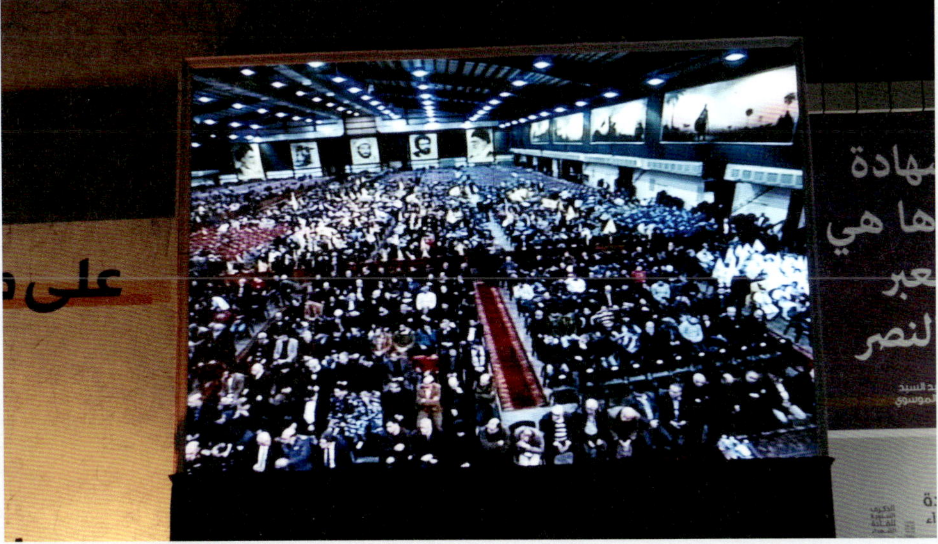

[Music and babble of voices]

 3' 45"

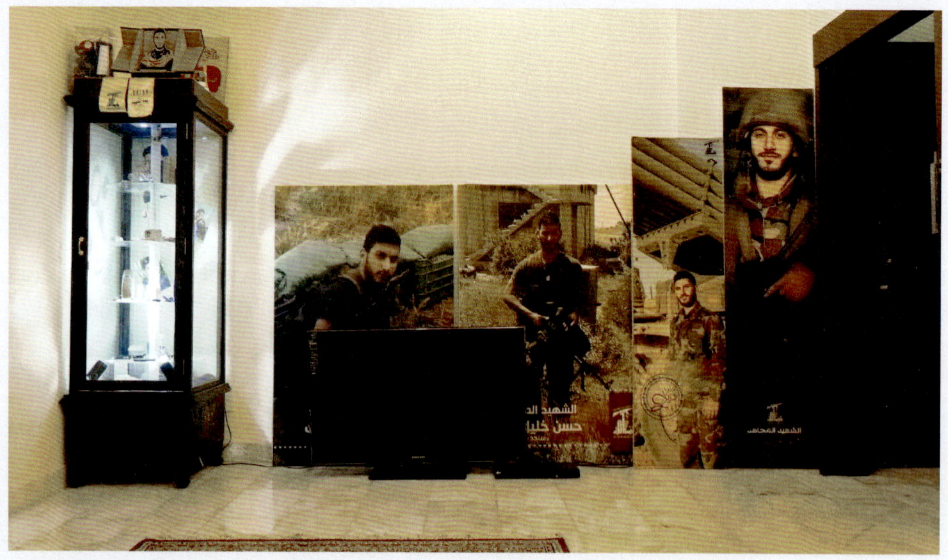

Hayat Gebara: "When did your son become a martyr?"
    Ibtissam Malak: "Two years ago."
Hayat Gebara:"How did he become a martyr?"
    Ibtissam Malak: "In the war against Syria."

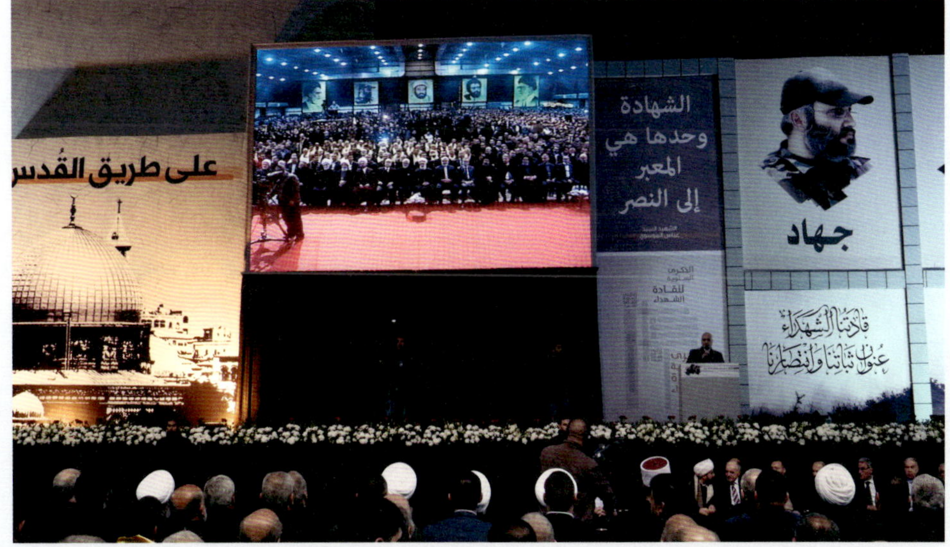

Speaker: "What was written for him is not comparable with what was written for others."

                                                                              5'23"

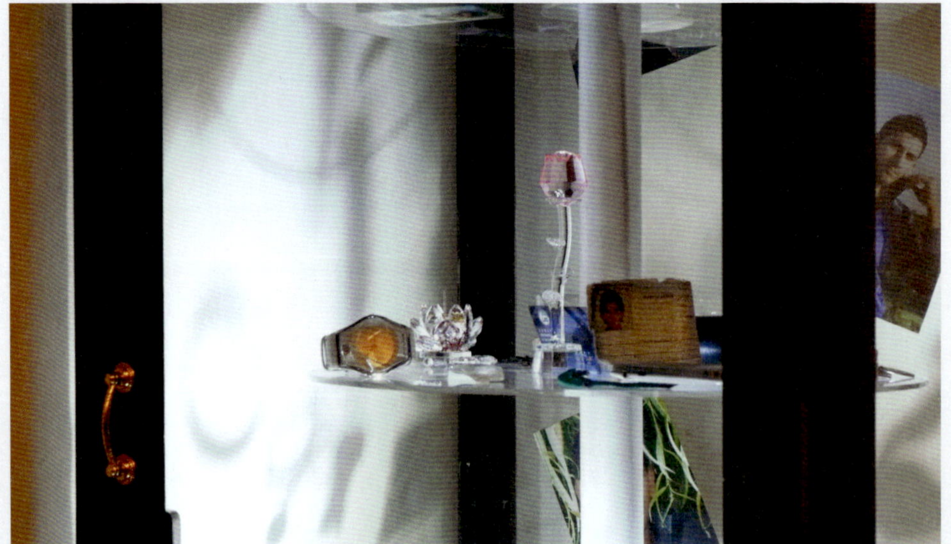

Ibtissam Malak: "Honestly, when we sacrifice our children, we don't mourn for houses. Nor
    furniture or anything else. Even if the war returns and our houses get destroyed again, and
    even if my second son goes too, we will remain loyal and will never leave the resistance.
    No matter what happens."

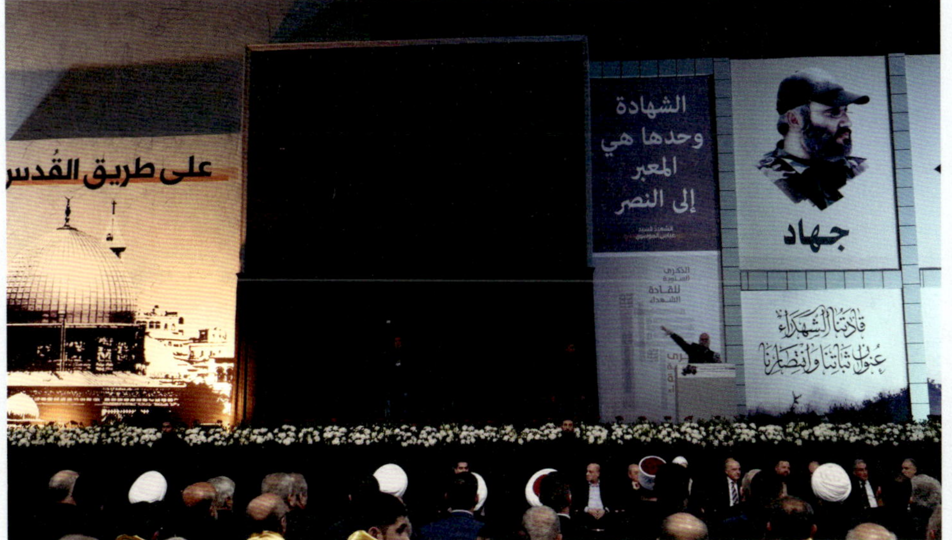

Speaker: "At this hour, the believers rejoice in his appearance."

Sequence A

5' 59"

                                                                    3'08"

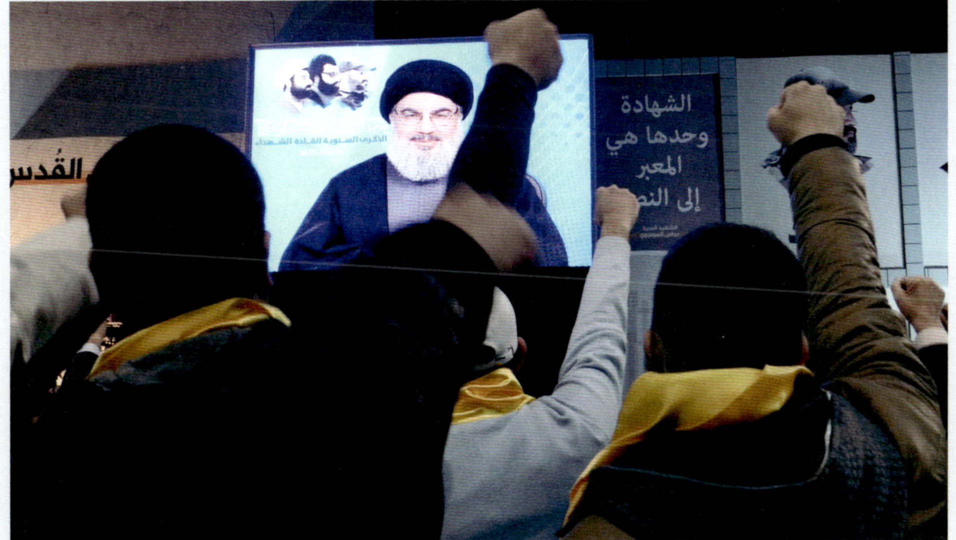

Crowd: "We are at your service, you, son of Fatima."

Sequence A

Sequence C

Sequence D   3' 29"

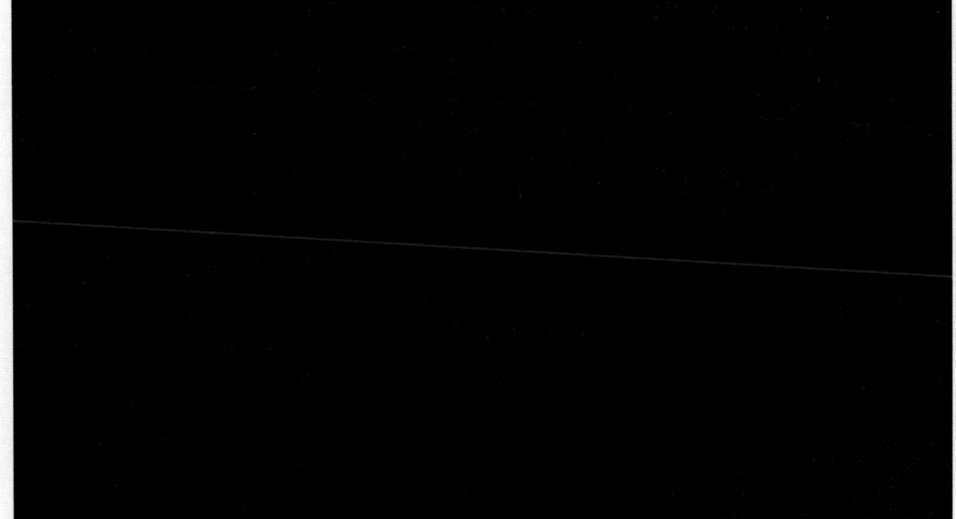

Sequence B

Acknowledgements

This book was written in exchange with many people. I particularly want to thank Jochen Becker, who accompanied the project from its beginning and patiently read many drafts of the text. Elske Rosenfeld for her feedback and structural advice. Walid el-Houri, whose texts about Hezbollah's use of the term "resistance" (some of which were written with Dima Saber) played an important role in my research and who also helped with Arabic translation. Adania Shibli, who spent all night editing the English subtitles for *Constructed Futures: Haret Hreik* and with whom I discussed semantic shifts as well as questions of visual representation. Adania also provided helpful feedback for some chapters of my writing. Volker Pantenburg, who sent me Jean-Luc Godard's *Que faire?* manifesto at just the right time, in the wonderful leporello published by the Austrian Film Museum in Vienna. Hanne Loreck, as part of the PhD programme at the Hochschule für bildende Künste (HFBK) Hamburg, and my PhD colleagues Katrin Mayer, Eske Schlüters, and Jana Seehusen for their reflections on our different approaches to artistic research. Katja Dieffenbach for an exchange that took place during accidental encounters in Berlin's Wrangelkiez, focusing on the visual representation of violence. Klaus Viehmann for the private lessons about the radicalisation of students in West Berlin and the US in the 1970s.

I owe particular thanks to Mareike Bernien and Achim Lengerer for joining me in watching militant films and discussing texts. Jörg Franzbecker for sharing texts about reenactment and repetition. The Frank B Wilderson III reading group for their thoughts and exchange. The "No Play—Feminist Training Camp" for screening *Bambule* by Eberhard Itzenplitz and Ulrike Meinhof. Thanks also to Jasmina Metwaly and Sherief Gaber from the Mosireen Collective for providing images from public screenings during the Egyptian revolution. Laliv Melamed for sharing her text *Sovereign Intimacy: Israeli Homemade Video Memorials and the Politics of Loss* and helping with Hebrew translations. Britta Lorch and Marga Tsomou for providing space for writing retreats in Switzerland and Greece. Mareike Bernien, Gerda Heck, and Kathrin Wildner for reading my text and providing helpful remarks and feedback. Britta Lorch and Maxa Zoller for discussing the title of the book.

I also wish to acknowledge Fouad Gehad Marei for sharing his experiences of working in Haret Hreik during a very early stage of my work. The film team in Beirut (Nadine Khayat, Hayat Gebara, Sandra Boutros,

Amer Mohtar, and Lama el-Masri). Monika Borgmann and Lokman Slim from the UMAM Documentation and Research Centre for providing access to films, photographs, and files in their archives. Janina Herhoffer for her dramaturgical advice throughout the different stages of the filmic work.

Special thanks also to Andrea Thal and Bonaventure Soh Bejeng Ndikung for supporting my project before it actually started. Stéphane Bauer from Kunstraum Kreuzberg for screening and discussing the video works in a preview. The Berlinale's Forum Expanded, where both works premiered and were made accessible to a wide audience. The artist Helene Kazan for screening *Constructed Futures: Haret Hreik* for the first time in Beirut as part of her great programme "Points of Contact". Sylvia Arnaout and the Goethe Institute Beirut for supporting my travel. Ahmed Refaat and Andrea Thal for showing my work at the Contemporary Image Collective in Cairo within the framework of the exhibition project "If Not for That Wall: Imagined Life in a Museum Vitrine". Berit Schuck for inviting me to kick off a workshop at MASS Alexandria as part of "Farocki Now: A Temporary Academy" and sharing my work in Alexandria through screenings at the Goethe Institute. I would also like to acknowledge all of the artists who participated in the workshop—particularly Assem Hendawi and Ash Moniz for making files travel from Cairo to Berlin.

My thanks also go to Harun Farocki, who joined this project at the beginning and whose unexpected death was experienced as a great loss. My thanks equally go to Michaela Ott, who accompanied and encouraged the project from its start, and Brad Butler, whose critical feedback and thoughts gave me great support during the writing process.

I wish to thank Ekaterina Degot and the Academy of the Arts of the World in Cologne for their financial support, which made the production of the video work possible. I am also grateful to the Rosa Luxemburg Foundation—without their funding I would never have been able to complete my PhD. Thank you to everybody who joined me during the process.

Many thanks to metroZones for including this book in their series. Thanks also to Spector Books and to Wolfgang Schwärzler for his graphic design, Diana Abbany for checking the Arabic words, and Bonnie Begusch for proofreading.

This text was written as part of a practice-based thesis in art, which I completed at the HFBK Hamburg. My supervisors were Michaela Ott, Brad Butler, and (until 2014) Harun Farocki.

Bibliography

858 Initiative
— n.d. "858. An Archive of Resistance". Online archive. Accessed 30 April 2018. https://858.ma/grid/title.

Ahmad, Eqbal
— 2002 (written 31 January 1999). "Religion in Politics". In *Eqbal Ahmad Reader: Writings on India, Pakistan, and Kashmir*, edited by Sarthak Tomar, 39–41. n.p.: thecominganarchy.

Ahmed, Sara
— 2004. "Affective Economies". *Social Text* 22 (2): 117–39.
— 2014. *Willful Subjects*. Durham and London: Duke University Press.

apr/dpa
— 2018. "Investoren planen offenbar jüdischen Freizeitpark in der Negev". *Der Spiegel*, 6 March 2018. http://spiegel.de/wirtschaft/unternehmen/israel-investoren-planen-offenbar-juedischen-freizeitpark-in-der-negev-wueste-a-1196746.html.

Arendt, Hannah
— 1958. *The Human Condition*. Chicago: University of Chicago Press.
— 1970. *On Violence*. New York: Mariner Books.
— 1992. *Hannah Arendt and Karl Jaspers: Correspondence, 1926–1969*. Edited by Lotte Kohler and Hans Peter Saner. New York: Harcourt.
— 2006 (first published 1963). *Eichmann in Jerusalem: A Report on the Banality of Evil*. New York: Penguin Classics.

Attac Koordinierungskreis
— 2001. "Auf Distanz zur Gewalt? Eine Kontroverse zur Frage der Militanz". https://sopos.org/aufsaetze/3b9919a8ac56b/1.phtml.html.

Bakhtin, Mikhail
— 1982. *The Dialogic Imagination: Four Essays*. Translated by Caryl Emerson and Michael Holquist. Austin: University of Texas Press.

Bayat, Asef
— 2010. *Life as Politics: How Ordinary People Change the Middle East*. ISIM Series on Contemporary Muslim Societies. Amsterdam: Amsterdam University Press.
— 2012. *Leben als Politik: Wie ganz normale Leute den Nahen Osten verändern*. Berlin: Assoziation A.

Becker, Jochen, Katrin Klingan, Stephan Lanz, and Kathrin Wildner, eds.
— 2014. *Global Prayers: Contemporary Manifestations of the Religious in the City*. Zürich: Lars Mueller Publishers.

Beit Beirut
— n.d. Accessed 22 May 2019. http://beitbeirut.org/english/thehouseen.html.

Benjamin, Walter
— 1999 (first published 1921). "Critique of Violence". In *Walter Benjamin: Selected Writings, Vol. 1, 1913–1926*, 277–300. Cambridge, MA: Belknap Press of Harvard University Press.
— 2003 (first published 1940). "On the Concept of History". In *Walter Benjamin: Selected Writings, Vol. 4, 1938–1940*, edited by Michael W. Jennings, 389–400. Cambridge, MA: Belknap Press of Harvard University Press.

Bitter, Sabine, and Helmut Weber
— 2016. *Front, Field, Line, Plane: Researching the Militant Image*. Edited by Hannes Loichinger and Ulf Wuggenig. Hamburg: adocs.

Brenez, Nicole
— 2014. "Light My Fire: The Hour of the Furnaces". British Film Institute. http://bfi.org.uk/news-opinion/sight-sound-magazine/features/greatest-films-all-time-essays/light-my-fire-hour-furnaces.

Butler, Chris
— 2009. "Critical Legal Studies and the Politics of Space". *Social and Legal Studies* 18 (3). https://papers.ssrn.com/abstract=1492087.

Butler, Judith
— 2009. *Frames of War: When Is Life Grievable?* London: Verso.
— 2013a. "Judith Butler: 'Ich bin tief verletzt'". *Die Zeit*, 1 November 2013. http://zeit.de/2012/36/Judith-Butler.
— 2013b. *Parting Ways: Jewishness and the Critique of Zionism*. New York: Columbia University Press.

Cohen, Greg
— n.d. "The revolution must (not) be advertised. The Players vs. Ángeles Caídos, the discourse of advertising, and the limits of political modernism". *Jump Cut*. Accessed 4 May 2016. https://ejumpcut.org/archive/jc56.2014-2015/CohenPlayersFallenAngels/index.html.

Daher, Ali
— 2015. Interview with the author on 19 February 2015.

Daher, Joseph
— 2016. *Hezbollah: The Political Economy of Lebanon's Party of God*. London: Pluto Press.

Daulatzai, Sohail
— 2016. *Fifty Years of The Battle of Algiers: Past as Prologue*. Minneapolis: University of Minnesota Press.

Deleuze, Gilles
— 1997 (first published 1983). *Cinema 1: The Movement-Image*. 5th ed. Minneapolis: University of Minnesota Press.

Deleuze, Gilles, and Félix Guattari
— 1986 (first published 1975). *Kafka: Toward a Minor Literature*. Minneapolis: University of Minnesota Press.
— 1987 (first published 1980). *A Thousand Plateaus: Capitalism and Schizophrenia*. Translated by Brian Massumi. 1st ed. Minneapolis: University of Minnesota Press.

Demos, TJ
— 2015. "The Post-Militant Image". In *The Militant Image Reader*, 41–46. Graz: Camera Austria.

Der Spiegel
— 1969. "Gesellschaft/Gewalt: Wann und Wie". *Der Spiegel*, 10 February 1969. http://spiegel.de/spiegel/print/d-45789182.html.

Derksen, Jeff
— 2015. "'Do Not Think One Has to Be Sad': Circulating the Militant Image". In *The Militant Image Reader*, 13–18. Graz: Camera Austria.

Draxler, Helmut
— 2016. "Traversing the Phantasm". Talk given at the 66th Berlinale, Berlin, 13 February 2016.

Ehmann, Antje
— 2016. "Working with Harun Farocki's Work". In *Harun Farocki: Another Kind of Empathy*, edited by Antje Ehmann and Carles Guerra. Barcelona: Fundación Antoni Tàpies.

Eshun, Kodwo
— 2007. "Drawing the Forms of Things Unknown". In *The Ghosts of Songs: The Film Art of the Black Audio Film Collective*, 74–99. Liverpool: Liverpool University Press.

Eshun, Kodwo, and Ros Gray
— 2011. "The Militant Image: A Ciné-Geography". *Third Text* 25 (1): 1.

Espinosa, Julio Garcia
— 1997. *For an Imperfect Cinema: New Latin American Cinema, Theory, Practices, and Transcontinental Articulations*. Edited by Michael T. Martin. Vol. 1. Detroit: Wayne State University Press.

Fanon, Frantz
— 1963. *The Wretched of the Earth*. Translated by Constanze Farrington. New York: Grove Press.
— 2017 (first published 1952). *Black Skin White Mask*. London: Pluto Press.

Farocki, Harun
— 2009. "Written Trailers". In *Harun Farocki: Against What? Against Whom?*, edited by Kodwo Eshun and Antje Ehmann, 220–41. London: Koenig Books.
— 2016 (first published 2008). "Einfüh-lung (Empathy)". In *Harun Farocki: Another Kind of Empathy*, edited by Antje Ehmann and Carles Guerra. Barcelona: Fundación Antoni Tàpies.

Farocki, Harun, and Philipp Goll
— 2016. "Interview mit Harun Farocki". In *Harun Farocki: Another Kind of Empathy*, edited by Antje Ehmann and Carles Guerra. Barcelona: Fundación Antoni Tàpies.

Fayad, Rahif
— 2015. Interview with the author on 4 February 2015.

Fischer, Joschka
— 1977. "Vorstoss in 'primitivere' Zeiten". *Autonomie: Materialien gegen die Fabrikgesellschaft* 5, 52–64.

Fisher, Jean
— 2007. "In Living Memory … Archive and Testimony in the Films of the Black Audio Film Collective". In *The Ghosts of Songs: The Film Art of the Black Audio Film Collective*, 16–30. Liverpool: Liverpool University Press.

Forensic Architecture
— n.d. "Forensic Architecture". Accessed 17 May 2019. https://forensic-architecture.org/.

Foucault, Michel
— 2003 (first published 1972). "Preface". In *Anti-Oedipus: Capitalism and Schizophrenia*, by Gilles Deleuze and Félix Guattari, xi–xiv. Minneapolis: University of Minnesota Press.

Franke, Anselm
— 2003. "Territories". In *Territories: Islands, Camps and Other States of Utopia*, edited by Anselm Franke, 10–14. Berlin: KW Institute for Contemporary Arts; Cologne: Verlag der Buchhandlung Walther König.

Free Osman Kavala
— n.d. "About Osman Kavala". Accessed 2 May 2018. http://osmankavala.org/en/about-osman-kavala.

Gabriel, Teshome H
— 1982. *Third Cinema in the Third World: The Aesthetics of Liberation*. Ann Arbor: UMI Research Press.

Getino, Octavio
— 2011 (first published 1973). "The Cinema as Political Fact". *Third Text* 25 (1): 41–53. https://doi.org/10.1080/09528822.2011.545613.

Getino, Octavio, and Fernando Solanas
— 1969. "Towards a Third Cinema". Accessed 8 August 2019. http://documentaryisneverneutral.com/words/camasgun.html.

Ghossein, Ahmad
— 2016. "When the Ventriloquist Came and Spoke to Me". Performance presented at the 66th Berlinale, Berlin.

Giefer, Thomas
— 2010. Interview with Sandra Schäfer and Jochen Becker on 18 October 2010.

Global Prayers
— n.d. "Global Prayers". Accessed 27 March 2018. https://globalprayers.info/about/index.html.

Godard, Jean-Luc
— 2016 (first published 1970). "Que Faire?" In *What Is to Be Done?*, edited by Österreichisches Filmmuseum. Vienna: Österreichisches Filmmuseum.

Halbwachs, Maurice
— 1980. *The Collective Memory*. 1st ed. New York: Harper & Row.

Hall, Stuart
— 1980. "Encoding/Decoding". In *Culture, Media, Language: Working Papers in Cultural Studies, 1972–79*, edited by Stuart Hall, Dorothy Hobson, Andrew Lowe, and Paul Willis, 128–38. London: Routledge.

Hantelmann, Dorothea von, and Carolin Meister, eds.
— 2010. *Die Ausstellung: Politik eines Rituals*. Berlin: diaphanes.

Haraway, Donna
— 1988. "Situated Knowledges: The Science Question in Feminism and the Privilege of Partial Perspective". *Feminist Studies* 14 (3): 575–99.

Harb, Mona
— 2010. "Story of a Name". In *Beyroutes: A Guide to Beirut*, 57–61. Amsterdam: Archis.

Harb, Mona, and Reinoud Leenders
— 2005. "Know the Enemy: Hizbullah, 'Terrorism' and the Politics of Perception". *Third World Quarterly* 26 (February): 173–97.

Harithy, Howayda al-, ed.
— 2010. *Lessons in Post-War Reconstruction: Case Studies from Lebanon in the Aftermath of the 2006 War*. London: Routledge.

Hartman, Saidya V, and Frank B Wilderson III
— 2003. "The Position of the Unthought". *Qui Parle?* 13 (2): 183–201.

Harvey, David
— 2012. "From Space to Place and Back
  Again: Reflections on the Condition of
  Postmodernity". In *Mapping the
  Futures: Local Cultures, Global
  Change*, edited by John Bird, Barry
  Curtis, Tim Putnam, and Lisa Tickner.
  London: Routledge.

Heinecke, Gabrielle
— 2017. "Hamburg G20—Das sagt der
  anwaltliche Notdienst". 8 July 2017.
  http://matrixchange.blogspot.
  com/2017/07/hamburg-g20-das-sagt-
  der-anwaltliche.html.

Holert, Tom, and Brigitte Oetker, eds.
— 2000. *Imagineering: Visuelle Kultur
  und Politik der Sichtbarkeit*. Cologne:
  Oktagon.

Houri, Walid el-
— 2012. *The Meaning of Resistance:
  Hezbollah's Media Strategies and the
  Articulation of a People*. Amsterdam:
  Rozenberg Publishers. https://
  academia.edu/1500422/The_
  meaning_of_resistance_Hezbollahs_
  media_strategies_and_the_
  articulation_of_a_people.

Houri, Walid el-, and Dima Saber
— 2010. "Filming Resistance:
  A Hezbollah Strategy". *Radical
  History Review* 106: 70–85.

ID-Verlag, and RAF, eds.
— 1997. *Rote Armee Fraktion: Texte
  und Materialien zur Geschichte der
  RAF*. Berlin: ID-Verlag.

Jeshi, Hassan el-
— 2015. Interview with the author on
  29 January 2015.

Jusuf, Windu
— 2014. "Beatriz's War and Us". *The
  Jakarta Post*. 21 December 2014.
  http://thejakartapost.com/
  news/2014/12/21/beatriz-s-war-
  and-us.html.

Lagasnerie, Geoffroy de
— 2016. *Die Kunst der Revolte: Snowden,
  Assange, Manning*. Berlin: Suhrkamp.

Lefebvre, Henri
— 1995. *Writings on Cities*. Edited and
  translated by Eleonore Kofman
  and Elizabeth Lebas. Oxford: Wiley-
  Blackwell.
— 2007 (first published 1974). *The
  Production of Space*. Translated by
  Donald Nicholson-Smith. Oxford:
  Wiley-Blackwell.

Loreck, Hanne
— 2006. *Eske Schlüters: Sehen als
  Denken sehen*. Edited by Eva Schmidt.
  Frankfurt am Main: Revolver.

Maasri, Zeina
— 2008. *Off the Wall: Political Posters
  of the Lebanese Civil War*. London,
  New York: I.B. Tauris.

Mafud, Lucio
— 2007. "Un ilamado a transformar la
  realidad". *Página 12*. 25 August 2007.
  http://pagina12.com.ar/diario/
  suplementos/espectaculos/subno-
  tas/7408-2455-2007-08-25.html.

Malak, Ibtissam
— 2015. Interview with the author on
  24 February 2015.

Mansour, Ahmad
— 2015. Interview with the author on
  25 January 2015.

Melamed, Laliv
— 2018. *Sovereign Intimacy: Israeli Homemade Video Memorials and the Politics of Loss*, PhD diss., Department of Cinema Studies, New York University.

Mende, Doreen
— 2013. *The Itinerant: On the Delayed Arrival of Images of Socialist Internationalism That Confound Contemporary Exhibiting Processes*. PhD diss., Department of Visual Cultures at Goldsmiths College, University of London.

Mignolo, Walter D
— 2012. *Epistemischer Ungehorsam: Rhetorik der Moderne, Logik der Kolonialität und Grammatik der Dekolonialität*. Vienna, Berlin: Turia + Kant.

Mohr, Reinhard
— 1996. "Intellektuelle: 'Revolutionäres Gewäsch'". *Der Spiegel* 33. 12 August 1996. http://spiegel.de/spiegel/print/d-9080434.html.

Montgomery, Nick, and carla bergman
— 2017. *Joyful Militancy: Building Thriving Resistance in Toxic Times*. Chico: AK Press.

Mosireen Collective
— n.d. "Mosireen". Accessed 8 August 2019. https://youtube.com/user/Mosireen.

neue Gesellschaft für bildende Kunst, ed.
— 2016. *No Play—Feminist Training Camp*. https://archiv.ngbk.de/en/projekte/no-play/.
— 2017. *No Play—Feminist Training Camp*. Berlin: neue Gesellschaft für bildende Kunst.

Nirumand, Bahman
— 1967. *Persien, Modell eines Entwicklungslandes oder die Diktatur der Freien Welt*. Hamburg: Rowohlt Taschenbuch Verlag.

O'Doherty, Brian
— 1976. *Inside the White Cube: The Ideology of the Gallery Space*. San Francisco: The Lapis Press.

Ott, Michaela
— 2011. "Unbestimmte Affekträume im Film". In *Raum und Gefühl. Der Spatial Turn und die neue Emotionsforschung*, edited by Gertrud Lehnert, 96–108. Bielefeld: Transcript Verlag.

Paola Yacoub
— 2013. "How to Fabricate Heroes?" In *Global Prayers: Contemporary Manifestations of the Religious in the City*, edited by Jochen Becker, Katrin Klingan, Stephan Lanz, and Kathrin Wildner, 322–27. Zürich: Lars Mueller Publishers.

Poitras, Laura, and Hito Steyerl
— 2015. "Techniques of the Observer: Hito Steyerl and Laura Poitras in Conversation". *Artforum* 53, no. 9 (May): 307–17.

Rizk, Philip
— 2014. "2011 is not 1968: An Open Letter from Egypt". *ROAR*. 25 January 2014. https://roarmag.org/essays/egyptian-revolution-working-class/.

Rogoff, Irit
— 2003. "Engendering Terror". In *Geography and the Politics of Mobility*, edited by Ursula Biemann, translated by Roger Buergel and Timothy Jones, 48–63. Vienna: Generali Foundation; Cologne: Verlag der Buchhandlung Walther König.

Rustom, Joseph
— 2012. "If You Can't Walk on Water I Never Get Out of the Boat". In *Faith is the Place*, edited by metroZones, 38–39. Berlin: b_books.
— 2014. "Ta'ifa". In *Global Prayers: Contemporary Manifestations of the Religious in the City*, edited by Jochen Becker, Katrin Klingan, Stephan Lanz, and Kathrin Wildner, 328–35. Zürich: Lars Mueller Publishers.

Russel, Enrique
— 2003. *Philosophy of Liberation*. Eugene: Wipf and Stock.

Safa, Mohamed
— 2018. "50cm Slab". In *Points of Contact*, edited by Helene Kazan. Exhibition brochure.

Schäfer, Sandra
— 2009a. "Documents". Online publication edited by Sandra Schäfer and Karin Rebbert. Accessed 17 May 2019. http://mazefilm.de/publications/online-publications.
— 2009b. "Passing the Rainbow". *Printed Project* 12: 88–94.
— 2009c. "Passing the Rainbow". In *Visuelle Lektüren–Lektüren des Visuellen*, edited by Hanne Loreck and Katrin Mayer, 37–54. Hamburg: Textem.
— 2009d. *stagings: Kabul, Film & Production of Representation*. Berlin: b_books.
— 2012. "on the set of 1978ff". In *Faith is the Place*, edited by metroZones, 245–65. Berlin: b_books.
— 2013. "'There is no answer to any of these things': Religious Street Politics in Tehran 1978ff". In *Global Prayers: Contemporary Manifestations of the Religious in the City*, edited by Jochen Becker, Kathrin Klingan, Stephan Lanz, and Kathrin Wildner, 300–13. Zürich: Lars Müller Publishers.
— 2015. "Making Film Militantly". In *The Militant Image Reader*, edited by Urban Subjects, 49–56. Graz: Camera Austria.
— 2016. "Facts are no more solid, coherent, round, and real than pearls are". In *Poetic Biopolitics: Practices of Relation in Architecture and the Arts*, edited by Peg Rawes, Stephen Loo, and Timothy Mathews, 209–20. London: I. B. Tauris.
— 2019. "Contested Frames: Short Histories of Afghan Films". *Katalog Forum,* 69th Berlinale, Berlin.
— 2020. "Whose Gaze? Stories Told between Kabul, Herat, and Berlin". *BioScope: South Asian Screen Studies* 11.1 (forthcoming).

Schäfer, Sandra, Jochen Becker, and Madeleine Bernstorff, eds.
— 2006. *Kabul/Teheran 1979ff: Filmlandschaften, Städte unter Stress und Migration*. Berlin: b_books.

Schlüter, Christian
— 2012. "Adorno-Preis: Ist Judith Butler Israel-Hasserin?" *Berliner Zeitung,* 29 August 2012. http://berliner-zeitung.de/kultur/adorno-preis-ist-judith-butler-israel-hasserin--6034150.

Scribner, Charity
— 2015. *After the Red Army Faction: Gender, Culture, and Militancy.* New York: Columbia University Press.

Seeßlen, Georg
— 1997. "Deutschland im Herbst". *Filmzentrale.* September 1997.

Sekula, Allan
— 1995. "Red Passenger". In *Fish Story*, 42–54. Düsseldorf: Richter Verlag.

Sheikh, Simon
— 2009. "Positively White Cube Revisited", *E-Flux Journal* 3. February 2009. http://e-flux.com/journal/03/68545/positively-white-cube-revisited/.

Shilleh, Reem, and Mohanad Yaqubi
— 2015. "Reflections on Palestinian Militant Cinema". In *Politics of Memory: Documentary and Archive*, edited by Marco Scotini and Elisabeth Galasso, 93–103. Berlin: Archive Books.

Silverman, Kaja
— 1996. *The Threshold of the Visible World.* New York: Routledge.
— 1997. "Dem Blickregime Begegnen". In *Privileg Blick: Kritik der visuellen Kultur*, edited by Christian Kravagna, 41–64. Berlin: Edition ID-Archiv.

Smith, Anna Marie
— 1998. *Laclau and Mouffe: The Radical Democratic Imaginary.* New York: Routledge.

Spivak, Gayatari Chakravorty
— 1988. "Can the Subaltern Speak?" In *Marxism and the Interpretation of Culture*, edited by Cary Nelson and Lawrence Grossberg, 271–313. Chicago: University of Illinois Press.

Stakemeier, Kerstin
— 2018. *Entgrenzter Formalismus.* PoLYpeN. Berlin: b_books.

Steinke, Ronen
— 2019. "Warum Deutschland die Hisbollah nicht als terroristische Vereinigung einstuft". *Süddeutsche Zeitung*, 31 May 2019.

Steyerl, Hito
— 2008. "White Cube und Black Box. Kunst und Kino". In *Die Farbe der Wahrheit: Dokumentarismen im Kunstfeld.* Vienna: Turia + Kant.
— 2009. "Is a Museum a Factory?" *E-Flux Journal* 7, June 2009.

Third Text
— 2014. "Third Text Mission Statement". *Third Text*, 18 November 2014. http://thirdtext.org/mission-statement.

Tieke, Julia
— 2014. "Das Deutsche Kaiserreich und der Dschihad". *Deutschlandfunk Kultur*, 19 November 2014. https://deutschlandfunkkultur.de/geschichte-das-deutsche-kaiserreich-und-der-dschihad.976.de.html?dram:article_id=303174.

Tollmann, Vera
— 2014. "Watching Powers of Ten in 2014: A Blueprint for Same Old Power Structures?". *Regarding Spectatorship.* http://regardingspectatorship.net/watching-powers-of-ten-in-2014-a-blueprint-for-same-old-power-structures/.

Tor
— 2018. Accessed 4 January 2018. https://torproject.org/.

Tunzelmann, Alex von
— 2009. "The Battle of Algiers: A
  Masterpiece of Historical Accuracy".
  The Guardian, 26 March 2009. https://
  theguardian.com/film/2009/mar/
  26/the-battle-of-algiers-film-histori-
  cal-
  accuracy.

UMAM Documentation and
Research Centre, ed.
— 2007. "Collecting Dahiye". Accessed
  8 August 2019. https://umam-dr.org/
  en/home/projects/14/advance-
  contents/54/collecting-dahiyeh.

Umoja, Akinyele Omowale, ed.
— 1999. "Repression Breeds Resistance:
  The Black Liberation Army and the
  Radical Legacy of the Black Panther
  Party". *New Political Science* 21 (2):
  131–54.

Urban Subjects, ed.
— 2015. *The Militant Image Reader*.
  Graz: Camera Austria.

Viehmann, Klaus
— 2007. "Militanz". In *ABC Der Alterna-
  tiven. Von "Ästhetik des Widerstands"
  Bis "Ziviler Ungehorsam"*, edited by
  Ulrich Brand, Bettina Lösch, and Stefan
  Thimmel, 124–25. Hamburg: VSA.

Vishmidt, Marina
— 2013. "Permanent Reproductive
  Crisis: An Interview with Silvia
  Federici". *Mute*. 7 March 2013.
  http://metamute.org/editorial/
  articles/permanent-reproductive-
  crisis-interview-silvia-federici.

Waad, ed.
— 2006. *Waad: The Uniqueness of
  the Experience. Workshop on the
  Reconstruction of the Southern
  Suburb of Beirut after the Israeli
  Aggression*. Beirut: Waad.

Wayne, Mike
— 2001. *Political Film: The Dialectics
  of Third Cinema*. London: Pluto Press.

Weizman, Eyal
— 2002. "Introduction to the Politics of
  Verticality". *OpenDemocracy*. 23 April
  2002. http://opendemocracy.net/
  conflict-politicsverticality/article_801.
  jsp.
— 2003. "The Air". In *Territories: Islands,
  Camps and Other States of Utopia*,
  edited by Anselm Franke, 114–17.
  Berlin: KW Institute for Contemporary
  Art; Cologne: Verlag der Buchhandlung Walther König.
— 2007. "The Politics of Verticality".
  In *Hollow Land: Israel's Architecture
  of Occupation*, 12–16. London:
  Verso Books.

Wilderson III, Frank B
— 2014. "Black Liberation Army and
  the Paradox of Political Engagement".
  Scribd. https://de.scribd.com/
  document/239904094/Wilderson-
  Black-Liberation-Army-the-Paradox-
  of-Political-Engagement-2013-READ.
— 2017. Talk presented in the framework
  of the exhibition *Klassensprachen*.
  District, Berlin, 16 September 2017.

Wisniewski, Stefan
— 2003. *Wir waren so unheimlich
  konsequent … Ein Gespräch zur
  Geschichte der RAF mit Stefan
  Wisniewski*. Berlin: ID-Verlag.

Yacoub, Paola, Joseph Rustom, and
Kathrin Wildner, eds.
— 2013. *O Syria! metroZones*. Hamburg:
  adocs.

Yaqubi, Mohanad
— 2012. "A Militant Cinema: Mohanad
  Yaqubi in conversation with Sheyma
  Buali". *Ibraaz*. https://ibraaz.org/inter-
  views/16.

Zelik, Raul
— 2014. "Wie revolutionär ist die
  Revolution? Zu Walter Benjamins
  'Kritik der Gewalt'". http://raulzelik.
  net/kritik-literatur-alltag-theorie/
  440-wie-revolutionaer-ist-die-
  revolution-zu-walter-benjamins-kritik-
  der-gewalt-woz-und-nd-juni-2014.

Zgeib, Ayman
— 2007. *Mawtin, kessat madina wa
  hareb.* Television series produced by
  al-Manar.

Films, Sound, and Installations

858 Revolutionary Archive
— https://858.ma/grid/title.

Akomfrah, John, and Black Audio
Film Collective
— 1986. *Handsworth Songs.*

Anonymous
— n.d. Videoclips.

Antonio, Emile de, Haskell Wexler,
and Mary Lampson
— 1976. *Underground.*

Bruch, Klaus vom
— 1977–78. *Das Schleyer-Band.*

Brustelin, Alf, Hans Peter Cloos, Rainer
Werner Fassbinder, Alexander Kluge,
Beate Mainka-Jelinghaus, Maximilane
Mainka, Edgar Reitz, et al
— 1978. *Deutschland im Herbst.*

Costard, Hellmuth
— 1978. *Der kleine Godard an das
  Kuratorium junger deutscher Film.*

Czenki, Margit
— 1987. *Komplizinnen.*

Djebar, Assia
— 1982. *La Zerda et les chants de l'oubli.*

Dziga Vertov Group
— n.d. *Jusqu'à la victoire.*

Eames Office
— 1977. *Powers of Ten.*

Farocki, Harun
— 1969. *Nicht löschbares Feuer.*
— 1988. *Bilder der Welt und Inschrift des
  Krieges.*
— 1995. *Schnittstelle.*

Gavras, Costa
— 1972. *État de Siège*.

Getino, Octavio, and Fernando Solanas
— 1966–68. *La hora de los hornos*.

Ghossein, Ahmad
— 2016. *When the Ventroliquist Came and Spoke to Me*.

Godard, Jean-Luc, and Anne-Marie Miéville
— 1976. *Ici et Ailleurs*.

Green, Sam and Bill Siegel
— 2002. *The Weather Underground*.

Jirmanus Saba, Mary
— 2017. *Shu'our akbar min el hob*.

Limonadi, Ali
— 1967. *Das Abonnement*.

Maldoror, Sarah
— 1969. *Monangambeee*.

Meinhof, Ulrike
— 1965. *Arbeitsunfälle, Reportage NDR*.
— 1965. *Arbeitsplatz und Stoppuhr, Reportage NDR*.

Meinhof, Ulrike, and Eberhard Itzenplitz
— 1970. *Bambule*.

Meins, Holger
— 1967. *Oskar Langenfeld*.

Minow, Hans-Rüdiger, and Thomas Giefer
— 1967. *Berlin, 2. Juni*.

Mosireen Collective
— http://mosireen.org/?page_id=6.

Périot, Jean-Gabriel
— 2015. *Une Jeunesse Allemande*.

Poitras, Laura
— 2014. *Citizenfour*.
— 2017. *Risk*.

Pontecorvo, Gillo
— 1966. *La battaglia di Algeri*.

Safa, Mohamed
— 2018. *50cm Slab*.

Schäfer, Sandra
— 2011. *on the set of 1978ff*.
— 2016. *Mleeta*.
— 2017. *Constructed Futures: Haret Hreik*.

Scheffner, Philip
— 2007. *The Halfmoon Files*.

Soueid, Mohammad, and Fadi Toufic
— 2006. *The Sky Is Not Always Above*.

Stephan, Rania
— 2006. *Lebanon/War*.

Trotta, Margarethe von
— 1978. *Das zweite Erwachen der Christa Klages*.
— 1981. *Die bleierne Zeit*.

Yaqubi, Mohanad
— 2016. *Off Frame aka Revolution until Victory*.

Biography

The artist Sandra Schäfer works with film and video installations. Her practice explores the process of unfolding and rereading documents, images, spatial narratives, and performative gestures. Her works are often based on extended research regarding the margins, gaps, and discontinuities of our perceptions of history, political struggles, and urban and geopolitical space. Her films have been exhibited at the 66th and 67th Berlinale, Berlin; Schirn Kunsthalle, Frankfurt; mumok, Vienna; Museum Ludwig, Cologne; Depo, Istanbul; and La Virreina, Barcelona. Schäfer is a professor at the Academy of Fine Arts Munich and a member of the feminist film organisation Cinenova in London. She has edited the books *stagings: Kabul, Film & Production of Representation* (b_books, Berlin, 2009) and *Kabul/Teheran 1979ff: Filmlandschaften, Städte unter Stress und Migration* (b_books, Berlin, 2006, together with Jochen Becker and Madeleine Bernstorff). For more information please visit: www.mazefilm.de

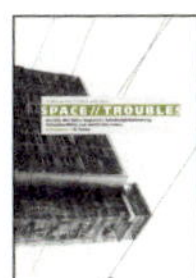

metroZones 1
Space // Troubles. Jenseits des Guten Regierens: Schattenglobalisierung, Gewaltkonflikte und städtisches Leben
Jochen Becker, Stephan Lanz (eds.)
2003, b_books, Berlin
ISBN 3-93357-51-8

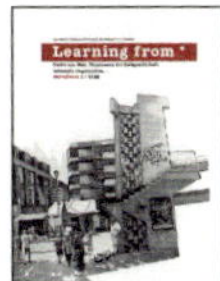

metroZones 2
Learning from *. Städte von Welt, Phantasmen der Zivilgesellschaft, informelle Organisation
Editing: Jochen Becker, Claudia Burbaum, Martin Kaltwaser, Folke Köbbeling, Stephan Lanz, Katja Reichard; Editor: neue Gesellschaft für bildende Kunst
2003, nGbK Berlin
ISBN 3-926796-86-3

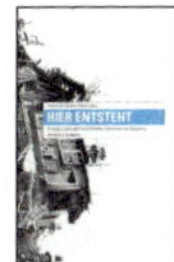

metroZones 3
Hier entsteht. Strategien partizipativer Achitektur und räumlicher Aneignung
Jesko Fezer, Mathias Heyden (eds.)
2004, b_books, Berlin
ISBN 3-933557-52-6

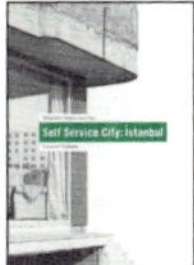

metroZones 4
Self Service City: Istanbul
Orhan Esen, Stephan Lanz (eds.)
2005, b_books, Berlin
ISBN 3-933557-52-6

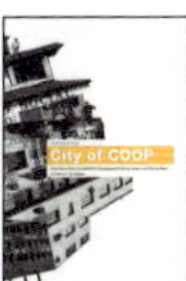

metroZones 5
City of COOP. Ersatzökonomien und städtische Bewegung in Rio de Janeiro und Buenos Aires
Stephan Lanz (ed.)
2004, b_books, Berlin
ISBN 3-933557-54-2

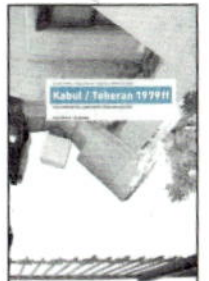

metroZones 6
Kabul/Teheran 1979 ff. Filmlandschaften, Städte unter Stress und Migration
Sandra Schäfer, Jochen Becker, Madeleine Bernstorff (eds.)
2006, b_books, Berlin
ISBN 3-93357-55-0

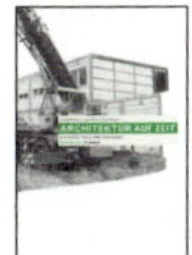

metroZones 7
Architektur auf Zeit. Baracken, Pavillons, Container
Axel Doßmann, Jan Wenzel, Kai Wenzel
2006, b_books, Berlin
ISBN 3-926796-66-6

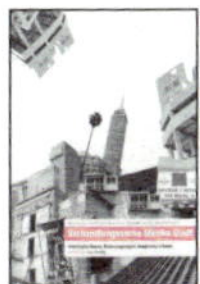

metroZones 8
Verhandlungssache Mexiko Stadt. Umkämpfte Räume, Stadtaneignungen, imaginarios urbanos
Anne Becker, Olga Burkert, Anne Doose, Alexander Jachnow, Marianna Poppitz (eds.)
2008, b_books, Berlin
ISBN 3-933557-89-6

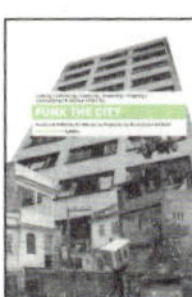

metroZones 9
Funk the City. Sounds und städtisches Handeln aus den Peripherien von Rio de Janeiro und Berlin
Stephan Lanz, Gese Dorner, Katharina Gaber, Nele Harlan, Nadine Jäger, Sigurd Jennerjahn, Birke Otto, Swantje Plähn (eds.)
2008, b_books, Berlin
ISBN 3-933557-91-9

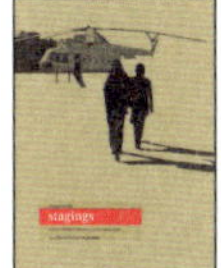

metroZones/media 2
stagings. Kabul, Film & Production of Representation
Sandra Schäfer (ed.)
2009, b_books, Berlin
ISBN 978-3-933557-99-5

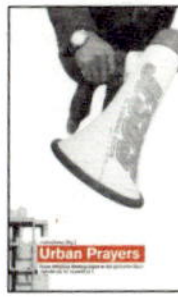

metroZones 10
Urban Prayers. Neue religiöse Bewegungen in der globalen Stadt
metroZones (ed.)
2011, Assoziation A, Berlin/Hamburg
ISBN 978-3-935936-78-1

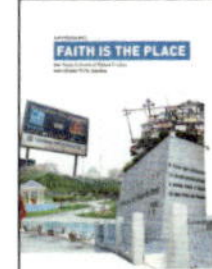

metroZones 11
Faith is the Place. The Urban Cultures of Global Prayers
metroZones (ed.)
2012, b_books, Berlin
ISBN 978-3-942214-04-9

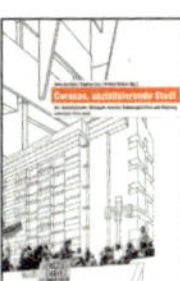

metroZones 12
Caracas, sozialisierende Stadt. Die „bolivarianische" Metropole zwischen Selbstorganisation und Steuerung
Dario Azzellini, Stephan Lanz, Kathrin Wildner (eds.)
2013, b_books, Berlin
ISBN 978-3-942214-13-1

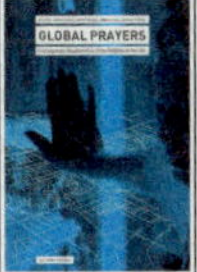

metroZones 13
Global Prayers. Contemporary Manifestations of the Religious in the City
Jochen Becker, Katrin Klingan, Stephan Lanz, Kathrin Wildner (eds.)
2014, Lars Müller Publishers, Zürich
ISBN 978-3-03778-373-3

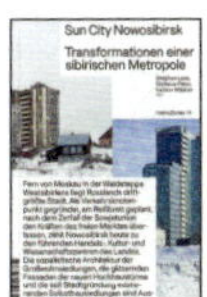

metroZones 14
Sun City Nowosibirsk. Transformationen einer sibirischen Metropole
Stephan Lanz, Stefanie Peter, Kathrin Wildner (eds.)
2018, Spector Books, Leipzig
ISBN 978-3-95905-165-1

**For more information please visit:
www.metrozones.info**

Imprint

Moments of Rupture:
Space, Militancy & Film

Written by: Sandra Schäfer
Serial Title: metroZones 15
Proofreading: Bonnie Begusch
Graphic Design: Wolfgang Schwärzler
Colour Correction: Siegfried Füreder
Printing and Binding:
Gutenberg Beuys Feindruckerei

Supported by the Rosa Luxemburg
Foundation

First Edition, Spector Books,
Leipzig, 2020
© this edition: Spector Books,
metroZones – Center for Urban Affairs,
and mazefilm

Printed in Germany
ISBN: 978-3-95905-391-4

www.spectorbooks.com
www.metroZones.info
www.mazefilm.de

metroZones
Zentrum für städtische Angelegenheiten | Center for Urban Affairs

Every effort has been made to contact
the copyright holders for the images
used in this book. Spector Books and
the author apologise in advance for
any omissions. Should we be notified,
these will be corrected in the next
edition of this publication.

For their kind permission to reproduce
images we would like to thank: Harun
Farocki GbR, Berlin; Donation Simon
Field, Collection Austrian Film Museum,
Vienna; Sherief Gaber, Mosireen;
Helene Kazan; Alexander Kluge and
Kairos Film, Munich; Hans-Rüdiger
Minow and Thomas Giefer; No Play;
Joseph Rustom and Guy Asmar;
Andrea Thal; Klaus vom Bruch; and
Stefan Wisniewski.

Distribution

Germany, Austria: GVA, Gemeinsame
Verlagsauslieferung Göttingen
GmbH&Co. KG, www.gva-verlage.de
Switzerland: AVA Verlagsauslieferung AG,
www.ava.ch
France, Belgium: Interart Paris,
www.interart.fr
UK: Central Books Ltd,
www.centralbooks.com
USA, Canada, Central and South America,
Africa, Asia: ARTBOOK / D.A.P.,
www.artbook.com
South Korea: The Book Society,
www.thebooksociety.org
Japan: twelvebooks,
www.twelve-books.com
Australia, New Zealand:
Perimeter Distribution,
www.perimeterdistribution.com